Seasons of Birth

A Year of Autonomous Birth Stories

Bree Moore

Innate Ink Publishing

Seasons of Birth: A Year of Autonomous Birth Stories

First published by Innate Ink Publishing 2022

Copyright © 2022 by Bree Moore

Ebook: 978-1-956668-09-4

Paperback: 978-1-956668-06-3

Hardcover: 978-1-956668-08-7

All rights reserved. No part of this publication may be reproduced, stored or transmitted in any form or by any means without written permission from the publisher.

It is illegal to copy this book, post it to a website, or distribute it by any other means without permission.

No information that is given in this book is intended as medical advice. The reader should take personal responsibility for their health and treatment.

Contents

1. Why I wrote this book — 1
2. Reverdie — 3
3. The Free birth of Jane Esther — 5
4. A Memorial Day to Remember — 11
5. Knowledge is Power — 15
6. The Wild Pregnancy and Freebirth of Phoenix — 27
7. Freedom through Surrender — 31
8. The Trampoline Freebirth Of Micah — 35
9. Bringing Tehani Earthside — 43
10. Freebirth of Mazikeen Riley — 45
11. The Ecstatic Unassisted Birth of Rya — 47
12. Unwavering Strength — 49
13. Cedar's Wild and Free Birth Story — 61
14. Advice for a Spring Birth — 69
15. Estival — 73
16. The Free Birth of Daisy Moon — 75
17. A Dream Birth — 79
18. The Birth of Sunny — 85

19.	The Birth Of Milo Septem Agape	89
20.	The Birth of Waverly Love	93
21.	Worth it All - The Birth Of Agatha Wren Sue	105
22.	Baby Jazmine's Birth Story	115
23.	We are Warriors	117
24.	Advice for a Summer Birth	121
25.	Tips on Beating the Heat While Pregnant	123
26.	Holistic Advice for Common Pregnancy Symptoms	125
27.	How to Talk to Your Husband or Partner About Freebirth	129
28.	Ruska	137
29.	My First Freebirth	139
30.	My Unassisted Home Birth	145
31.	Truly Biological Birth	149
32.	My 23-minute Birth	157
33.	The Birth of Ledger Wolf	161
34.	In Denial	165
35.	The Incredibly Long Birth of Theodore Ignatius	167
36.	Freebirth of Elijah Sage	173
37.	Advice for an Autumn Birth	179
38.	Unpacking Pain-free Birth	181
39.	My Favorite Books, Blogs, and Podcasts about Birth	185
40.	Apricity	187
41.	Birth of Ivy Arabella	189
42.	A Thanksgiving Freebirth	201
43.	Everett's RV Birth	207
44.	Born Free and Breech	211
45.	Yacuruna Storm's Free birth Story	215
46.	Lavender's Birth Journey	221

47.	The Freebirth of Yusuke Pierce	225
48.	A Life-Changing Christmas Freebirth	233
49.	Warming Postpartum Recipes	241
50.	Chicken or Vegetable Stock	242
51.	Ginger Tea	245
52.	Beef Stew	247
53.	"Pudding" Oatmeal	249
54.	Postpartum Belly Binding	251
55.	Advice for Winter Births	255
	Also By Bree Moore	259
	About the Author	261

Why I wrote this book

SIX YEARS AGO, MY freebirth journey began with an insightful homebirth midwife who looked at me, after hearing the interventions I was planning to refuse, and said, "It sounds like you want an unassisted birth."

I'd never heard that term before, but her words opened a portal to this incredible world of autonomy that I had been craving but had never known existed.

During that pregnancy, and each pregnancy since, stories of freebirth have been an essential part of my journey. I've had four successful unassisted pregnancies and births now. I'll forever be grateful for the midwife who helped put me on this path and the women who wrote their stories online and in print for me to find that shaped my journey.

Now, I work to share the stories that inspired me by publishing these collections. Between having my own babies and homeschooling, having a career as a fantasy author and postpartum belly binder, I make time to bring these collections together. Even when they're short. Even when there are only a few stories.

Because stories matter. Beginnings matter. And each time you embark on a pregnancy and give birth, it's a new beginning. Full of hope. Full of life. Full of promise. My hope is that by reading these stories, you will plant the seeds of hope and vision for your pregnancy and birth and allow them to grow into a fruit that you can pick with joy and confidence. That you'll be prepared for birth and what comes beyond.

I hope the stories these women have shared will inspire and uplift you in your own birthing journey, wherever that may take you.

I want to encourage you to stimulate the power of belief in your life.

Believe that you are part of a bigger source of unlimited power within the universe. Believe that you can give birth to this baby on your own, no matter who you choose to have at your side, no matter your circumstances. Believe in the women you serve, if you're a birth attendant, and trust in them and their bodies.

Whatever you choose to believe, I think we can all agree that birth is a unique sort of magic, and that magic can be found in abundance when women free themselves in birth.

Reverdie

Reverdie: to become green again
Derived from a 14th-century French verb ("reverdir")

The Free birth of Jane Esther

By Kathryn Sullivan

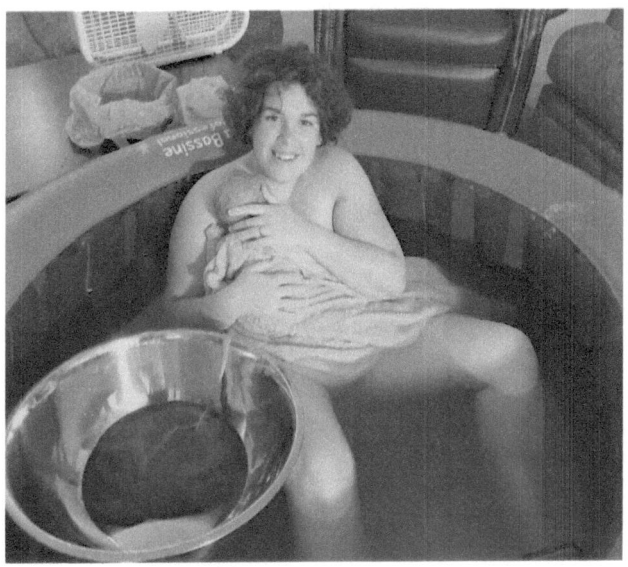

MY FIRST BIRTH HAD gone quite awry in plans for a natural birth at a Birth Center. My water had broken at 41 weeks and 2 days, and labor had started for a few hours, but due to having to drive to the Birth Center when I was not ready to go yet, my contractions completely stopped. I feel like due to performance anxiety, they never started again.

We ended up transferring to the hospital on the third day after my waters had released and augmented labor with Pitocin. It was honestly a terrible experience. I labored for 24 hours, and it took a very long time for me to dilate. I was in very hard labor and had just barely gotten to 4 cm, when I felt so overwhelmed by the nurse yelling at me to get out of the shower, my Doula telling me to be quiet and to lay down in the bed and try to rest without making a sound, and feeling so incredibly overwhelmed after 14 hours of hard contractions made by the Pitocin, that I finally decided on an epidural.

Even after the epidural, It took 10 more hours for me to be completed. My poor little girl just was not comfortable with coming into this world with everyone watching her! When it was time to push, for a while everyone was very respectful of me wanting to sit up more and to gently bear her down. But once the doctor came in, they couldn't find a heartbeat as she was crowning, so he threatened an episiotomy if I did not push her out with the next contraction.

At that point, they laid me down on my back and made me push extremely hard to get her head out. She had meconium all over her, and my husband was supposed to catch the baby, but the doctor pushed him aside and grabbed the baby, had my husband instantly cut the cord, and took her away to get cleaned off and deep suctioned.

All I remember after that for the next 10 minutes is bawling and begging for them to let me hold my baby. But I was ignored, and after a quick deep suctioning, they proceeded to keep cleaning, weighing, and diapering her. It was honestly the longest 10 minutes of my life. When they finally gave her to me, I bawled like crazy, and just held onto her. We tried to get her to latch in that one hour that they let me hold her, but my nipples were so flaccid and I was shaking and so anxious after the experience, that she wasn't able to latch.

They then whisked her away to go get tested for about an hour and a half and poked her with needles to make sure she had no infection from me being GBS positive, with my waters broken. I once again cried, and made my husband go with her so I knew that they didn't do anything else to her while I wasn't there. When I finally got her back, we were finally able to latch.

I hated being there, especially with nurses constantly checking us, one of them getting mad for nursing baby on demand, and of course the heel prick which the nurse was so incredibly rough on baby girl, that she was screaming and screaming, and I was bawling my eyes out yet again. After two days during discharge, we did not have a pediatrician at the time, because I thought I was going to deliver at the birth center and didn't feel pressured to have one yet. The nurse basically talked to me for over an hour about how much I was an idiot, and finally, after bawling yet again, she let me leave the hospital, with the hospital pediatrician technically as our provider.

Once we got home, the postpartum anxiety was so intense that I didn't sleep at all for days. I kept thinking scary and violent thoughts and was so worried that my baby was going to die. When my milk came in, I was a disaster. After that whole experience, everything eventually got better, our breastfeeding journey was great, and I got much healthier in my eating habits and running habits.

I very slowly gained my confidence back as a woman. I ended up reading a lot about homebirth, and when I became pregnant with our second baby on our first try, I knew that we were giving birth at home this time. There was no way anyone was going to make me leave my house again in labor.

At first, we hired a midwife, but due to her being sneaky and lying about weird things, and us not connecting to her, we fired her by 19 weeks. That went on with lots of drama back-and-forth and trying to get some of our money back. After suing her in small claims court, we finally ended up getting our refund. We are so glad that we followed our intuition and got rid of her.

I ended up reading lots of books about unassisted birth and felt like that was what was right for me. Pregnancy was filled with lots and lots of prayer, keeping myself healthy, and having faith that we would be able to do it on our own at home, with our amazing and open-minded Doula.

It all started on Wednesday night when I had a small gush of fluid come out along with a little bit of mucus plug. I thought that it was my complete bag of waters, but it turned out it was only the first layer of the amniotic sac. So after a couple days of stressing that labor wasn't starting, I settled back into being okay with going past 42 weeks of pregnancy. When we finally got to 42 weeks and two days, (which I'm so glad that we just waited and didn't go in for any intervention anywhere), my contractions started off very light and every 10 minutes starting at 9:30 a.m. on a beautiful Sunday during the Coronavirus quarantine.

I tried to ignore them and just relax and watch a show for a few hours. They started ramping up and getting closer together by 11 a.m., so I decided to send my husband and my daughter off to go bring the sacrament to his mother and to visit so I could have some time alone to prepare the house and to try to build up to labor without anyone watching me. It was just the trick! They arrived back by 2 p.m., and I had all the birth supplies and birth pool set up.

I was starting to low moan through my contractions. They were about two to four minutes apart at this point. We laid our baby down for her nap, and started filling up the pool with lukewarm water, so it was at least halfway filled up by the time I was ready to temp it and get in. Within half an hour, I jumped into the pool and didn't want to get out! By 4 p.m., we called my mom to come and get our daughter after her nap, and we called our Doula. At first, I was unsure of calling her because I didn't want to waste her time. But the moment she came, things started progressing really nice and fast. From about 4:30 to 6 p.m., I was in nice active labor. My husband and Doula were amazing and just let me do whatever I wanted and go wherever I wanted in the house. When 6 p.m. hit, transition began. I started getting in and out of the pool, on and off the toilet, and in and out of the bed. I was kind of spinning around like a crazy person and kept getting in some crazy positions that I felt intuitive to do.

I finally sat on the toilet and checked myself, and could feel her head still around my cervix but getting closer to being in the canal. What an amazing experience! I felt so empowered by that. That's when we moved back to the birth pool, and the next four to six contractions were her head descending into my birth canal. Wow. Talk about intense! I let FER *(fetal ejection reflex)* kick in and let my body bring baby down through my canal.

I moaned and screamed that entire time, as I honestly felt like that was the only thing I could do to get past that intensity! Once she crowned, that ring a fire was real! But I let my body stop and take a couple minutes of breath, and I let my husband feel the head. It was such a special time! Then with one uncontrolled push from my body, her head and body slipped out into the water.

We pulled her out, ended up having to unwrap the cord once away from her neck, and were so elated to have a baby at 8:06 p.m.! Only 11 hours, and half of that actually intense! My sweet husband was nervous about her breathing, even though she was perfectly fine and had great color, so I did a little bit of suction with my mouth and with a little Nose Frida in her nose. I reached down and felt that there were no balls.

I could have sworn it was going to be a boy the whole pregnancy, so we were shocked that it was a girl! It was amazing. I kept telling her sorry for calling her a boy. The placenta flew out of me by 12 minutes postpartum, and it was enormous! It was bigger than our baby was! I had Daddy hold her skin to skin with the placenta while I got out of the bath, and we laid down in bed and burned the cord around 10:30 p.m.

She eventually got an amazing latch and she nursed for two hours straight. I had no postpartum anxiety, and felt so calm and tranquil after this amazing and healing birth! So grateful for everything I learned through prayer, intuition, and amazing resources from other women! The healing of my perineum has been incredible, I had no tearing this time, and baby was perfect! Despite being 42 weeks and two days, she was only 7 pounds and 14 ounces! A whole 1 pound and 1 ounce less than our other baby! Fortunately, her head was much smaller as well, so I was grateful for that. At this writing, we are now just three days postpartum, I and feel amazing! I will never go back to birthing anywhere but home, if I can help it.

A Memorial Day to Remember

By Amanda

Contractions started in the early morning hours of Sunday, May 24th, at around 1:00 a.m. We had just got home from my parent's house about an hour earlier, and my husband and our 18-month-old son were asleep.

Just a few hours before, I had a feeling that I would go into labor that night.

At first, I thought I had gas, and I didn't want to get too excited, so I tried to get sleep. But every time the feeling of a wave would come and pass, it made it difficult to sleep. All I could think about was meeting our baby!

I texted our doula and told her I was having some light inconsistent contractions and that it wasn't time yet, but I wanted her to know my progress since she lived an hour away. She called me and asked for details. I filled her in and let her know I would be trying to get some sleep.

I did eventually fall asleep, but not for long since I was woken several times to light, wave-like contractions and having to pee. I labored off and on inconsistently all of Sunday. Contractions varied from every five minutes to every hour and weren't very intense.

I set up the pack and play, and then went out to lunch with my husband and son. After we drove back home at around 2:00 p.m., I crocheted an umbilical cord tie for baby.

I lost my mucus plug throughout the day. Around 6:00 p.m. contractions started to be a little more consistent, but they still felt light. My parents came to pick up our older son for the night since labor time had arrived.

At 9:00 p.m. I knew it was time to have the doula come. The contractions were much stronger, and I needed to lean on my husband. She arrived at 10:00 p.m., and contractions were somewhat strong, but they had slowed down a little bit. We were burning lavender incense for relaxation.

We played King's Corner for about an hour and then decided to go on a walk to try to move things along. The night was warm, but it felt nicer outside than in our hot one-bedroom apartment. We had not put the window air conditioner in yet, so we had to open all of our windows.

The walk helped to progress the contractions, as they started to be five minutes apart consistently and were usually strong enough that I could not walk or talk through them. I leaned on my husband through each contraction, and we would continue to walk and have casual conversation after each wave.

We turned around from our walk after about a half-hour, and headed back to the apartment. When we got home things were more heated. We all talked for a while, and my husband gave me a Larabar to keep my energy up. I ate it, but I wasn't very interested in food.

I began to lean on my birth ball through each contraction, as sitting up became too difficult. The sensations were very strong by this point, and I knew our baby would most likely be in our arms within the hour. My husband and our doula took turns massaging my hips and lower back. Light pressure felt so good!

I kept feeling like I had to poop as I was leaning over my birth ball on my hands and knees and I did end up pooping, but I knew I was using the right muscles and was making room for the baby.

At one point I really felt like the baby's head was crowning. The doula told me he wasn't just yet, but I didn't believe her. Then I felt the baby slip backward a little bit. I tried to take the pushes slowly, even though my body was doing the work without my conscious effort to push for the most part. The doula was helping with counter-pressure, which my husband was going to do originally, but it didn't end up that way since he was holding my hands and encouraging me. My husband gave me rejuvenating sips of cold water through a straw periodically.

My water broke at around 1:40 a.m. About a minute later, our son's head was crowning. The doula asked me if I wanted to try to touch his head. I tried but I wasn't able to reach comfortably in the position I was in, so instead, she took pictures for me of his head crowning. The pressure was very intense and it hurt, but I knew it wouldn't last long. I asked our doula if the baby had hair, and she said he did. I was excited for another baby with a head of hair!

Another contraction came and his head was out! The doula took a picture of our baby's face and showed me. I said he looked just like his daddy! Another contraction came, and with one more involuntary push, our baby was born on May 25th, Memorial Day, at 1:46 a.m.

I picked him up for the first time and said his name. "Hi, Bishop."

He was so beautiful!

My husband came to my side to see our beautiful baby, and our doula took pictures of us together during the golden hour. The doula helped to lay down some Chux pads on our bed of blankets made out on the floor, and I laid down with Bishop to try to nurse, get skin to skin, and wait for the placenta to come out. Bishop was more interested in sleeping than nursing, which I was fine with.

I gently massaged my own belly and uterus off and on, and relaxed. I was so tired, but so at peace. After about an hour the doula suggested that I sit up on my knees to try to let gravity bring the placenta down, and I did. As a small cramp-like contraction came, I pushed gently, and out came the placenta! The doula and I inspected it together, as my husband got a bowl to put it in. It was amazing to be able to analyze and see this organ that God had designed my body to make specifically for Bishop to keep him alive and healthy. Everything was intact and beautiful.

After birthing the placenta, my husband poured me a warm bath and then held Bishop while the doula helped me into the bath. It was so relaxing to sit in the warm water and get clean.

I relaxed in the bath for what felt like maybe a half-hour, and then our doula helped me out of the bath and into my postpartum underwear. She told me I looked sexy, which made me laugh a little and made me feel good because postpartum underwear is not the prettiest thing in the world.

When I finished in the bathroom, we came out and my husband tied the umbilical cord, which by this point was white and limp. He clamped and cut it while I held our son. Then we weighed him and measured him. He was 7 lbs 12 oz, 20 inches long, with a head circumference of 13 and 3/4".

Our doula held Bishop for a little bit, and I took pictures of her with him. I was worried that I wouldn't be able to pee because I had a hard time peeing after the birth of my first son and was catheterized. I asked the doula to stay for moral support until I was able to pee, which she did, and I ended up peeing as soon as I tried.

A little later my husband brought out some orange juice and crackers and cheese. I tried to eat to replenish some energy, but I was not hungry at all, only thirsty and tired. The doula cleaned up all the Chux pads, and the bathtub, and put all of the clean towels and birth supplies away, and she assured me if I needed anything else to give her a call.

Then she left, and my husband and I laid down with our new baby to sleep.

The atmosphere of this birth was very different from my first birth. It was intimate, peaceful, homey, free, and empowering.

I didn't feel limits, I didn't have distractions. I was respected and did not feel coerced into doing anything. I was able to take things slow and was not subjected to painful uterine massage, catheters, stitches, or vaginal exams. I had a small tear that barely bled and healed in a week.

I was able to sleep the next day away, in bed with my husband and our son, nursing, bonding, healing, and relaxing. No interruptions, no baby exams, no beeping machines, and no nurses trying to tell me what to do with my beautiful baby boy. I would never choose a hospital birth after having such a perfect experience at home.

I thank God for His perfect design, and I am thankful for my husband and our amazing doula who both helped to make this a perfect birth!

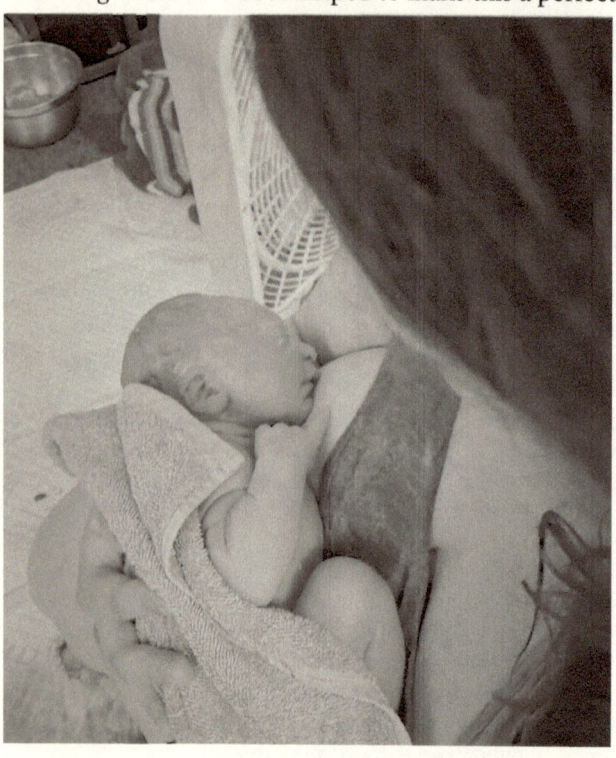

Knowledge is Power

By Keely Pogue

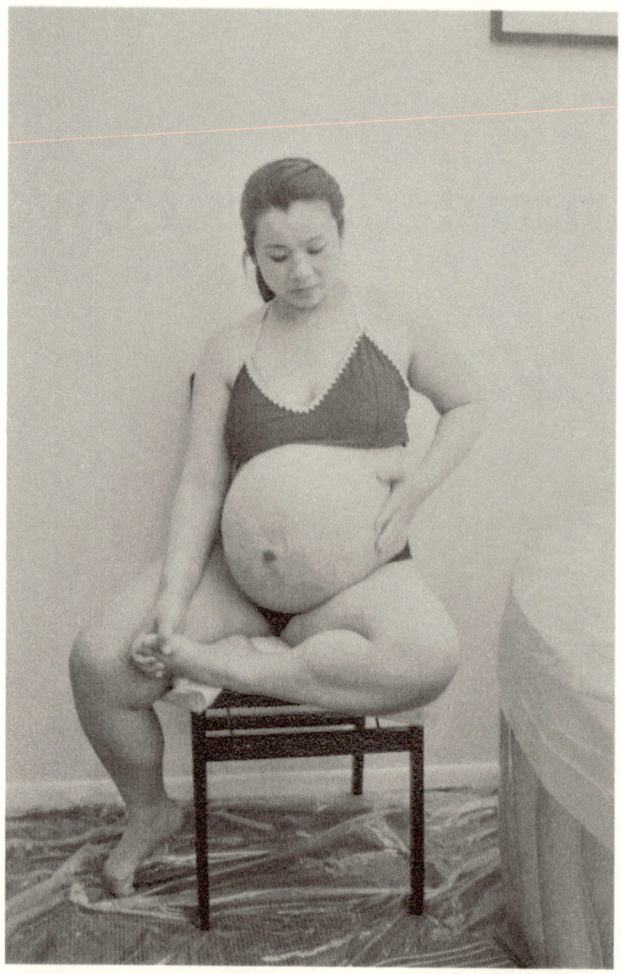

My unassisted birth journey began with my first child. At the age of 22, I found out I was pregnant and I had no idea what to do. I went on Yelp looking for a provider to help me navigate this new and exciting unknown part of life. The first search result was a CNM (*Certified Nurse Midwife*) group. They had lots of good reviews so we thought we would give them a shot. The first "get to know you" meeting was great, and I liked what they had to say about their practice. I was intrigued by their emphasis on the woman being in charge of her birth experience. I guess up until then I hadn't really considered that as being how it should work, but that resonated with me.

As I got closer to birth, my husband and I went to a typical hospital birthing class to educate ourselves. At the time it was very informative, and it helped to solidify the path I wanted to take. I knew I wanted a natural birth for several reasons. First, with what we learned in the birthing class, I knew I did not want to experience the side effects of an epidural or any other pain medication.

Second, I'm a small person, and people tend to underestimate me a lot. As a result I can be a bit competitive, and I don't like being told I can't do something. I love rising to the challenge, beating all expectations, and sometimes even trying to do things that others say they can't. With so many women these days shrinking at the thought of natural birth, it almost begged the challenge.

Third, and this is with some influence from my husband and a little bit of a tie-in to the second reason, natural births have been a defining part of womanhood since time began. It's our birthright to experience it, and so the thought of having a natural birth gave me a sense of connection to all the women who came before me; of being part of a fraternity of amazing, capable women. And I also took comfort in the idea that "If they can do it, I can do it too." My CNM was also helpful in encouraging me that I could go all natural if that's what I wanted.

December 24, rolled around and my water broke. It was go-time. I called the CNM office and they gave me instructions on what to do. I downloaded a random birthing app to help me keep track of my contraction patterns. Several hours went by, and we decided to call the office back. I wasn't too uncomfortable, but as a first time mom I wasn't sure if it was time to go to the hospital. I didn't want to be like one of those moms who got sent home for not being ready.

We called the office several times, but no one answered. We then decided to call the hospital. They reached out to my CNM and it turns out that they forgot to roll over the phone. They had ended their day early because it was Christmas Eve. Thankfully they asked me to come into the hospital even though I wasn't at the '5-1-1' contraction rate.

While I was laboring at the hospital, I really started to feel like I wanted an epidural at 4cm, even though my goal was to have no intervention. The pain was too much, I barely could move, and I was progressing extremely slowly. My husband was supportive of whatever route I chose to take, but despite that he knew that I really wanted a natural birth and was thankfully extremely supportive in reminding me of what I wanted, and telling me that I was strong and I could do it. Up to this point I was mostly laying on the bed in a reclined position, so my husband encouraged me to stop doing that and use the laboring tub that they had at the hospital.

The laboring tub was awesome! The pain was now very manageable, and when I got out of the tub I had progressed very quickly compared to when I wasn't in the tub. Two hours in the tub took me from 4cm to 8cm vs the stuck at 4cm for 3 hours previous to that. Simply amazing! I was forever sold on using a tub after that. Unfortunately, the hospital did not allow women to give birth in the tub, so I eventually had to get out.

The CNM then asked me if I wanted any Fentanyl, I said no because, thanks to the tub, at 8cm I felt great! Not being in the tub, though, things slowed down a tad, so when I was at about a 9cm I was starting to doubt myself a bit and asked for Fentanyl and, thankfully, my CNM said it was too late. I basically had no choice but to endure to the end, which I was okay with.

At this point, everyone was cheering me on. The support was great. I did try a lot of different positions and stools and such, but settled on the standard back-laying for the final position because I didn't have the strength to hold myself in any others. Despite that, everything which came after was everything I could have hoped for: no tears, no hemorrhaging, no complications, husband helped catch the baby, delayed cord clamping, and skin to skin for about two hours with my beautiful 7lb 3oz baby girl. It was all-in-all a wonderful first time experience, but ever since I got a glimpse of a water birth, became my dream birth plan.

About five months after my first birth, I found out I was pregnant again. I had a friend who had a home birth, and she told me about her experience with it. It sounded so magical! Unfortunately, a home birth would cost more than we could afford despite our great insurance at the time. Also, my husband was anti-home birth. He liked the security of a hospital.

We decided to go with the same CNM group and hospital since I loved the experience I had with my first. This time around we did not go to any birth class because we felt like we knew everything about birth, having experienced it once already. Plus, it hadn't been too long since I had given birth (14 months!). Little did I know, it was going to be a whole different experience.

When it was go time, I was at home with my 14-month-old daughter who wouldn't watch T.V. or leave me alone. After only two hours I was already experiencing heavy contractions. I told my husband he needed to come home ASAP because it wasn't going to wait until he got off work, but I had to wait another two hours for my husband to come home (because he had to wait for his on-call co-worker to relieve him) and for my sister-in-law to come watch our daughter. When I got to the hospital, I struggled to relax and feel calm due to the high stress I was experiencing at home. Upon arrival, they said I was already at 10cm. This was after just 4.5 hours or so.

I couldn't use their birthing tub because I was already at 10cm, which was too close for them to allow me in. Since they don't allow birthing in the tub, they said I would at best get to be in it for about five minutes because tubs are magical and anything beyond that would be sure to result in a birth in the tub. I didn't want to get in then get out, so instead,

I used their shower. It was very relaxing, but I couldn't stay there for very long.

I was only at the hospital for 1.5 hours before the birth, so it was only 6 hours from start to finish, making it literally half the time of my first birth. Pushing was much more difficult this time around. I couldn't move as much because when I did the baby's heart rate would drop into the 80's, which no one in the room liked. After I got the head out they said that he had shoulder dystocia (stuck shoulders) and was starting to get a little blue, so while shoving my legs upwards as hard as they could to open my pelvis as much as possible, with another nurse simultaneously pressing down right above my pubic bone to help dislodge the shoulders, they gave him a bit of a yank to get him out.

Due to that 'complication,' and him "turning blue," we were not able to do delay cord clamping or immediate skin to skin. With how fast everything was going, with the agonizing waiting for my husband to take me to the hospital, with not getting to use the tub that I had been looking forward to for hours, with everyone bustling around me due to arriving at 10cm, and one thing after another while laboring, this was a very stressful birth. On the bright side, I again received no interventions and no tears with the back-labor of my whopping 9lb 2oz baby boy. Though I wish I had been more prepared like I was with my first.

18 months after my second birth, I found out we were pregnant with our 3rd. This time we were not in sunny California anymore. We were in a state that is well known for families with lots of kids—Utah. With my third, we were on Medicaid, so birth and prenatal care was free. This time around I pushed hard towards home birth or birth center. I had two natural births with no complications, so I was an ideal candidate. I knew a home birth or birth center would be best for me, especially since I was considered low risk. I wanted to relieve the experience I had with my first: I wanted to labor in a birthing tub.

U of U was the only hospital I knew of that allowed moms to labor and deliver in a birthing tub, but it was 45 minutes away. Not knowing how fast baby would come and with two little kids and no family or close friends nearby, we decided to pass on U of U. I then began my research of all the birthing centers and midwives nearby. I did tons of research as to why a home birth was better for me. I would always share my findings with my husband hoping he would change his mind. Miraculously my husband came around and agreed with all the information I found. He became anti-hospital for low-risk patients! I was getting closer to my dream birth!

We looked into a midwife or birth center, but we really couldn't afford it. At the same time, I wanted my kids to be at my birth and having two toddlers at a birth center doesn't quite work. We were still new to Utah, with no close friends and with our families in a different state and unable to fly over to help us, and I just didn't like the idea of having a stranger watching our kids without us present.

Financially, we really could not afford a homebirth midwife either. Then one day my husband brought up the idea of going unassisted. Yup! The person who was super pro-hospital birth suggested going unassisted! I nervously jumped on board. If that was what it would take to get my dream birth, then unassisted it would be!

We educated ourselves on all the what-ifs and what to do in every situation. This time around we decided to take the Hypnobabies birthing class to better prepare ourselves. After that class, I couldn't believe all the information I did not know about birth! I thought I had known everything about birth. We had most of my prenatal care with another CNM we found at a local hospital to make sure everything was okay but to avoid any negativity we never told them we were planning an unassisted.

When it was almost go-time, we had decorated our spare room into a beautiful birthing room with beautiful string lights, lanterns, and words of affirmations. It felt very homey and peaceful.

Starting at 37 weeks, I was seeing my hospital midwife weekly and receiving an NST. She was great and flexible with me throughout my prenatal care. When I was at "41 weeks" and not seeing any signs of action starting, my husband was even able to convince her that the expected due date was not accurate, and she moved it back a week. However, then she had to go on vacation and one of the other CNMs in the office, we'll call her CNM-B, was going to be the next one to see me. My CNM warned me that CNM-B didn't like mothers going past 39 weeks and that she may give us a hard time, but also started me on weekly ultrasounds to monitor the placenta to help prevent some of that. It worked—or so we thought.

At the next appointment, which was at my new 41-week mark, CNM-B was nice. She said everything looked great on the last two ultrasounds ("the placenta doesn't look old like we would expect, it looks younger, so that's great"), and that the NST looked perfect, even showing it to my husband and pointing out everything that showed it was great with nothing to worry about. This was on Monday. Everything was fine.

That Friday (42 weeks) I had an NST again. They had me hooked to the NST machine for about 3x the normal length because all of a sudden "baby was no longer fine." During the first round of the NST, she reviewed it and said my numbers were lower than the results from the beginning of the week. CNM-B claimed that the placenta was aging and the fetus was under distress, based on the NST, since there was not enough variation in the heart beat and that it was in a range that was too low. I had my husband and kids with me, but they were in the car waiting.

I was literally in tears because she claimed that I needed to be induced, and I've never been induced before. I knew that one intervention can lead to another. I had no complications or interventions with my other two births. I wondered, "Why would it be different with my third?"

This was my healthiest pregnancy. I ate more cleanly compared to my previous two pregnancies, and I had worked out a ton. I did lots of squats and weighted workouts at least twice a week until I was about 40 weeks. I wanted what was best for baby and me, but I was so confused.

CNM-B kept on saying "The hospital is ready for you. Baby isn't doing well." I was an emotional mess. I know that baby comes when baby is ready, and there's no need to induce if it isn't a true emergency. I had no idea what to do, I was really torn. I had to call my husband to come in and talk to her. My husband was just as confused as I was, but for a different reason.

He has a near-photographic memory. He said Monday's and Friday's NST were nearly identical. He even asked CNM-B why the line she was pointing to was "Bad today when it was perfect on Monday." She didn't really have an answer. He was livid with the situation and the stress they were causing me. They even had the OB-GYN that the CNMs work under come and speak with us. He was less worried than CNM-B was but said since we were over 38 weeks he would induce anyway "just because.

After he left it took us over two hours in the NST chair to discuss our battle plan. I took pictures of as much of my NST tape as I could, and my husband told them, "My wife is very stressed and being induced would be counterproductive because the body's natural response to stress is to stop labor. We will let you know what we decide tomorrow, an extra day shouldn't hurt, and we don't have anything ready. No babysitter, hospital bag, etc."

They seemed fine with the idea of us getting things in order so the birth could be less stressful. We headed home with no intention of going to the hospital the next day (Saturday). My regular CNM was due home on Sunday, and there was no way we were going to have CNM-B be the one to oversee the birth.

When we got home, we googled "How to read an NST." We found the training manual from the manufacturer of the NST machine. We learned that not only is it normal for the numbers to drop as the fetus ages, and that our NST was in the exact perfect range for a healthy baby at our gestational age, but we also learned what the distress CNM-B claimed the baby was experiencing actually looks like on an NST tape. I'll give you a hint: NOTHING like my tape at all. Not even close! It didn't look anything like any of the issues that an NST is able to reflect. It did, however, look exactly like a sleeping baby, which is what we had been told at the Monday appointment. Either CNM-B was lying to try and scare me into doing things her way, or she had no clue what she was talking about when it came to NSTs: either was completely unacceptable.

We then ignored all contact with them because they were stressing me out. My husband kept telling me baby was okay and healthy. I, obviously, was pulled in two directions. I wanted baby to be healthy. I was fine with induction as long as it was medically necessary, but he kept reassuring me that everything was okay and homebirth was the route to take.

He grounded me and helped me attain my dream birth.

Monday came and it was go-time. 3:30 a.m. contractions started to appear. I could not sleep. My husband decided to stay up with me to keep me company. We didn't have any major action through the morning, so we still went out to run errands. By about noon things started to get more serious, so we headed home. Birthing pool was filled up with warm water, snacks on hand, dim lights, and birthing playlist on repeat. This was it.

With every contraction, my husband squeezed my hips, provided me with cool compress, and encouraged me through the whole process, even during my doubts. Hours went by and so did the contractions. Finding a comfortable position was a challenge. I moved back and forth from the birthing pool to the couch throughout the day. I was grateful the kids were happily watching TV and popping their heads in and out of the birthing room.

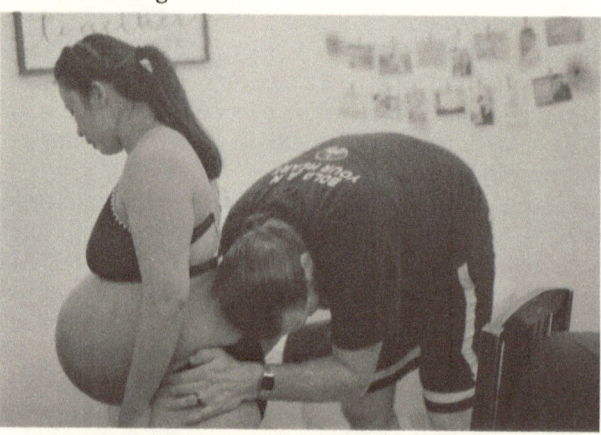

It was getting late, around 8 p.m., and still nothing. I knew that the third kid was normally a wild card in terms of birth, but I had expected a quick labor. We had a neighbor we had gotten to know since we got pregnant that we had as an on-call sitter. My husband called her and she was happy to put the kids down for the night. To my surprise, my kids were okay with someone putting them down other than us (it was the first time that had ever been tried).

My water did not pop until around 10:00 p.m. I was filled with joy knowing that there was no meconium in the sac. I couldn't handle being in the pool any longer, so I moved to the ottoman where I was on my hands and knees hanging off the ottoman with every contraction.

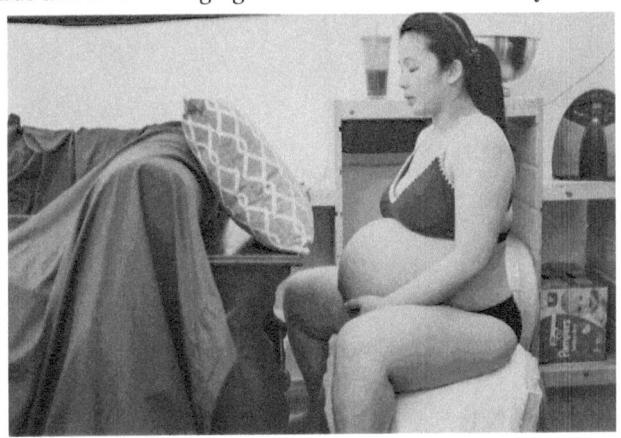

By this time I had been awake for almost 24 hours. I was so exhausted! Between every contraction I would rest my eyes and head. It was almost 12 a.m., and I had to get the baby out. I wanted to have an Earth Day baby, and I was running out of time. I was confused as to why baby wouldn't come out. I was in the most optimal birthing position.

With lots of heavy, strong pushes, baby started crowning. More strong pushes, and we had the head totally out! But as hard as I tried, I couldn't get any more of the baby out. Having experienced this before with baby #2, my husband knew what was happening.

This time it was a true shoulder dystocia. I was in an optimal birthing position and environment and he truly was stuck.

While I was pushing, my husband saw that baby's head was turning blue from lack of oxygen.

My husband quickly took action, told me what position to get into over the edge of the ottoman, and guided him out with a firm, gentle tug. And with that, at 42 weeks and 3 days, at 11:56 p.m., after 22 hours of labor, I gave birth to a healthy 10lbs 3.2oz baby!

My husband had coached, reassured, supported, cheered me on, and now had delivered my baby, and baby came out perfect.

There was nothing wrong with him; CNM-B had been totally wrong about baby being in danger. And again, I had no tears. I did, however, bleed longer than we knew I should, and my placenta wasn't coming out, so we made a quick call and had a stress-free postpartum transfer to a hospital (not the one the CNM I had been seeing worked at).

This was one place where our preparation really helped. We had read everything from our Hypnobabies course book, read through emergency situations and procedures, and knew exactly what to "worry" about, and what not to.

Turned out I had an undiagnosed Placenta Acreta, which isn't always noticeable during prenatal care. But again, because we were prepared, the whole transfer was calm, collected, and stress-free.

It felt really good that we stuck with our instincts. It was a very empowering experience!

I know that if I had delivered at the hospital I would have had "failure to progress" and had some kind of intervention foisted upon me. I wasn't failing to progress; I just had a big baby, especially for my size (you see, I'm only 4'11).

I also know that without the birthing pool and the low-stress environment it wouldn't have ever happened. It may have been my longest labor (22 hours vs 12 & 6), and my biggest baby (10.3lbs vs 9.2 & 7.3), but we did it on our own, on my terms, exactly the way I wanted it. Even though the baby was not born in the water, it was still a dream come true!

The Wild Pregnancy and Freebirth of Phoenix

By Hannah

TWO WEEKS BEFORE PHOENIX came earthside, my fiancé, Bill, tested positive for COVID. I was around 37 weeks pregnant and knew that if my baby decided to come a little early that my birth plan was not going to be what I had originally planned.

Bill had to quarantine for 10 days, and because I tested negative, I had to quarantine for an extra 14 days. I originally planned to have my photographer friend take pictures, and my mom was going to take our kids because my 3-year-old is a wild child.

I went into labor at 39 weeks and 5 days.

On the early morning of March 7th, I kept getting woken up by very light but noticeable contractions. I was still sleeping through them but feeling that they were there. When I got up for the day, I was still having consistent contractions. Because they were light and not getting stronger, I convinced myself that it was prodromal labor. I went about my day as normal, tending to my older two boys and keeping the house clean.

I started preparing my birth supplies that were in a box I kept under the crib and really tidying up the house. That should've been a sign for me that I was in fact in labor. But it wasn't, I was still convinced it was prodromal and would go away.

Around 3 p.m. my contractions started getting stronger, so I started timing them. They were 1-2 minutes apart and lasting for about 40 seconds. After going to the bathroom and seeing my mucus plug with bloody show, I knew this had to be labor. I then told Bill that I thought it was the real deal.

He called his parents and asked if they'd be willing to take their chances with us just getting over COVID and pick up our older boys. They were! But they lived an hour and a half away. I went upstairs to get into laborland, and Bill kept the boys occupied downstairs.

I knew I wanted to give birth in our bedroom, so I turned on my birth playlist and bounced on my birth ball in our room. I also knew I wanted to labor in the bathtub for a little to see if what they say about water being "nature's epidural" really was true, so when the contractions started getting stronger I hopped in there. My belly wasn't submerged even a little bit, so I still don't know how nice it feels to get in the water while in labor.

While in the tub, I knew transition was coming. Contractions were really ramping up in strength and length, but I was still getting one minute in between. I decided it was time to get out since I've seen myself give birth in our bedroom throughout my whole pregnancy. I got four chux pads out and laid them on the bed. I had 14, I don't know why I only grabbed four. I also didn't see myself giving birth in our bed, but that's where I wanted to be. Being in bed just gives me cozy vibes.

Contractions were really uncomfortable at this point. I was screaming like an animal to get through them. Bill turned on the GoPro and left me to be with the kids. On the bed, I kept moving from hands and knees to my back to hold on to the headboard through contractions. When Bill came in to check on me after a little while my water burst out all over our bed the whole way to the floor.

There was meconium in my waters, and I reassured Bill that although sometimes it could be a bad thing it's usually just a variation of normal, and we'd just have to check out the baby when he came. The next contraction my body just started pushing, and baby's head was coming out.

I tried to hold back and let him come into the world slowly, but my body took over and out came his head. When his head was about halfway out is when I felt the ring of fire for the first time, and everyone was right in telling me the contractions are way harder than the actual act of getting the baby out.

I waited for the next contraction and he was here! Bill got to catch our third son which was probably the best feeling in the world for him. As soon as Phoenix was born he immediately cried and went from purplish to pink/red quickly. It was the most amazing experience in our lives.

No nurses to take our baby away and poke and wipe down, just immediately placed on my chest with all of his birth goop greatness. No bright lights or loud noises other than his older brother jumping up and down in excitement. It was exactly how birth should be for every woman. I stressed hard with having COVID, not being able to have my photographer friend take pictures, and struggling with finding someone to take our older kids.

It really wasn't as bad as I thought it would be with our older boys here. Grandma and grandpa got there shortly after Phoenix arrived and took our two older boys to New Jersey for the night so that Bill and I could have at least a little bonding time with Phoenix.

It's funny because when I was first planning this birth, I wanted it to be a family birth with my fiancé and our children present, but over the course of the pregnancy I was talked into sending my kids away because they're "a lot," and then I chose to have a photographer.

I do believe the way it worked out with having COVID and having my birth plan kind of fall through was just the way it was supposed to be. After going through it, I couldn't imagine having anyone else here with us. I think I would've been really uncomfortable with the extra energy.

And so my birth ended up being exactly what I wanted in early pregnancy.

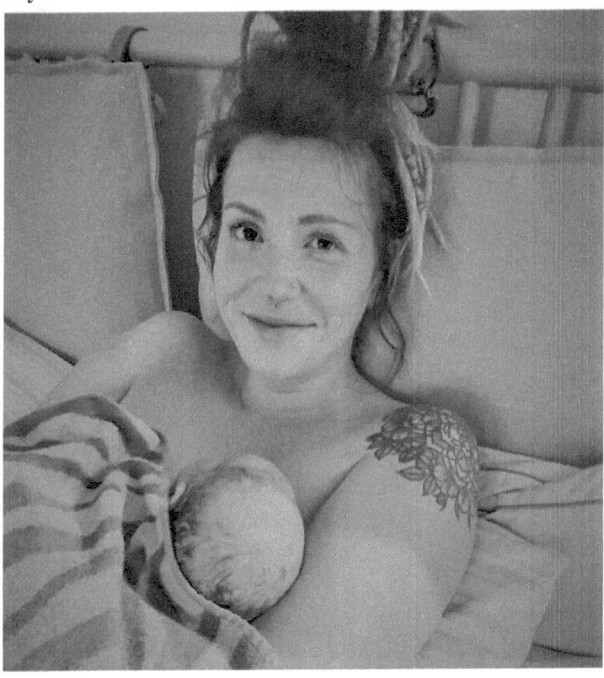

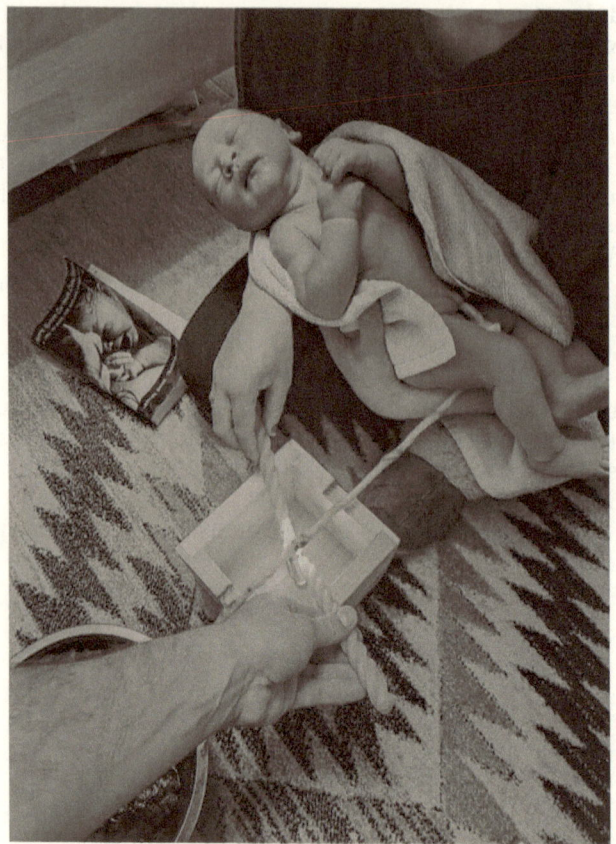

Cord burning

Freedom through Surrender

By Moriah Austin

SPRINGTIME BIRTHS—I CAN'T THINK of a more pleasant time of year to celebrate emerging new life. This was my eighth pregnancy. It had been exactly two years ago since my last, which had been a beautiful, long, calm, nearly painless labor and delivery at the hospital. I had reached euphoric levels in the last hours, experiencing God's love perfected at the height of contractions.

My first freebirth was different. While I had enjoyed the springtime those last couple of weeks, relaxing in the warm sun and scent of wild Carolina Roses in the breeze, the season did not factor much in the birth. Actually, there wasn't a whole lot that did factor in! Obadiah came quickly during the night. Almost by magic. Almost as if a stork had set him on our doorstep. At least it must have seemed to the little kids who went to bed that night and woke the next morning to meet their new baby brother.

I routinely slept the second part of the night on the couch where I could get a bit more comfortable. This early Thursday morning, I jolted awake from the pop! of my waters breaking. It felt like I had been kicked from the inside out. I grabbed a towel and went to tell my snoozing husband. I asked if we should start filling the birthing pool which had been leaning up against one wall in our bedroom for two weeks. He told me that we would wait for the contractions to become close and then fill it up. I agreed and went back out into the living room.

So I sat alone on a birthing ball while the contractions started. The ball had been wonderful throughout my last labor but it quickly became uncomfortable this time. I tried to draw on the goodness of God that I had experienced so clearly during my last labor. But I didn't have the same concentration. I didn't have the time. I knew the baby was coming fast. I went to my husband and told him it was progressing fast. He got busy filling up the pool. And I tried to focus on breathing, anticipating the relief of the hot pool water.

When I got into the water it was the best feeling. The pain was almost completely eliminated. The only concern was keeping the water hot enough. He was going back and forth to the kitchen. I relaxed in the dim room, the only light coming from the closet. I knew I transitioned when there were long intervals in between the contractions. This was when I started to get unsure. I've always been okay with laboring but the final pushing is what I'm afraid of. I thought I needed to find a better position and got up on my knees.

I tested a couple little pushes and suddenly my body was hit with the FER! Something so powerful, completely out of my control, like a miniature, yet mighty freight train crashing through my body, a guttural, primal utterance, and the baby's head was out. My husband remained calm and reassuring throughout, my rock.

I wish I had the presence of mind of some women who catch their own babies. But I go to a different place in my head, eyes closed, I feel totally out of it. The next contraction I cocked my left leg up and pushed one more time. The baby dipped into the water just for a second, my husband later told me. I heard him say, "Hello, Obadiah" and immediately I turned around to see the warm slippery perfect body. He started squalling right away. He was covered in thick vernix and I started trying to rub it all in. I was surprised to see a bluish mark near his mouth. But other than that, he looked just like his siblings.

My husband helped us out of the pool—no easy feat! We got into the bed, baby wrapped in a towel. I don't really remember if he nursed much at this point or not. I think we were just marveling at him; I was especially intrigued by the umbilical cord as it was the first time I had been up close and personal with one.

Everything was a new experience, and at the same time, I felt completely comfortable with it all, like an old pro. That is right up until I started to try to birth the placenta. I was unprepared for that part of birth. We had cut the cord after 20 minutes or so. We were not sure of specific times (I think labor was around 1 1/2 hours). And then I thought I should try to see if the placenta was ready to come out.

Dad took the baby into the living room and I took my bowl into the bathroom. To no avail. I tried the edge of the bed. Nothing. I finally asked for the baby back and just laid down on my side to nurse him. Then suddenly a contraction had me pushing and whoops! here it was. I barely caught it with a chucks pad and called for my husband to help. Little did I know how uncomfortable he was with this part. He said he examined it then disposed of it. I was saddened by this later because I really would have liked to have seen it for myself. Next time!

We moved to the living room where I tried to relax in a chair. The jitters hit and the cold flashes. I drank a lot and ate a bit. My bleeding was heavy and I felt like taking some shepherd's purse just for the peace of mind. I texted my mom and she reassured me that it usually looks like much more than it is. She was right. I woke my older girls up for school around 5 am. I turned the light on and said, "The baby's here." I got disbelief at first then exuberance! I let them stay home if they chose.

My in-laws and Mom came to visit around 7 and we woke the other kids up. This was one of my favorite parts of having a baby at home. Everything felt so natural, so normal, so just a part of life. There were no pokes and prods, no questions, no answering to anybody, no interruptions. It was absolutely peaceful. The house was in order (my older daughter had cleaned the night before while I took the kids to church). My husband had started the washing machine.

It was as if nothing had changed, yet here was this miracle wrapped in a towel. Perfectly knit together in my womb. No doctors, no ultrasounds, no strange hands touching me, no strange hands touching him. Just surrounded by love. And rest. And all the comforts of home.

Obadiah Charles means "servant of God" and "free man," which has many layers of meaning for me. On the top layer is the fact that by giving up control over my family size, I experience more depth and character development than anything else I could have done in my life. It is one thing to say, "Yes, God, I trust you and I will follow you," and a whole other thing to say, "I will have as many babies as you choose to bless me with." All glory and honor and praise to our God. For it is in Him that we live, and move, and have our being.

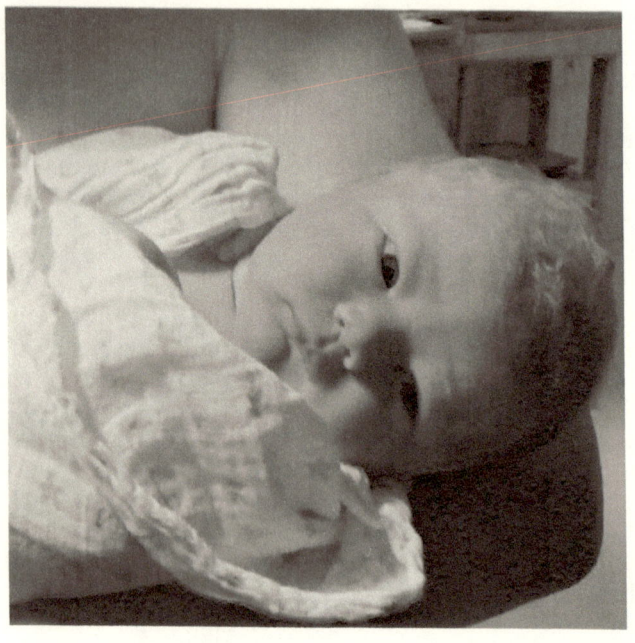

The Trampoline Freebirth Of Micah

By Taylor Bland

Photo credit Sara Hunter Photo LLC

For years I have had the privilege to bear witness to and support over 100 labor and births, the majority of them successfully occurring naturally. The most special to me tend to be the unassisted, untouched, primal births. Until I gave birth to baby Micah, I had never experienced that level of magic and power in my own mind, body, and soul. I was absolutely majested by it, and so honored to be accepted into that sacred space. And now I'm fascinated by it on a whole new level because I have transcended into that realm, thanks to my beautiful rainbow baby boy.

Here is my story.

I woke up around 5:30 a.m. on Feb 16th with cramping and lots of energy. A very peaceful feeling. Noah and Joshua could feel my vibrations and woke up in good moods as well several hours later. I had blueberry oatmeal for breakfast, went to Target to pick up some staple grocery items, got an iced coffee from Starbucks, and came back home.

Noah and Joshua spent most of the day outside. After a pumpkin soup lunch, I laid down for a few hours, rotating positions, feeling very sleepy but could not sleep. Around 4:30 p.m. I got a slight burst of energy and did dishes, swept, did some laundry, and then around 5:20 p.m., I felt overwhelmingly hot and suffocated in our house and went outside.

It was about 65 degrees outside and a lovely cool cloudy day, as the sun began to set. Noah was watching a movie and Joshua was working on his car, I went to rock in the hammock, feeling light surges every so often that would bring nausea, sweating, and mid-to-lower back pain. Baby movements were wonderful and frequent, he shifted several times from LOA, ROA, and OA, kicking me lots in between, but I enjoyed feeling him.

The surges went away for a bit after sunset, but I could not stomach dinner except a couple of bites, and my pelvis was in quite a bit of pain, more than usual. I knew labor was coming that night or the next day! I cleaned the house some more obsessively until Noah went to sleep, then laid down, having occasionally strong cramps that were sporadic but deep.

Around 2 a.m. on Feb 17th I could not sit or lay down any longer and decided to take a nice shower to see what would happen with them. They did not slow, but instead slightly intensified after the shower. I paced around the house and easily breathed and squatted through them for the first hour. I put on delta waves and felt very euphoric.

It wasn't until about 3:33 a.m. I remember looking at the clock, enjoying the fact that it was 3:33 and thinking wow these are pretty uncomfortable and seem to be coming non-stop. This was also the time that the song on my birth playlist "Hear You Me" came on and it made me feel very warm and relaxed knowing my spirit baby Elian was with me. I did not see or feel any other spirits the entire time except his though I did hear words of encouragement that my friends had spoken at my mother blessing and otherwise! It was so helpful hearing their kind words in my mind to keep me on track, like I was wrapped in their love and not alone, even though I was physically alone!

I began to strongly need to be COLD but did not want to go outside even though it was in the 50s and would have cooled me down, because of the neighbors. I didn't want anyone to look at me or talk to me, not even something positive, I desired to be completely alone, in total darkness, naked, and accomplish this birth. I stuck my head in the freezer and would lay it down on the freezer door during contractions while I rocked and tip-toe swayed and stomped my feet to get through the pressure.

I found it very cathartic to watch the clock as I had contractions, noticing that most of them were two minutes apart and a minute long. I don't know why this was relieving to me, perhaps because it felt like progress. I was also utilizing the rebozo to press into my butt and give myself counter pressure as baby descended.

Around 4:45 a.m., I thought it would be wise to get into my bathtub. Even though the water being hot/warm was nauseating, the water lifting my belly did bring some relief. However, I couldn't fully relax because my bathtub was too small. Noted—always have a birth tub on hand even if you strongly don't desire a water birth. I was desiring a soft birth tub to lay down in so bad but ultimately glad I got to experience the land birth I desired initially. I lasted about 10 minutes in the tub.

Throughout this process, my bowels kept clearing, and I was able to pee very easily which was so nice. I don't know why that was a concern of mine prior to labor that I wouldn't be able to do either but it didn't end up being an issue. However, I HATED the toilet in labor, the contractions on it were awful and my bathroom is not labor-friendly, I have found.

I went back to my freezer/clock station and continued my stomping and rocking and during some contractions, I felt I could have ripped the freezer door off its hinges. To pull on something sturdy felt so good. Low soft growls were my only vocalization. I felt like a lioness or a bear in labor, pacing, growling, getting close to the ground with my contractions.

At this point, it was coming up on 5:15 a.m. I was in full distress mode because my water hadn't broken and I thought I still had hours to go. I had never had a labor with my water intact. I was not sure how I could possibly continue on like this for even another hour. I just wanted to lay down and get a quick nap and then felt I'd be okay to continue but there was no laying down or sitting down possible!

That was when my next contraction came with a gentle bearing down, and I was so thrilled. I knew either my water was about to break and I would get some relief or baby was coming out en caul. I called my birth photographer (my phone says I called her at 5:28) hoping she would make it as baby was crowning, thinking I still had another half-hour plus to go probably. I was very wrong! Only five involuntary pushes and he shot out. Right before he crowned I ran from my standing freezer station to our small in-home trampoline, knowing I didn't have the strength to catch him and that even if I called for Joshua he wouldn't have made it in the few seconds I had to make a decision.

I squatted on the trampoline and braced myself on the wall and felt my pelvis completely expand. The sensation was unbearable yet oddly comforting. I felt a strong burn as his head emerged, my water broke with it, not stopping to restitute at all, just a steady "here I come!" and his body was born in the same push. FER (*fetal ejection reflex*) is powerful as hell.

I let out my one and only deep primal scream, and he was born into the trampoline covered in a soft wool blanket. Joshua woke to my scream and baby cries, and I asked for the time quickly, 5:42 a.m.

I picked him up and was shaking so badly, all I could say was "Oh my god, hi!" over and over again. It was hard to breathe and collect myself, so surreal that it just occurred. He had zero crowning, molding, any discoloration, or anything, he was absolutely perfect. Thank you to my chiropractor for obviously having him in the perfect position so he came out so effortlessly. I checked right away to see if the sneak peek test had accurately depicted a baby boy, and he in fact has a penis! And it's staying whole #YourWholeBaby, thank you very much!

Joshua cried, rubbed my back, stared at baby and back at me, and told me I was so brave and beautiful, that I made a healthy big boy, got my goal and I should be proud. That this was MY birth and I didn't need anyone and hoped I felt powerful. He tried to get Noah to come out but Noah wasn't ready to wake up. Joshua got me water, a blanket for baby, and went to lay back down.

Baby pooped all over me and himself SEVERAL times, luckily I had warm washcloths waiting for me in the crockpot to clean us up.

My birth photographer entered about 15 minutes after birth, took lots of pics of the first latch, baby, and me processing trying to get the placenta out. The placenta took about an hour, maybe slightly over. It was highly irritating and I wanted it out super bad, I couldn't even enjoy holding my baby fully because it was so obnoxiously sore and crampy, and I lost quite a bit of blood. I had never experienced an unmanaged third stage before.

Photo credit Sara Hunter Photo LLC

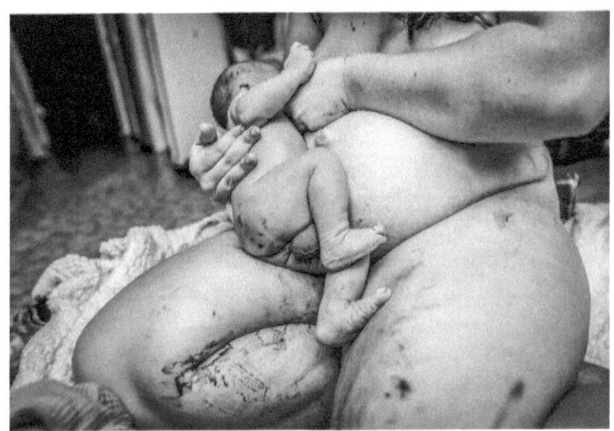
Photo credit Sara Hunter Photo LLC

Photo credit Sara Hunter Photo LLC

I gave myself very gentle cord traction and massaged my belly to work it out as quickly as it could safely come.

When it came out, I felt so much relief but was exhausted and asked my photographer to come back at a later time when I was rested to do the other postpartum photos I wanted like baby weighing and family photos. She agreed, and we said goodbye!

I got to bed, carrying my baby and placenta bowl, and Joshua made me soup, tea, and more upon my request to help rejuvenate me. We rested, then Noah woke up to snuggle and meet his brother, then Joshua and Noah burned the cord together and we went back to sleep.

Many say during their births they don't recall a lot and went off to a different realm; I did not experience this. I felt very present and conscious the entire time and aware of my every move, feeling fairly rational and connected to my surroundings. I remember it all very well as I write this and can play it back in my mind easily. This was my first natural birth, home birth, and unassisted birth all in one.

It was very different from my previous experiences, but I have to say I don't blame anyone for not wanting to go natural. I feel it takes a lot of self-control, trust, mental preparation, and strength. It's a brutal but beautiful process. I feel it paved the best way for my second son's health and brought me peace as a woman to heal from my birth trauma and know that I can give birth, physiologically.

If there was one thing I could change I would have been recording myself throughout the process. I was really loving my birth playlist and didn't think to get my laptop or camera or anything to record, but I wish I could see myself as he was born. I also would have definitely desired a postpartum doula/Birthkeeper to help clean up, and do the newborn evaluation stuff for me so that could have been captured on photo. It was such a chill, independent experience but sometimes you just desire that feminine energy and understanding after from someone you trust, and I would have really loved that even if just for an hour.

Micah is such a little blessing, coming in hot at 7lbs 3oz (I for sure thought he was bigger!) and 15-inch head. Now that's what was big—I felt that! At 42 weeks gestation.

Stay tuned for articles on what I did with my placenta, tips for cord burning, how Joshua nourished me postpartum, advice for heavy blood loss like mine, and more that stemmed from this amazing freebirth experience!

Bringing Tehani Earthside

By Tiaja Trice

At 12 a.m. on March 22, 2021, I started to experience contractions that were about 30 minutes apart. I chose to continue resting because I knew today would be the day. The contractions were already painful, and I was woken out of my sleep every time I had a contraction. I woke up my husband to let him know of my contractions, and he started prepping our bedroom as I was going to labor there.

Around 1:30 a.m., I asked my husband to do a cervical check. I was about 2cm dilated. The contractions grew stronger and started to become more frequent, coming every 20 minutes. I slept for a few hours as my body started to grow more and more tired from the contractions

I woke back up around 11 a.m. with more consistent contractions. They were 10 minutes apart and lasting a minute long. I had my 40-week ultrasound scheduled for 1 p.m., so my husband and I got our two sons dressed and heading out the door for the appointment. I chose to sit and bounce on the pregnancy ball.

After about 10 minutes of being on the ball, I suddenly had the feeling of pressure in my bottom, and my water broke! I knew at that moment I was not going to make it to my ultrasound appointment. I contacted my doula to let her know that my water had broken and my contractions were more frequent, averaging about five minutes apart for one minute long. She grabbed her things and headed my way.

I knew I would labor fast, as this was the third baby, her head being very low the last few prenatal appointments and I was past 40 weeks.

Our family was also contacted. The contractions grew stronger and stronger.

While I labored, my husband was the BEST doula ever. It was like he knew what to do without saying anything. He was PERFECT! oxytocin was definitely being released. I lost my mucus plug around 2:15 p.m., and then I entered my transition phase of labor. FER (*fetal ejection reflex*) started to kick in as I allowed my body to push for me. This caused her to move further down into the canal, and I felt her crowning. I changed positions to get more comfortable because she would be here any minute.

I gave one big push and her head was out. I inhaled, and she was birthed at 4:40 p.m. My doula and husband moved me and baby to the room so I could start immediate skin to skin and allow the placenta to be birthed. I latched my daughter on, which kicked in some REALLY intense contractions. I birthed the placenta 45 minutes after baby. Everything was intact and looked perfect. We then clamped and cut the umbilical cord. I continued to breastfeed and rest with baby while my husband got dinner ready for us.

Tehani Kobey Trice
March 22, 2021
7lbs 8oz
19 1/2in

Freebirth of Mazikeen Riley

By Kelly S.

I WOKE UP AROUND 4 a.m. to use the bathroom. I felt a little crampy but had been having contractions on and off for weeks so I didn't pay much attention to it. After using the bathroom, I noticed some bloody show when I wiped. Knowing that my labors have always been fast, I decided to wake my husband up to let him know.

We had been planning a water birth, so we decided to start filling the bathtub. Contractions still just felt like cramps at this point so we put on some music. I got in the tub and checked my cervix. I was about 6cm and could feel baby's head. Knowing it wouldn't be long, we just hung out together talking and singing while I relaxed in the warm water.

Around 5 a.m. our 2-year-old, Freyja, woke up and came to check on us. Contractions were getting a bit stronger. I never timed them but could tell they were getting closer together as well. Freyja sat next to the bathtub and rubbed my arm as I breathed through the contractions. She kept saying "You okay, mama?"

Once I assured her I was okay, she decided to go watch tv. My husband took her place next to the bathtub. I had a few strong contractions that I need my husband to do counter pressure on my lower back. After that my body started pushing with contractions. I got up on my knees while pushing and at 6:08 a.m. my water broke followed immediately by baby's head being out at 6:09 a.m.

I took a slight pause and rubbed her head while I waited for the next urge to push. At 6:10 a.m. the rest of her body slid out and Mazikeen was born. My husband handed me a towel to put over her to keep her warm, and I sat back against the tub with her in my arms.

After a few minutes, I decided I wanted out of the tub. As I stood I could feel the placenta coming out. My husband handed me a bowl. I kneeled over the bowl and pushed the placenta out into it. My husband helped Mazikeen and me out of the tub and helped us move to the futon we had set up right outside the bathroom in our bedroom.

We relaxed for a bit as we waited for the older kids to wake up for school. They had slept through the entire labor and birth. We called my mom to let her know that we had the baby, and she came right over.

The older kids woke up around 7 a.m. and got to meet their little sister before getting on the bus to go to school. Around 7:15 a.m. we decided to separate the baby from the placenta. I placed the clamps and let my mom cut the cord. Mazikeen and I laid down, snuggled, and relaxed next to my husband on the futon the rest of the day.

Mazikeen Riley
March 8th, 2021
41 weeks + 4 days
7lbs 3oz 18in

The Ecstatic Unassisted Birth of Rya

By Britney

I FELT MYSELF START to have contractions on May 14th (my birthday, lol). They increased in number and intensity throughout the day and into the night. I tried to sleep as much as I could, although occasionally during the night I had to get up and move around because it felt relieving to do so (for me personally). By the time it was like 9 a.m., I couldn't sleep much anymore and was walking around quite a bit and doing a lot of supported squats (holding onto countertops, my man, etc. for support).

Once it was around noon, I felt much too tired to keep moving around, so at that point, I knew I needed to rest more. I lay on my sides (switching sides between contractions) and got into a verrryy deep dream-like state but still conscious of the room to a certain extent.

I felt her head start to come down into my vagina, and it felt a lot like a heavy ball slowly moving down. At that point, I felt inside my vagina and got some extremely sticky mucus on my hand when I touched her head (*this was the mucus plug*). The mucus had like strings of blood in it, so I went to the bathroom and peed. I felt like that really sped things up because I felt some extremely powerful contractions come while sitting on the toilet.

I went to lay down and relax again, and after only about 30 minutes I could feel her head coming down very close to the opening of my vagina, and then it started to burn really really bad (*this sensation is commonly known as the ring of fire*).

It felt like the opening of my vagina exploded. I reached down to touch it, and it was all perfectly fine! There were no rips or even any microtears whatsoever. I was feeling her head right there at the opening, and it was amazing. The most incredible thing I have ever felt in my hand. The amount of energy and life I could feel running through her head was totally otherwordly and SURREAL.

I did my best to relax while I waited for the next contraction. Once the next one got there, I tried to kind of hold it and ease the baby out.

During the next one, I gave a little push and kinda rolled onto my back from my side, but not all the way flat on my back. Her head came out, and then I was like "Okay, one more contraction and little push, and her body will be out!" And on that one, when I gave just a little push, she flew out of my vagina the rest of the way and landed on my bed about three feet away from my vagina!

I lifted up my blanket and said "Baby!" to Mat, and he got up and ran to the bathroom because he thought there was something wrong because she was blue. I had seen a video of what to do when the baby hasn't yet taken a breath after being born, so I knew what to do. All that was needed was for me to pinch the cord for just a second and immediately release it, and she took a breath and cried a little bit.

I picked her up and held her in front of my face and softly said: "Hellooo, welcome to the world!" She just stared at me with so much love and wonder. Then I held her on my chest. She had her face on my breast, and I tried to feed her a little bit. She was so sweet from the moment she was born. It was such a beautiful and life-changing experience. I am so eternally grateful to have had it with her.

Britney is an unassisted birth Keeper and Menstrual Maven serving women worldwide virtually and in person.

You can contact her on IG: @britnybirthkeeper
Facebook as Britny Birthkeeper
or her website: https://linktr.ee/Birthanewearth

Unwavering Strength

By Karlee Smrstick

TRIGGER WARNING: KARLEE AND Merryn's story is one of incredible power. She starts out with a medical history at higher risk than most mothers, chooses home birth, chooses freebirth, transfers to the hospital, then ultimately gets the freebirth she always knew she needed to have.

For those extra sensitive to medical terminology and hospital staff coercion, this story may have a stronger impact than others.

As I lay here, looking at our beautiful daughter, I can't help but reflect on our crazy journey into and throughout pregnancy and the labor and delivery process. I want to share our experiences, not just to shed light on everything I stand for, but to document for Merryn.

I have PolyCystic Ovarian Syndrome (PCOS). Which is a hormonal disorder that affects menstrual regularity/flow, affects weight fluctuations and hair growth, causes infertility, depression and cysts on ovaries, among other symptoms and signs. I was diagnosed at the age of 19 years old.

I've been told by many medical experts since my diagnosis that I would not likely ever carry a child full term, and if I ever get to be so lucky, I would have to deliver via cesarean section. I used to believe that. I used to doubt my body and hate all that my body was.

Fast forward to 2016-2017. Brandon and I bought our home in October of 2016. We started to talk about a family and slowly worked towards what steps we would need to take to make it there. Neither of us had high hopes in conceiving. We spoke about adoption, fostering, etc. All while slowly trying for our own little miracle without much success and facing devastating loss.

In February of 2018, I went in to see my doctor. I worked HARD for months on diet and exercise. I went to the gym daily, changed my eating habits and did all I could to get down to a perfect BMI. I met my goal late spring/early summer of 2018. I was SO proud and excited. I felt confident and ready.

Brandon and I continued our efforts to conceive and raise a child. So many months in a row with negative pregnancy tests, irregular periods, not an ovulation in sight. I was feeling defeated. I settled into my negative headspace. I went back to the doctor. She ended up prescribing me with three rounds of Clomiphene (Clomid).

I took the first dose, nothing. Then dosed with Progesterone to start a period, another round of Clomid. Nothing. Again. Frustrated and angry with my body, I decided to give up. I still had one more round of the medication and decided to just leave it in the medicine cabinet and forget about it. Which is precisely what I did.

My doctor, whom I'd been seeing since age 19, ended up retiring. I decided to start on with another practice and get back on track. July of 2019, I began my care with a new women's health clinic. I had a well-woman check-up on July 1st of 2019. I explained my situation and told the doctor that I decided to take my final dose of Clomid during my last period. I had pretty low expectations but I tracked my ovulation the very best that I could and made sure to time everything correctly.

In the middle of July 2019, Brandon and I hit up Street Care Takeover every year at Bandimere in Colorado. Before we left on our trip, I researched all I could about how to successfully manage implantation and do all I can to ensure a successful conception. I did EVERYTHING that I could, yet still just knew that it didn't work. I ate green leafy vegetables, kept my feet super warm, drank tons of water, etc.

On July 22nd, 2019, I took the pregnancy test. It was 12 days post ovulation, (2-3 days before you should expect to test usually) I saw the faintest second pink line. I didn't believe it. I jumped on Brandon (who was still in bed that morning) and called my mom! I was in awe! On my lunch break, I stopped the grocery store and picked up several more tests.

EVERY. SINGLE. ONE. POSITIVE!! I called the doctor and they were unable to get me in until the middle of August for the first prenatal. In the meantime, I went into the walk-in clinic and had them blood test several days in a row so that I could rule out an ectopic pregnancy, false positives, etc. Each test came back with double+ HCG hormone numbers. It was official!!!

August came and we had our first prenatal and ultrasound. It was incredible to see this tiny, strawberry-sized jelly bean on the screen. Brandon and I were absolutely over the moon. Each month after came more appointments, and blood draws on the side. Never an issue in sight. Everything was progressing fantastically. Merryn was as healthy as an ox the entire pregnancy!

At my 25-week appointment, it was time to discuss birth control after delivery and the upcoming standard glucose test. After bringing me to the room, the first words out of the nurse's mouth were, "sooo let's talk sterilization!" I was so taken aback, I assumed she was talking about cleaning! I mean, I was 26 years old, at the time uncomplicatedly pregnant with my first baby, and I was pretty sure I wanted at least one more! Looonnngg story short, the clinic asked me several times if I was sure that I wanted to decline sterilization after delivery.

During the same visit, I was also told about the standard Glucose test. I told the doctor that I wouldn't be drinking the glucose drink and would be doing organic jelly beans or the equivalent in organic fruit juice, etc. The doctor proceeded to tell me that I did not have that option (which was a lie) and that the glucose drink mixture was simply corn syrup! (She was misinformed.)

After I explained that the ingredients in said drink have multiple ingredients, corn syrup being the least of the problem. Sodium Benzoate, a chemical compound known to affect reproduction capacity and cause fetal harm and a list of red and yellow dyes, as well as a flame retardant! All LISTED ingredients in the Glucose drink! No thanks!

The doctor began speaking to me as if I were a child and didn't have the capacity to understand the test. She gave the option of just testing my sugars 3-6 times per day through the remainder of pregnancy, which is not even how the original test works.

I left that appointment feeling frustrated and anxious. I called my doula and worked through it with her. She helped me to understand and empower myself. I was the one in charge of my and my daughter's care! It's my responsibility to make sure that it goes my way. After discussing it with Brandon that night we decided we would fire our OB doctor and hire a midwife. The next business day, I called the OB clinic and let them know that their services were no longer needed. I also called a midwife and set up an appointment to meet.

After going over my records, doing a physical exam on me, and discussing our birth plans with the midwife, she agreed to take on our care! We decided to move forward with home birth. I saw our midwife in our home about twice a month at first and then gradually increased to once weekly during the later weeks of pregnancy.\

Around week 34 of my pregnancy, my fundal height and weight fluctuated upwards a little quicker than expected. Our midwife was concerned about a condition called Polyhydramnios, which is excessive amniotic fluid surrounding the baby, or Large For Gestational Age baby (LGA).

She requested an ultrasound sound be done so we could gauge Merryn's fluid sacks and approximate size. Since she's my first baby, the midwife erred on the side of caution. She didn't want to continue with a home birth without being able to 100% know that we would be safe with the outcome. I appreciated that.

We had the ultrasound. Merryn had a perfect amniotic fluid index. She was measuring in the 95th percentile. The midwife decided after that appointment that she would be a candidate safe for a home birth if we could do one more scan in the following 2 weeks, to gauge Merryn's growth pattern and rule out the LGA diagnosis. Two weeks later, we had the scan. At that point, Merryn measured in the 63rd percentile. All systems were a go!

Because Merryn was measuring a bit bigger than most babies, my midwife did give us a time limit for delivery. Otherwise, she would need to transfer our care to a Family Practice for a hospital delivery. I was terrified! Our timeline was 40 weeks + 3 days, which seems practically impossible for a first-time mom and it definitely proved true for me!

We just continued to bake our little girl and work on natural ways to ready my body for labor. I ate 6-8 dates per day, drank 20-30 ounces of Red Raspberry Leaf Tea, walked, ate pineapple, did nipple stimulation, the whole nine yards!

During this time, and currently, there's a global pandemic happening. On March 20th, 2020, the city we live in ended up with the first case of COVID-19, and the number has been actively climbing ever since.

At this point, my midwife no longer felt it was safe or necessary to have me continue to work and risk myself or my daughter, as I work with dirty money all day. Policies were and continue to rapidly change throughout essential businesses and things are super hectic, with stress piled a mile high.

The day before our due date, March 27th, 2020, we had our last prenatal visit with our midwife. We attempted a membrane sweep but unfortunately, I wasn't dilated enough to have it be effective. At that point, I was feeling pretty down. I went home that day and worked and worked on as many natural induction techniques as I possibly could. My due date came and went. Aside from some intermittent Braxton Hicks contractions, I felt no different. Nothing was going to get Merryn out of the womb.

40+3 came around the corner and my midwife ended up needing to transfer my care to the Family Practice. I had a virtual visit with him over a zoom meeting webinar, due to the COVID crisis. He was a very nice man and was happy to allow me to be the "captain of my own ship!" I appreciated him in the fact that he knew that my views were extremely unconventional but also mega important to me and for my daughter's health, safety and well-being.

We called the hospital to check for their current policy on labor and delivery visitors. We were informed that I would only be allowed ONE support person for the duration of my stay. It was one of the most difficult decisions Brandon and I had to make for our daughter.

To give birth with our Doula as my support, as she is knowledgeable, experienced and a wealth of support and help, especially during a time like this when the hospital is on high alert and can easily not follow the birth plan with no recourse. And take that experience away from my husband, where he wouldn't be able to see his new daughter for up to days! I couldn't bear to do that.

Every living piece of me screamed that I could NOT deliver in the hospital! I needed my husband to be with me and I needed my Doula for support. I discussed it with Brandon and my Doula.

Brandon had a really hard time coming to terms with attempting an unassisted birth but he understood my fears and took into consideration the whole picture. I couldn't be more grateful to him for his grace and allowing me to do what I felt was best. He didn't downplay my Mama Intuition and although he was absolutely horrified, he agreed that we would do it.

A few days later, I received a phone call about another midwife that was willing to look at my case and possibly take on our birth! We were ecstatic, such an answered prayer! After reviewing my records and visiting on the phone, the new midwife decided she would like to take us!

In our state, midwives are only legally allowed to assist in home delivery up to 42 weeks gestation, no exceptions. At that point, I was 41 weeks + 4 days pregnant so time was closing in on us and I still felt no signs of labor.

On Friday morning, April 10th, 2020, at 41 weeks + 6 days, the midwife sent me a text asking how I would feel about naturally inducing. I was huge, uncomfortable and desperate.

There was also a pretty gnarly storm headed our way in the next 24 hours to pass. The midwife and her assistant lived 2 hours away so they hit the road heading to our house.

In the meantime, I made a milkshake with castor oil, peanut butter, and chocolate ice cream. I called my mom and my Doula, both got here around 11:30 a.m. We decided to go for a walk and wait for the midwife to show.

Around 12:45 p.m., the midwife showed up. She gave me a couple different herbal tinctures to start labor and then left for a couple of hours to let them begin to work. She came back a few hours later and things were slowly moving along. We decided to do a membrane sweep and that really kicked it into high gear!

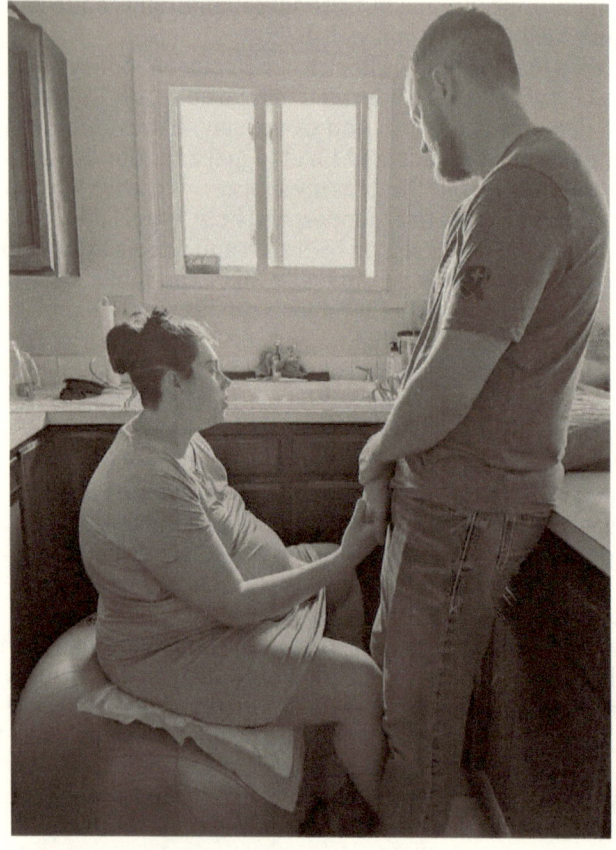

Contractions started getting more intense and coming regularly. Around 9:00 p.m., I went to the bathroom to urinate. I came back out to wash my hands, and as I was standing at the sink my water broke. Labor was really moving steadily at that point, and I was in quite a lot of pain. We got the birthing pool set up and started to ready everything for the next stage.

The midwife was very hands-off and would occasionally come over to me to check my temperature, blood pressure, pulse, and Merryn's heart rate. Everything seemed to be going well.

Since my water broke around 9 p.m. on Friday night, we were on a time crunch AGAIN! In our state, midwives can legally assist in the delivery for up to 24 hours after the rupture of the waters unless given the pushing stage has begun already. At 6 a.m., the midwife checked my cervix for dilation which at that point I was hovering between a 5 and a 6cm. I had been awake for about 22 hours and laboring for about 18-19 hours. I was absolutely exhausted.

Brandon and I decided to see if we could just lay down and try to get some rest between contractions. It wasn't easy, but we were able to snuggle in for a few minutes here and there while dealing with these intense surges of pain and sensation.

A couple hours had passed and we had to get up and move around. My Doula, mom and I went for a walk and I bounced on the yoga ball.

My midwife checked my cervix again around 10 a.m., and I was at a 6. She cautioned that if I didn't dilate soon that she would have to transfer me to the hospital because she wanted me to have a shot at a vaginal delivery and have time for Pitocin to kick in at the hospital. She was worried that I was teetering on the brink of exhaustion as I wasn't able to eat or drink anything the whole time I labored. Anything I took in, including just sips of water, would just come right back up during the next contraction. Again, terrified and feeling stalled out, I felt as if I couldn't take it anymore.

We did another round of the herbal tinctures, bounced on the ball some more, and went for more walks. During the last walk, I could barely take three steps without needing to stop. This was transition, and I had absolutely no idea. Around 2:00 or 3:00 p.m. my midwife came in and informed us that "my body just wasn't progressing."

She didn't think we were going to be able to have this baby at home and we needed to strongly think about heading to the hospital. She offered to check my cervix one more time but because the labor and delivery team at the hospital was going to check me as well, I wanted to avoid too many or unnecessary cervical checks. I declined and decided to shower and get ready to head into the hospital.

I felt an all-time low, like the absolute failure of a mom and the complete opposite of everything I stand for. I couldn't stop replaying the horrific feelings in my head about not having Brandon by my side and being forced to be on Pitocin and just dealing with the hospital environment altogether.

At around 5:30 p.m., we arrived at the hospital. I gave Brandon hugs and kisses while feeling the absolute worst I've ever felt. My Doula and I headed inside. We got checked in to labor and delivery, got all hooked up to the monitors, and tried to settle in. When I was being checked in it was right at shift change so everything was a bit chaotic. I had four different people check my cervix. I was 100% effaced and dilated to a TEN!!! Merryn was at a +1 position in my pelvis. We were so close to being able to push. I didn't need the Pitocin to kick start labor into higher gear! Things were sort of looking up. I was still extremely disappointed and upset to be away from my husband but thought what we were doing was for the best for our daughter.

Then the shift happened...one of the doctors came in to offer me IV antibiotics because it's their standard of care since I was in labor for so long after my water had already broken. I declined. He insisted, I declined again. He basically dropped it because I wasn't budging. Then they sent the next doctor in. She was going over standard care and my birth plan.

I explained that I would not consent to Pitocin after delivery unless there was a medical need, like a hemorrhage. She told me that I wasn't allowed to decline. I explained that I know my rights and that I would be declining. She argued.

She then brought in several nurses and doctors to help her try to get me to change my mind. They told me I would be forced to stay for 48 hours after delivery. I told them, I wouldn't be doing that and that I would sign an Against Medical Advice document if need be. The doctor then said, "What if I told you that you can't?"

I explained to her that she wasn't allowed to tell me what I can or can't do and that she's only allowed to give her opinion and recommendation. Several times back and forth with bringing in people to stand over me in the bed, arms crossed and attempting the intimidation tactics. They then told me that if I didn't give in to their standard of care, then they would put a hold on my daughter and take medical custody!

My Doula spoke up and said, "You mean like medical kidnapping?! So you're saying we should get a lawyer and speak with the patient advocate?"

The doctor replied, "You can do whatever you want but because of the state of the nation we can and will take her. You will not be able to sign her out."

Then the charge nurse piped in with, "If you're not going to consent to what we tell you, then you might as well just go home because we're going to do our job anyway."

Back and forth, round and round, we went through this. I informed them of my right to consent and bodily autonomy and they declined any and all of my rights to my body and to my daughter's.

My Doula then told them to round up the discharge papers because we were out of there! She yanked the cords out of the monitor and helped me get everything off and my clothes back on.

The doctor came back in and joked sarcastically that they were at the nurses' station laughing about my situation and thought it would be just hilarious if I went home and delivered my child with no issues whatsoever. I signed the Against Medical Advice document, even though the charge nurse specifically told me to just go home if I was going to stick to my guns which completely voids the purpose of the document, and we fled.

We were only at the hospital for approximately an hour and a half but it felt like an eternity. I couldn't wait to get home! My Doula and I were completely in shock over the entire experience.

When we got to her jeep, my contractions were getting a little more intense, and I was just ready to be back at home in my husband's arms and ready to have this baby. We pulled into my driveway around 6:35 p.m. Everything felt so much better. More at peace, at ease, and ready to progress into the final stages.

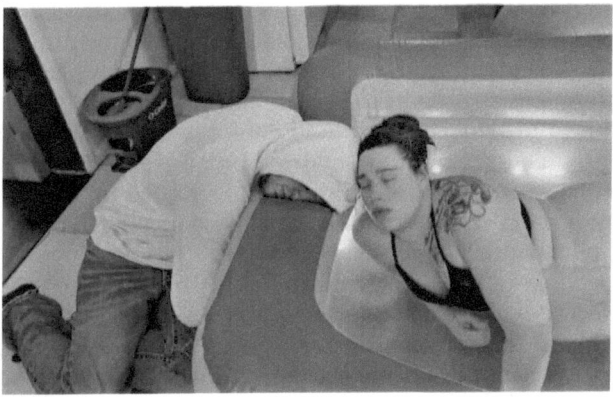

I stripped my clothes off and then got into my birthing pool. My Doula coached me through some intense contractions and helped me listen to my body's cues on how and when to push. I was feeling everything in my hips and tailbone. It was the most intense sensation I've ever been through. I kept begging Brandon to apply pressure to the area but after doing some googling, my support group showed me that they couldn't do it anymore because it was stopping my bone in my back to retract and allow Merryn to pass through.

I labored in the pool for a little bit. Every two contractions I would switch to a different position.

After about 12 contractions I got out and went to the bedroom to labor Merryn down in bed. That's when the pushing reflex started. I did my best to just bear down and work her down and out. After being in my bed, I got up again and went back to the kitchen. I was next to the sink, and my mom and Brandon took turns being my support on the other side of the counter.

I would hold on to their hands and just squat down and push. I did that for maybe an hour to two hours, or so it felt! I'm not entirely sure any of us really know. Time was just blending together.

Eventually, out popped Merryn's head! Completely covered in meconium, it was squirting out of her nose, etc. The cord was wrapped around her neck TWICE! The cord got flipped up over her head both times so she could be delivered. With just a couple more pushes, the rest of Merryn's body was out! She was limp. My support team wrapped her in a towel and began rubbing her vigorously to get her to come to.

Finally, I heard her little voice after we frantically searched for the suction and got her breathing. It was such a relief and the most beautiful sound I have ever heard. While I waited for my placenta to be delivered, Merryn and I got into the birth pool. I began to bleed. My Doula fed me 9 or 10 dates and fixed me some Red Raspberry Leaf Tea.

I started to try to get Merryn to latch to stimulate my uterus to contract. I could feel large blood clots making their way out and into the water. No more than 15 minutes had passed and my placenta came out with one decent contraction. I grabbed it out of the water and handed it to my Doula, as my mom took Merryn so I could get out of the pool and get dried off and the blood cleaned off. Brandon, Merryn, and I went to the bedroom and cuddled up together for a while after about an hour of Merryn being connected to her placenta, and Brandon cutting her cord.

The next day, our original midwife came to the house to examine both Merryn and me. Merryn passed her APGAR tests with flying colors. My uterus was contracting exactly the way it was supposed to, and surprisingly I didn't tear or rip! My bleeding even tapered off to basically nothing that night. Merryn was starting to get better and better at latching. Two days after her birthday, we had another appointment with the midwife. Merryn passed her newborn screening! The midwife even commented on her being advanced for a newborn!

All in all, our sweet rainbow baby is here. She is healthy and I'm just relishing in the surreal experience from start to finish. So many moments to remember and I'll never forget the way she makes me feel. Being Merryn's mama is everything to me. She is my beautiful rainbow after so many storms. I will do everything in my power to keep her safe and healthy.

I'd claw the eyes out of someone that had the nerve to hurt her.

Mama loves you, Merryn Cedar. We went through hell and back to get you here. I hope you know how much you mean to your Daddy and me.

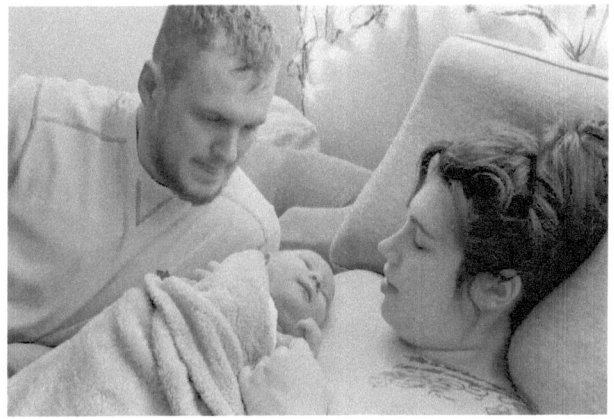

Cedar's Wild and Free Birth Story

By Kersti Smith

Part 1: Why Freebirth?

My decision to freebirth was a slow and gradual one.

I'd been drawn to the power of freebirth for a while, but I wrote it off as something Steve would never be on board with. Little did I know. We found out we were pregnant with Sprout a couple months into the COVID pandemic.

We knew we were likely to move before they were born, which meant we wouldn't be able to use the midwife we had used and loved with each of our previous home births.

Once we realized we'd be looking for a new midwife, I started thinking more seriously about freebirth. I listened to hundreds of birth stories through my pregnancy. In my heart I knew this was my path. It was the next step: full responsibility for my baby and myself.

Casually, I just kept bringing it up in conversation, slowly familiarizing Steve with the idea and the what-ifs.

"When we freebirth..." I would say as if it had been decided already, and he would laugh and shake his head "no," because of course, it was just too crazy.

I talked to a couple of local midwives and even found one I really liked—but I just could never commit.

It felt silly to spend thousands of dollars on care that I didn't really want and would hardly use, just to have the false sense of security that nothing could go wrong if she were here.

We kept talking. We kept not making a decision. But I think we both knew. Steve saw me taking ownership of my pregnancy in a new way.

Leaning into my intuition, and trusting myself and my baby, he saw the beginning of what could be and he saw the difference in me. Choosing responsibility, choosing autonomy. Could it really be so brilliantly simple?

I was well into my third trimester before we officially decided on freebirth. That was after trying to find a midwife to be on-call for us should we decide we wanted assistance... which we couldn't find anyway, thanks to licensing and regulations.

I don't think Steve was ever 100% comfortable, but he made a decision to trust me and actively chose faith over fear. After we had made a choice, he didn't talk to me anymore about his fears and I appreciated his positive energy.

Once we decided we were really going to do it, I occasionally would have moments of nervousness. I'd never taken such complete responsibility before and it felt...new.

I had the choice to run from that feeling or lean into it. I'd never gone into birth with any trepidation and this time was feeling a little different. I felt so much confidence in birth and in my baby and in my body's Knowing, yet doing something new came with some new feelings to sit with.

I didn't know anyone in real life who had made this counter-culture choice, but I was comforted by the stories I read and listened to of like-minded women choosing to birth outside the system and on their own terms. Through them, I was reminded that I wasn't crazy: that freebirth was just birth.

When I had moments of worry, I reminded myself of my truths and let myself be ok with all the feelings. Everything within me pulled me back to freebirth, to myself, to my baby's divine wisdom, to owning my power, over and over and over again. It was a dance and my intuition was leading. My Learning was to follow.

The weeks leading up to labor were filled with regular contractions.

The week of my due date we had a pretty epic winter storm and were snowed in all week.

There were a few nights where the contractions felt different, and I thought it might be the night.

For all of February, I had felt that Sprout would come on the 27th, yet the constant contractions had me thinking maybe they would come sooner (my actual "due date" was the 15th).

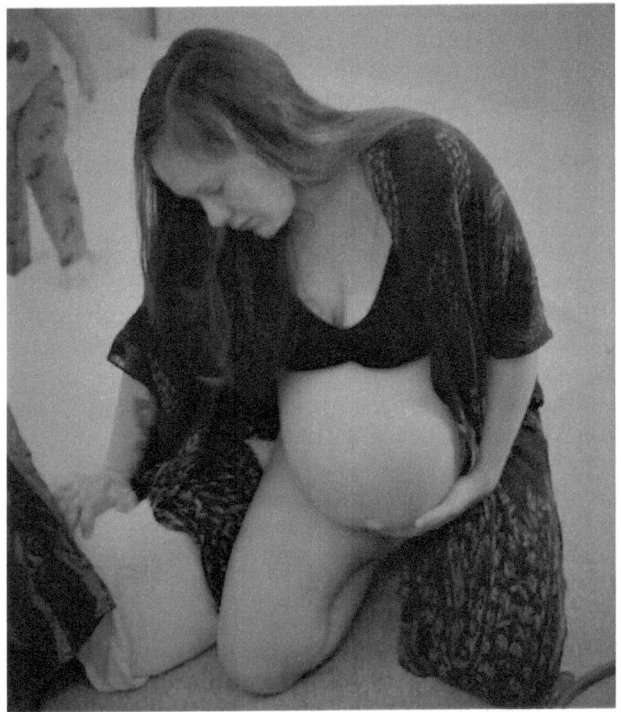

Part 2: Birthday

I woke up at 3:30 a.m. on February 27th under the full moon and had a few contractions in bed. I knew right away that it was different. They were 5-6 mins apart, but a totally different sensation that wrapped and pulled, and I was pretty confident it was the real deal.

I laid there for about 15 minutes and enjoyed a few moments of being quiet with my babe and being the only one who knew what was coming. Me and Baby. Together and a team.

Sprout wiggled in between contractions as if to say they were ready and coming, and I told them I couldn't wait and that I trusted them completely.

Steve heard me get up to go to the bathroom, and when I didn't come back immediately he checked on me, assuming it was time. It was the 27th, after all.

I texted my mom at 3:50 a.m., and she was on her way shortly after. Laying back down in bed, the contractions were still about 5 minutes apart. Steve made a pot of coffee and started getting the birth tub ready. My mom arrived. It was 4:15 a.m.

Shep was sleeping in our bed, so I tried to move him back to his room so we could get our room ready without waking him. I held his chubby little hand as I rocked through the waves that continued to roll through me, closer now although I had stopped timing them. It was 4:25 a.m.

Once Shep was sleeping again, I snuck out of their room. Mom helped me make up the bed with a waterproof layer and an old bedsheet.

The tub was filled up with as much warm water as our apartment hot water heater could give us and Steve added a few pots of boiling water as well. It was about ¾ filled, so we waited, hoping the water would have time to reheat. Spoiler alert: that's as much water as was going to get in the tub.

I turned on my worship music playlist. The first song that played was "Who You Are to Me." The lyrics sang,

"You're amazing, faithful, love's open door
When I'm empty You fill me with hunger for more
Of your mercy, Your goodness
Lord, You're the air that I breathe"

I was kneeling on the ground in our bedroom next to our bed, where I spent the entirety of my short labor, when Shep came out of his room. It was 4:40 a.m. He gave me snuggles and stayed close to me the rest of my labor, looking up for kisses and playing on the bed next to me. I was happy he was awake and pleasant and got to experience it with us.

My mom woke Violet up at 5:00 a.m., and she said, "I've been waiting for this day!" She came to my arms with bleary eyes and a huge smile.

We gave each other love and she settled in as my little doula, rubbing my back and my arms as I continued to work through the now ever-intensifying surges.

As I stayed put on the spot of the ground I had rooted to, I remember feeling the energy of my loves all around me.

My mom taking photos, witnessing us, holding our space with tender care and total trust. Steve behind me, supporting me, rubbing my back and my aching legs, telling me how strong Sprout and I were together—bringing only Love. My littles right beside me, showing me love in the way they know how, with their peaceful presence and sweet baby touches.

It felt holy and powerful and intimate and fierce...and yet it also felt so normal. Just birth. In its true simplicity. Family supporting family as the Body and the Baby work in tune with the divine to do exactly what they know to do. It's magic, it's miraculous, it's normal. It's just birth.

The waves required my full attention, as I gently moaned through them. I began to feel the first hint of the pressure that meant Sprout was descending, and I decided to get in the tub. It was 5:13 a.m.

The water felt wonderful as the waves intensified again, taking all that I had. I moved and moaned in the water, following my body's leading. I felt our baby's soft bag of waters about two inches up and knew they'd be here soon. My waters opened on the next contraction with a little pop.

There was one point that felt like too much and it didn't seem like it would stop...but it did, like it always does. I had one or two contractions in the tub like this and then they changed as I felt the urge to push.

This is my least favorite part of labor, every time. I can relax through intense surges like a champ, but pushing takes me to a different place where I get to be a more active participant in bringing my baby.

I remembered back to Shepherd's birth, where I resisted the urge to push for a couple contractions because I knew I wouldn't like it.

I decided not to do that this time and met the intensity full force. I worked with my body and not against it.

I yelled loud with one contraction but overall felt much more in control than I have with my previous births – where I was quite loud.

I had two pushing contractions and they emerged – their head first, facing my left side. I held their head in my hands under the water and said, "I love you."

Steve stayed close, rubbing my back, and reminding me to stay low in the water to keep Sprout fully submerged.

Mom guided the kids through what was happening, as they watched closely from the edge of the tub.

Another couple pushes and the shoulders were born. From water into water, they came to me, floating up to the surface.

The cord was wrapped around the back of the neck and Steve helped me unwrap it before I pulled them to my chest.

I rubbed their back and spoke gently to them, as my spirit called to theirs. About 10 seconds later they took a breath and just after that let out their first cry of life.

Violet cheered, "Mommy, you did it!" I held them close, filled with the biggest joy.

Meeting your baby after the work of labor is just the most indescribable feeling on the planet—this wet and warm and wiggly being that is part of you and yet their own. It is its own special kind of magic.

The baby pushed back to look at me as I spoke, and we just took each other in for a moment filled with such purity and innocence.

So sure that this baby was a girl, I said to Steve, "do you want to see what she is?" before correcting myself to, "do you want to see what they are?" I flipped Baby around and burst into laughter as I announced, "it's a boy!" We couldn't believe it. We had felt so strongly it was a girl and we were all in a little disbelief. We all laughed so loud we startled the poor guy and made him cry! He was ours and he was perfect and he was just who he always was—who our family needed.

"Communion" was the song that was playing when he was born. It was Shepherd's nap song for many months, so it's a song that Cedar must have been familiar with. It's a long song, but as we pulled him up from the water, the lyrics sang,

"This is where I'm meant to be
Me and You, and You and me."

We hung out together in the tub, soaking in all the Love and Joy of the moment. He latched on his own, about 20 minutes after he was born. I delivered my placenta about 50 minutes after the birth and then we were ready to get out of the tub. I hardly bled at all.

The next several hours consisted of everything good and perfect. Skin to skin, lots of nursing, tying and cutting his cord after two hours, weighing and measuring him, snuggles with Daddy and big siblings, and lots of kisses all over his perfect little face. It was heaven.

It felt so beautifully simplistic. While the birth was about the same length as Shepherd's labor, it felt so much less rushed to me. The energy felt more calm and peaceful vs frantically trying to prepare. Steve was able to be with me even more and his presence was reassuring and safe.

I never had a moment of fear or doubt about anything during labor. Everything felt so completely right and natural. I loved having the big kids be such a part of the experience of welcoming their brother to our family. I felt so proud of all of us—WE had done it.

We had done it wild and free, Trusting and Following the divine design of birth. Not unassisted at all, but completely assisted by my intuition, my Creator, the women who have gone before me, my spirit, my baby, my family's support. I had claimed my true power and been held and supported by the ones who love me. Cedar was the culmination of it all, our most perfect gift. His pregnancy and birth taught me so much about myself and what I'm capable of. It taught me that I can trust myself. It taught me to sit with the discomfort of growth. It taught me that I can create new stories and truths for our family. It taught me freedom. It taught me true Trust.

The whole day was bliss. We snuggled and nursed and all just loved on each other. That night as we were reading bedtime books to the kids, a thunderstorm boomed outside. Violet is usually afraid of thunder, but this night she didn't seem to be. We talked about it and decided it must be heaven celebrating Cedar's birth. This inspired us to read him "On the Night You Were Born" before we all went to sleep for the night. As the thunder clapped around us, we read,

"Heaven blew every trumpet and played every horn on the wonderful, marvelous night you were born."

Cedar Everett Smith
5:20 a.m.
9lbs 5oz
22 inches long

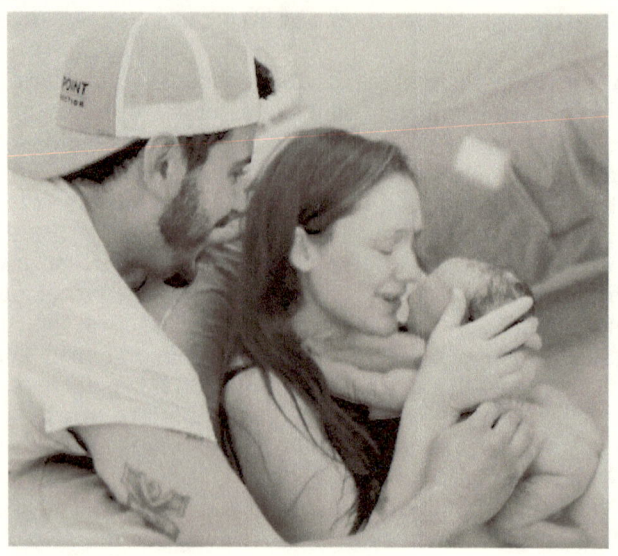

Advice for a Spring Birth

From the women who wrote the stories in this collection

Connect deeply with your body and nature's flow.

Embrace the seasonal changes that represent new life in all forms!

Listen to your body, work WITH your baby.

Don't buy too many seasonal clothes because who knows what the weather and size of baby will bring during that time of year.

Prepare as much as you can. Never wait until the last minute to get educated and gather items. Be prepared for ANYTHING.

Remain stress-free and positive.

Enjoy the time with your new little one, it's an incredibly special time to have a new soul come into the world.

Relax, sit outside, soak in the sun, appreciate the beauty of spring. Be thankful.

Don't let other people's fears and negativity into your headspace. You got this mama! You were made for this!

Knowledge is Power. It makes all the difference. So does having someone who's on the same page as you, supporting you, cheering you on, whether a Doula, your spouse, your BFF or whoever helps more than you would think. Having consistent affirmation of your ability, your power, and your prowess strengthens you.

Make sure to reserve/buy your birthing pool early! It's a busy time for births, so you don't want to miss out on the magic!

If you haven't already, take a Hypnobabies birthing course. You'll be amazed at how much you didn't know that you didn't know.

Having warming tea and foods prepared if it'll still be cold is so important.

It's even easier to become "cold" in your postpartum during the months transitioning from winter to summer.
Look up Ayurvedic or traditional Chinese medicine warming foods and herbs!

Estival

Estival: of or appearing in summer.
from the Latin word aestus, or "heat."

The Free Birth of Daisy Moon

by Mariah Boyer

On Wednesday night, September 12th, I went to bed hoping like every other night in the last month that I might wake up in labour. I hadn't really felt like eating dinner. I put the boys to bed, and my husband gave me a foot massage so I laid down and fell asleep quickly.

I woke up to a large surge at around 1:18 am. I got up and went to the toilet. When I looked down, I realised I had a bloody show and instantly felt excitement. I knew it was time, as I could feel more small surges coming.

I went in and woke my husband to let him know it was starting. I couldn't believe the day had finally come, and I was going to do it all at home in the environment that I wanted.

As the surges continued, I felt a wave of nervous energy take over, and I called my mum to let her know I was in labour and to get ready and come. She was bringing my sister as well. I then called my doula, Bec, and told her today was the day.

She asked how I was feeling and I said a little overwhelmed, remembering the experience I was about to go through for the third time. She was very calm and reminded me that I knew what I was doing and that I was safe.

When I got off the phone with her, I lit my candles, brought out my birth box, took some Rescue Remedy to relax my nerves, and sat down on my yoga ball. I pulled out my affirmation cards and laid them on the table in front of me and began reading through them and finding which ones were resonating with me in that moment.

I am safe, my baby is safe.

I trust my body.

I started to feel very calm and relaxed and then fully surrendered to the journey ahead.

My mum and sister arrived 45 minutes later, at about 2 am. There was a beautiful excitement and stillness in the air. They came in and we hugged and checked in with how I was feeling. By that point, I was much more calm and happy to just continue sitting on my yoga ball, so I told my husband to lay back down and rest as it might be a while.

My mum and sister both also tried to get some rest I attempted to lay down, but as soon as I did the surges got more intense so I hopped back up and sat back on the ball. I labored quietly on my own for a few hours and woke my mum up when I was feeling a little nauseous. We stood outside under the waning crescent moon with the sun slowly rising and talking about how today would be the day I would meet my daughter. It was a beautiful moment.

My two sons woke around 6 am, and they could feel the excitement and couldn't wait to meet their little sister. My sister took them to get breakfast and when they got back, I asked them to go over to my mother-in-law's house next door to us so I could focus.

I laboured in my bedroom in the dark for a while after the sun came up. It was the most intense part of my labour. It felt as though there was hardly a break between contractions. I asked my mum to call my doula, who arrived around 7 am. She came in to check on me when she arrived.

I told her I felt as though there was no break in between my surges, and I was quite tired. She suggested I have a drink or something to eat to give me some more energy. After a big drink and a small amount of carrots and hummus, I came out of the bedroom and hopped into the shower.

I went between the toilet and the shower for a while, and then really felt the urge to poop, so I got out and sat on the toilet. It was about 8:45 am. I felt a big gush and my waters burst into the toilet. There was a small amount of meconium in the waters.

I called Bec to check in, and she reminded me it was just a variation of normal. I felt good after that. All my intense surges went away, and I had a break to gather my thoughts. Then the pushing surges kicked in, and I got on the floor in the bathroom and began connecting with my baby to bring her down.

My husband stood by me and offered to set up the bedroom for the birth. After about five minutes he helped me onto the bed. I could feel she wasn't far away and waited patiently for each pushing surge. She descended and went back up a few times. I was happy to know I could slowly breathe her out to make sure I didn't tear. I held a warm cloth over my vulva and felt I needed to lay on my back to push out her head.

Once her head was out, I moved into the lunge position and birthed the rest of her body onto the bed at 9:11 am. I quickly picked her up and saw her beautiful face. I noticed she had quite a bit of mucus and sucked out the excess from her nose and mouth. She let out a cry immediately after and pinked up. It was such an incredible moment.

She was covered in vernix, which none of my babies had ever been. She latched on to feed quite quickly. We let my mother-in-law know, and she and my boys arrived soon after. Such a magical feeling to have my loved ones in a sacred birth space.

I then asked to have some quiet so I could birth the placenta. It took around two hours and 40 minutes. I took placenta release tincture twice and managed to do two big wees, but we ended up cutting the cord so I could hop into the shower to squat down and push it out myself. I was so happy once it was out and very relieved to have hardly any blood loss at all.

It was such an incredible experience, and I am so thankful for all the support from my friends and family. We are totally in love with our Daisy Moon.

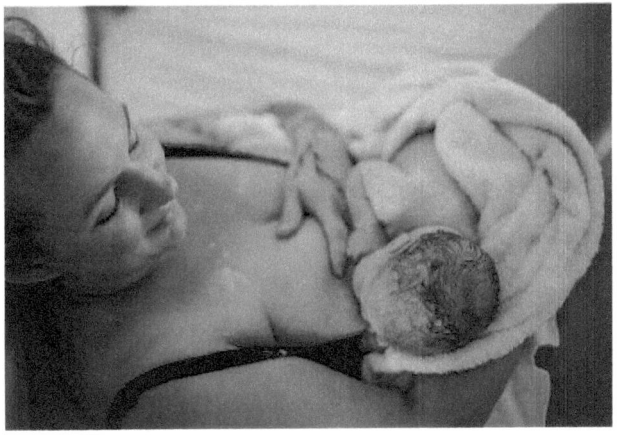

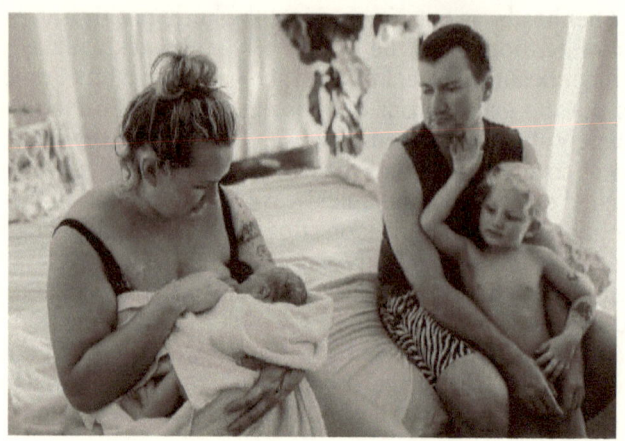

A Dream Birth

by Alexandra

I was 41 1/2 weeks, and I was so ready to give birth. My other pregnancies were 39 weeks, so I was surprised to carry him for so long. I decided to try every induction method I knew, and if I didn't have him by Saturday August 7th, I would take castor oil as a last resort.

I tore so badly with my other two, so I was really freaked out by how big this baby was getting! I did all the usual at home things: primrose oil, 5W, long walks, sex, semen, orgasms, nipple stimulation, spicy food, pineapple, magnesium and calcium, curb walking, a long drive on a bumpy road....on and on. On August 4th, I got acupuncture to induce, and on the 5th I asked my chiropractor to induce me. Well, baby came the next day, on August 6th! No castor oil! Thank Goddess!

I woke up at 4 am having strong surges. I had about five in 30 minutes, and I felt the baby corkscrew his way down into my pelvis! It was so incredible! So I KNEW it was finally happening! I woke my husband. We had lots of skin to skin time and made love. The moment his semen hit my cervix, the intensity of the surges doubled. I was so grateful!

My cousin and her husband had been staying in our guest house next door to help on our farm. When our two boys woke up, ages 8 and 10, I told them our baby was coming that day and sent them next door as we had arranged so I could birth in private.

We had a friend who was supposed to act as our doula, but we couldn't get a hold of her, so I called another doula friend and asked her to come and she did. (I'm a doula, and I have a lot of doula friends.) She was such an angel! I'm so glad she was with us. My cousin was also with us, handling all the practical things. She layed out the supplies, filled the tub, fed everyone, brought drinks out, and took photos and videos. Her husband was next door with my kiddos. I feel like I had the most perfect birth team!

I took a shower and then labored outside in the grass for a few hours.

Walked around a bit, but I really needed to be on my hands and knees for every surge. My husband checked my cervix and thought I was about 5-6 cm. I felt kind of pushy, so I was thinking I might be farther than that. But it was several more hours till my water broke in the grass and I felt REALLY pushy. I got in my outdoor clawfoot tub. I could feel that I had a cervical lip. The pain was so sharp. I kept saying I couldn't do it anymore. It was so much more painful than I remember. I hope it's over soon, etc. I was thinking "I'm never doing this again."

I was moaning and growling all day. With my other births I was SO QUIET, but with this one, I tried to hold it in at one point to direct my energy down, but I absolutely could not do it. I had watched lots of birthing videos with my sons to prepare them for the birth, in case they decided to be present. But we only watched quiet, peaceful births! When my 8 yr old son came over to see me, he got scared because of all my growling and went back next door. It's ok. I had told them both if they choose to be here or not, it's ok with me. Just go by how they feel in the moment.

I had set the goal to wait for FER *(fetal ejection reflex)* to do the work for me. I tore both times before because of coached pushing. I had never really felt FER before. I tried holding the lip back and giving some little pushes when I felt the urge, but didn't feel much movement. My doula suggested that I may be resisting a bit. I told her I was feeling fearful about tearing. She said "ok, now we've named the fear, and you can release it. Let it go."

That's all I needed to hear. She said to really let go and give it a big push to see if it felt good. So I did, and it felt amazing. I could still feel the water bag bulging. Even though my water broke earlier, I had only lost a trickle. So, I ripped the bag open and felt my baby's sweet hairy head. It was so motivating. I pushed harder and felt his head slip past my bones and into my vagina.

I started to feel slight burning, so I tried to push so slow. With one contraction I thought "oh no! I can't stop it now! My body is just pushing on its own!" And his head came out. One surge, 3 pushes. The burning was only slight, so I felt like I probably did not tear. I finally got to experience the Fetal Ejection Reflex!

My husband seemed surprised to see his head! He told me "Sweetie! The head is out!" As if I didn't know! He burst into tears holding baby's head.

With the next push, I figured his body would slide out like my other boys, but he did not. I had to push SO HARD to get his shoulders out. It was almost as hard as the head. And then his body slid out.

He was pretty well tangled in his cord around his armpits and neck. He had absolutely NO VERNIX at all and long fingernails. He did not cry. He was purple. I rubbed his back and he started up. I asked our doula to go get the boys and they came really fast. Baby was a bit gurgly, so Papi sucked out his nose and mouth with his mouth.

I stayed in the tub for about 10 minutes to try to push the placenta out, but baby was getting cold, so we decided to move inside. As soon as I stood up, I felt the placenta sliding out, so our doula put the bowl under me. The placenta seemed HUGE.

I sat down on the couch to nurse him, and he latched immediately and stayed latched for an hour on each side—2 hours!—before he finally fell asleep.

I took a shower and went pee. NO BURNING! NO TEARS! We all thought he looked like a really big baby, so we cut his cord at that time and weighed him. 9lbs 2oz! My biggest baby by far! And a 14 inch head, 19 inches long.

Our chiropractor came to the house and gave the baby his first adjustment. When he had his neck adjusted, he spit up a bit of amniotic fluid.

Another friend came by to pick up the placenta to encapsulate it.

My sweet husband keeps kissing me and thanking me for having his baby. This is his first child. We laid the baby between us in bed and stared at him until we fell asleep. Baby woke up a lot to spit and cough up amniotic fluid. When he finally had his first pee and poo in the morning, and we changed him, he cried a good cry for the first time. I thought it was good because it sounded like it cleared his lungs.

His latch is great! He's a very content baby. Big brothers adore him. I feel fantastic. Barely any blood loss. I had my cousin and best friend take care of my farm and house today. The neighbors heard me give birth outside, so they brought food over. We are so well cared for! And I feel so empowered! We had our absolute dream birth with no complications whatsoever.

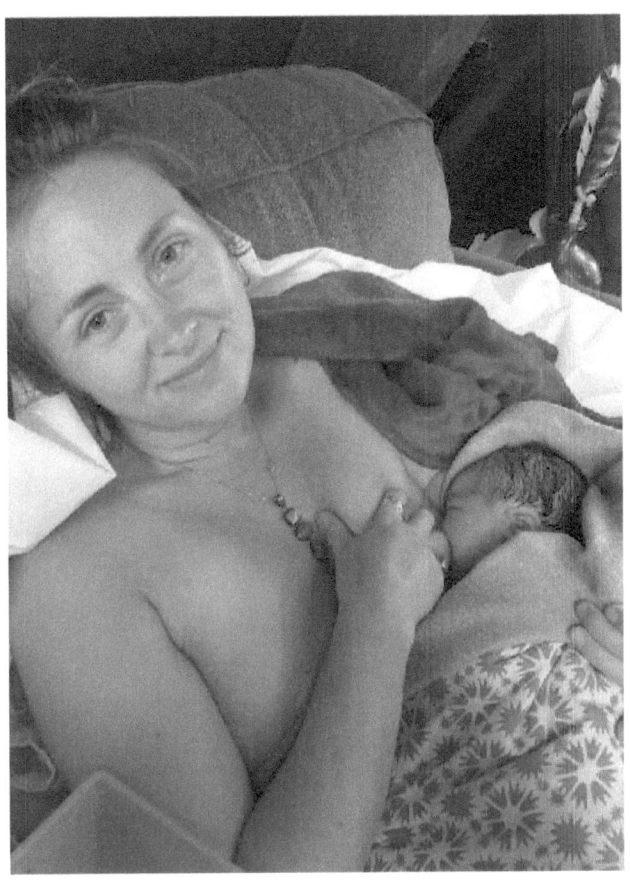

The Birth of Sunny

By Breanna Mooney

ON THE MORNING OF August 6th, I had gone to bed at about 1 am. I woke up about two hours later to light contractions. They were very irregular, spanning 20 minutes or longer apart. I laid in bed just breathing through them, wishing I could change positions, but my hips and lower back hurt so bad that I couldn't.

My husband soon woke up to my breathing and asked me what was wrong. I told him I was having contractions, but they were about 20 minutes apart. He was very excited and wanted to go get his mother who we agreed would be our "doula." He went and got her and we timed the contractions, which were still very irregular.

By 6 am, my mother in-law had called my husband's two sisters who were very anxious to see a home birth. One of my sisters-in-law had shown up that morning to check things out, but we decided that the baby wasn't coming just yet and she left to go to work. We let my other sister in-law know that if she wanted to come over she could. She was working so she would come after she got off work.

I spent that day eating beef jerky, making my other kiddos popcorn from our popcorn maker, walking around our property, and pulling weeds with my husband. My contractions stayed consistently irregular all day long.

Both my sisters-in-law showed up in the afternoon. They started reading the information I had posted all over my walls. The information was things like what to do if the baby was breech or if the cord was around the neck, etc. After that they checked out my emergency birth kits that I had ordered. I had ordered two of the same kits that had the very basics of what the doctors would use.

We waited for quite a while for baby to make his appearance. The contractions started to get more intense by night time. I could feel baby moving down more and more, I knew it wouldn't be much longer.

I was positioned on my back in my bed. The contractions were hard and the baby's head was right there, but he seemed to be stuck or something. I reached in myself and felt the baby's head. I decided to flip over and get on my hands and knees. In the motion of turning over, my water broke. I went about 15 minutes after my water broke and about four or five big pushes, and the baby was here!

My mother-in-law had delivered the baby, suctioned his nose and was wiping baby off with the receiving blankets that were in the kit. We left baby attached to the placenta for a short time, but everyone was too excited to wait for the placenta to deliver so we decided to clamp the cord and cut it, then deliver the placenta. I immediately began breastfeeding while the placenta was delivered.

Soon after the placenta was out, my mother-in-law took it to bury on our land. My other children had come to meet their new baby brother and were so excited.

I can't say my free birth happened the way I imagined it would, but I am happy with how it did go. I was surrounded by family and everybody had their own roles. Everybody was very hands off and my son was greeted into the world by his grandmother who was very happy to deliver him.

We named our son Sunny Dwain Mooney. He was born at 11:06 pm, weighing about 8 lbs.

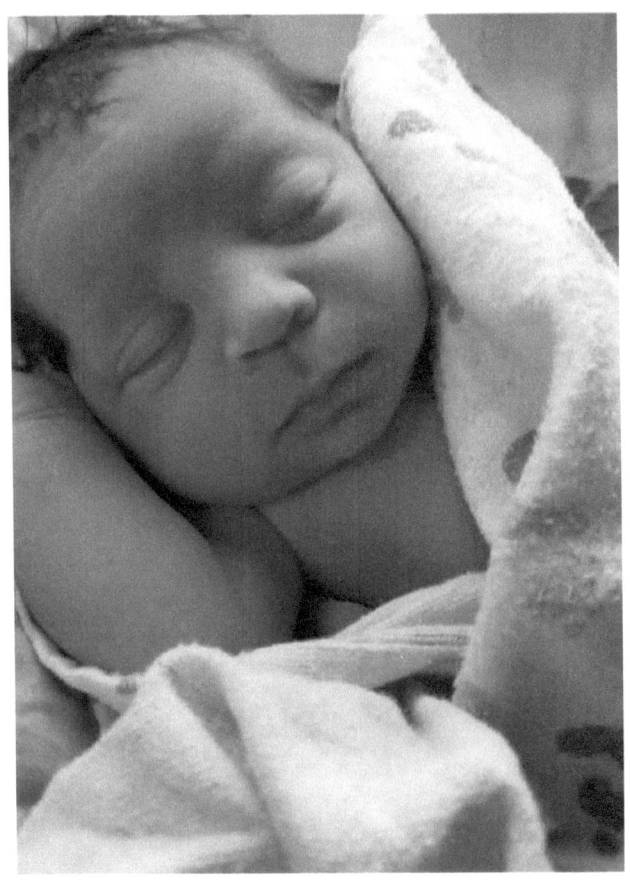

The Birth Of Milo Septem Agape

By Braydon Gordner

EARLY IN THE MORNING on July 3rd, I started feeling slight cramping sensations. I worked on my birth affirmation sheets and finished the last touches to my sacred birth space. I had a dream that night of my baby emerging from my womb at night under the full moon on the 5th.

July 4th was my "due date," but I knew and trusted that my baby would come on their own divine time. I rested as much as I could, as I did feel the baby was coming soon. But with all the fireworks, a huge thunderstorm, and back pain, I just tossed and turned and honestly was overflowing with excitement about meeting my baby soon!

On July 5th I started slowly losing my mucus plug in pieces, and my cramps were more consistent. I did some gardening work, walked around the lake with my dog, and tried to get more rest.

On July 6th, I lost even more pieces of the plug. We went to the health food store a little before noon to get some bulk foods, as I was in early labor. When we got home, the sensations escalated, and I knew it was time. I went out to the garden and said some prayers for my baby's safe travel to earth and gave thanks to Mother Earth for all the support, reassuring myself we were protected and guided from our ancestors and all the womban who have come before.

I picked flowers from the garden and set the vases in my birth space. Cameron, my partner and wonderful birth support, started a fire to heat water for the birth pool. I kept switching between walking through the garden, bouncing on the birth ball, squatting, swaying my hips, sitting in the warm water, and every so often Cameron would apply pressure to my back to ease the pain.

For a little I listened and sang sacred songs that empowered me, but shortly after that started to feel like a distraction, and I was being called deep within myself-to be present, silent, and just breathe through each rush of energy opening my body to allow my baby to come through.

Time seemed to be nonexistent. I just flowed through all the feelings. All I knew was that the sun was setting and the sensations were becoming greater and greater with each one.

As nightfall approached, the intensity grew greater with each rush of energy that opened my body, allowing my baby to come through. I didn't time the "contractions," how long they were or the length in between each one. I surrendered in complete trust of the natural process of birth. I trusted my body, I trusted my baby.

A few months before the due date, I had a dream of my baby telling me to release all the fears I had surrounding labor and birth and that I had to fully trust my baby and allow the process to unfold in its divine timing. I allowed the physiological and biological sequence of natural mammalian labor to unfold, undisturbed.

There came a point where I couldn't be standing still, I had to move and keep the energy flowing through me. I tried laying on the bed to get some rest and once my body hit the bed the pain got so intense there was no way I could lay down. So back walking through the garden I went.

When I would bend over and breathe into the rush, my dog Rosco would come running over to me and give me a big kiss.

As I walked back and forth through the garden and the driveway, the first time in many months I heard multiple owls making loud beautiful sounds. I felt as if they were there supporting me. Cameron was amazing at keeping me hydrated, making me raspberry leaf and stinging nettle tea, chaga mushroom tea, keeping the fire going for comfort to stand by and to heat water for the birth tub. The warm waters were the only place I could sit still and just breathe through the rush. It also felt very good on my aching back pains.

A few hours before I birthed Milo, Cameron said he needed to go lay down and get a little sleep. During those few hours before Milo came, I rested in the tub. Every time I would shut my eyes, I would see bright swirling colors and a deep sense/feeling of peace embodied in my being. I felt so safe, loved, empowered, at ease, and honestly so naturally high on life. I was riding the waves of each rush bringing me closer to meeting my baby. In those hours while Cameron slept, the rushes were the most intense indescribable feelings I have ever felt in my life, and I breathed right through them.

I was very quiet, not making any sounds the whole labor, and now as each rush came sounds vibrated out of my being with no control. Cameron soon after woke up as he said he started to hear my tones change and knew it was time.

Cameron came outside, and I was walking back and forth taking deep breaths, in such a blurry fuzzy yet focused state of mind, I couldn't even say anything until a surge came and moans and other wild sounds came from my being. I quickly walked to where Cameron stood and turned around pointing at my lower back for him to apply pressure there. He started, then suggested going to the birthing tub and leaning on it for support, and he would rub my back.

As I got to the tub my intuition told me to feel my yoni, and right as I did I felt something hard bulging out of me!

"Ah, their head!" I expressed to Cameron, and he helped me into the tub. I sat in the tub just breathing and blowing. Cameron rubbed the warm water on my back and reminded me a few times to blow and that I got this.

I asked Cameron to grab the flashlight and shine it in the water. As he turned around, I could feel more of the baby dropping, and when I touched them again it felt like a hard balloon. I said with great excitement that I could feel the tiny little ears on each side of the head. I realized when I felt the baby they were coming out En Caul, still in the sac, as my water never broke!

Right as Cameron walked back with the flashlight, without even pushing, the baby slid right out into my hands. He was shaped like an egg all curled up in his sac. It was such an instinct-intuition-primal thing, gently poking the sac and pulling it off of him. I then noticed he had the cord wrapped around his neck once, and once again instinctively, gently unwrapped it and he let out his first little cry to the world.

Born at 3:22 am on July 7th, 2020. Wow, just writing this out I am crying! This was the most powerful, transformative, blissful, yet excruciating experience in my life. I am so grateful. I sat in the water for a few minutes holding his little body so close to mine crying, hugging, and kissing Milo, laughing because I couldn't believe I had just done it! I was still in this high on life daze. I just kept repeating "I did it! I really did it!"

I moved to the bed Cameron made for us in our outdoor kitchen and fed Milo for the first time, he latched right on. About 35 minutes later, I felt I needed to squat, and out came Milo's placenta into the bowl Cameron held for me. After the three of us connected for a few hours and had a hydrating strawberry coconut water smoothie, we peacefully went to sleep for the first time as a family. I am forever grateful for my intuition that led me through this sacred rite of passage and for the trust and support from my partner, my ancestors and the land I birthed on.

The Birth of Waverly Love

By Alexandra Burries

AFTER THE INCREDIBLE UNASSISTED birth of Lennox last year, Zackary and I both knew that any more babies would be born in the safety of our own home. We were so at peace and in control that we couldn't imagine giving away that power by going into a place of assistance. Just four months after Lennox was born, we conceived baby Burries #4!

Yes, we know how that happens, but we had no idea it would happen so fast, especially with the long journey it took to conceive Lennox.

This pregnancy was wild and free–no checkups, no doctors, no ultrasounds. Just my intuition and connection with my body and my baby. My "prenatal care" included eating intuitively, an intense fitness routine, and paying close attention to the baby's movements everyday. During the first trimester, I also ordered an at home blood test to find out the sex. We were going to have another baby girl!

I was never certain of my "due date" (as if there is such a thing), but I determined it to be somewhere between mid to late June. Not having a specific date to fixate on was so freeing!

It was an extremely busy pregnancy, and Lennox was still so young that it seemed to fly by (until the very end of course). I continued to nurse throughout the pregnancy and never had any issues with milk supply.

I focused on taking care of the other kids and staying active. Like all my other pregnancies, I struggled with severe nausea and threw up almost daily the entire time.

The most preparation I did for my free birth was listening to and reading birth stories. It was a great way for me to see all the different variations of normal that are treated as "abnormal" or "emergent" in a hospital setting.

It was solidifying the fact that birth, when left alone, works as a physiological process of the female body. Zackary and I discussed what would be a true cause for concern during labor and birth and how to address those at home, as well as when we would seek assistance.

I began manifesting the birth I wanted early on in the pregnancy. Once we realized that we would be moving back to Tucson and buying a home, I imagined being able to labor in a beautiful backyard.

Once we moved, we lived with Zackary's parents for a couple of months and I began to worry that I would be giving birth there. But God's favor was over our entire home buying process, and we closed on our first home when I was about 36 weeks along!

We moved in and quickly started doing all the upgrades and renovations we wanted in order to make the house our own.

We worked nonstop for weeks and everything turned out amazing! It felt like a race against the clock to get everything done before the new baby arrived.

Of course, once the projects were completed, it felt like time stopped! I was so ready to have my baby in my arms.

As we got closer and closer to birth day, I decided to set up a shelf area in our closet for Zackary. The "birth shelf" had everything he would need to set up the birth space. We kept things simple and minimal for birth supplies.

We had a couple of plastic table cloths to keep the floors clean and a soft (but cheap) blanket to lay on top of the table cloth to make sitting/kneeling more comfortable.

I had a stack of towels/wash cloths to keep us warm right after birth and to clean up any fluids. I had a comfortable bra and underwear to change into and labor in.

My "medical supplies" consisted of two tinctures: Angelica and Wombstringe (both to help with postpartum bleeding).

I didn't anticipate needing them, but we had them on hand in case I was uncomfortable with the amount of blood loss.

We also had a shelf for the supplies needed after birth: blankets for the baby, a luggage scale and ring sling to weigh her, a soft tape measure, and some cloth diapers. Our birth cost us about $15. Once that shelf was set up, everything felt so real and we were both ready!

June 26: The beginning of early labor! My husband, Zackary, was at work and I was at home with the kids. My mom and sister, Addison, came over to hang out. My mom and I scrubbed the house from top to bottom (our favorite thing to do).

I experienced strong contractions throughout the day, but nothing particularly consistent. At 4:30 pm, they began to get very intense and stayed about three minutes apart.

I knew things were happening, but also knew it could be days (or weeks) before it was really time. Being patient with my body at the end of pregnancy is one of the most difficult things. The contractions continued at the same interval and intensity until about 2 am, when I finally got some sleep.

June 27: Contractions continued throughout the early morning while I nursed Lennox. They were painful, but very spaced out.

Zackary and I decided it would be best for him to stay home from work so I could try to relax. However, we found a great deal on a couch an hour away, so he took the boys for a little drive while I stayed home with Lennox.

My best friend, Beth, came over to keep us company, and it was amazing to have her there to distract me through the continuing labor sensations. Again, the contractions picked up and stayed approximately two minutes apart from 9pm to 3am before they stopped, allowing me to get some sleep.

June 28: By this time, I knew my body was close to starting true active labor, but the contractions were still sporadic. Zackary and I spent the day cleaning and working in the backyard. In the afternoon, I met my mom to get our nails done–some much needed self care!

The contractions picked up in intensity on my way home from the salon, around 5 pm. They continued until about 4 am before fizzling out once again.

June 29: Our 8th wedding anniversary! I woke up feeling crampy and uncomfortable. I told Zackary that I could not do another night of the pain without waking up with a baby in my arms.

He encouraged me and reminded me that I am strong and my body was doing exactly what it needed to do to prepare to bring our baby girl into the world.

My mother-in-law came over to watch the kids while we went out to lunch to celebrate.

Contractions were nearly nonexistent throughout the day. I had some intense contractions after the kids went to bed for a couple of hours, but they stopped pretty quickly and I got a full night of sleep for the first time!

Looking back, it's incredible that my body knew I needed a good night's rest before the day to come.

June 30: At 3:27 am, I shot out of bed. I had been dreaming that I was having an exceptionally painful contraction–only to realize moments later that it was not just a dream. Two minutes later another one came: intense, painful, and exciting all in one.

Zackary jumped out of bed more quickly than I'd ever seen before. He assumed I had been laboring all night again and the baby was about to come. Unfortunately, it was just the beginning!

As I worked through the contractions and got into the bathtub, Zackary texted my birth team. Even though I wasn't yet convinced, he knew this was the start of the real deal! Despite me telling him that it wasn't real and no one should come over, he let Beth and Addison know it was a good day for a baby.

I labored in my bathtub for a short time while Zackary started filling the birth pool with hot water (set up outside on my back patio).

I got up to go to the bathroom and finally started feeling some hope–there was my bloody show! I told Zackary and my mood instantly lifted. I finally saw an end in sight after all these days of early labor.

I got into the birth pool for the first time and felt immediately relaxed. The older kids were still sleeping, it was a gorgeous temperature outside, and the sun was still not fully risen. Perfection.

Beth arrived at around 6:30 am with breakfast in hand for the family. She's a real life superhero.

Addison arrived with a smoothie for me around 8 am–the team was all there, the kids were awake, I felt so at peace. This was exactly how birth should be. I was surrounded by people willing to labor with me, hold space, and love on my kids while I did the work.

The intervals between contractions were constantly changing. They remained painful and intense, but I did have some breaks throughout the day.

My older kids Kingston (5) and Maddox (3) played and watched movies and mostly did their own thing. Lennox (1 year old) was fairly clingy and nursed frequently. I told her she's lucky that nursing her helped to make my contractions more productive!

Once it started warming up outside, I decided I wanted to be back inside. Zackary set up an area on the floor in front of the couch and we all sat together, laughing and joking with each other in between contractions. We had worship music playing in the background and Nerf bullets flying around our heads. Words can't describe how at peace I felt laboring in my home surrounded by real life.

Around 11:30 am, Lennox asked to go take a nap. I reluctantly left my yoga ball and my circle of support to nurse her for her nap in her room. The contractions intensified, but she fell asleep quickly and I was able to return to my little nest on the living room floor. I thought it would be perfect to have the baby while Lennox napped so I wouldn't have to worry about nursing her. Spoiler alert: this did not happen; the baby was not born during nap time.

I bounced around between the living room and the birth pool outside, struggling to find a comfortable place to labor. The birth pool felt great, but we live in Tucson–it was hot out! Zackary provided some extra shade with an umbrella and even used our pressure washer to create a nice mister (my hero!). Once I got too warm and uncomfortable in the water outside, we moved back to the living room.

The boys were watching movies on my bed, and Zackary suggested that we switch places with them so I could be in our (carpeted) bedroom. I gladly accepted and he went to set up some space on the floor in front of our bed. The boys came out to watch movies and run around the house while I continued laboring in my bedroom.

I got in my bathtub for a short time as the contractions intensified. It didn't provide the relief I was hoping for so I ended back up on my bedroom floor.

At around 1 pm, Lennox woke up from her nap, just in time for labor to really intensify. I spent the time in between contractions nursing her, changing positions, and searching for some sort of relief. It was at this time that we all knew she would be arriving soon!

Leaning over the bed, both in a kneeling and standing position, was the most comfortable for me. It wasn't long before contractions became unbearable, and I needed to vocalize through them. I moaned and roared and worked through them.

After about an hour and a half longer, I was beginning to feel discouraged–I was not finding any relief from the pain and I saw no end in sight.

Finally, at 2:36 pm, my first bit of water started leaking. It wasn't a huge gush, but it was enough for me to finally see some progress! The intensity grew and the contractions continued getting closer together.

Addison started a video chat with my older sister, Angela, so she could be a part of the experience. It was so amazing to feel her support virtually, from all the way in South Dakota.

At 2:55 pm, I felt my first urge to push. My body started bearing down uncontrollably while I stood leaning over the side of the bed. Zackary knelt beside me, hesitantly looking for signs of a baby coming. (He was rightfully hesitant because at about this time with Lennox's birth, my water popped, startling us both.)

As anticipated, it happened again–my waters burst, and he jumped back. Lennox was also standing nearby and just barely missed being splashed. Luckily, we have that great moment on video!

A couple of minutes later, the next contraction came ripping through me and my body began to push. Zackary called for the boys to come in so they could be part of the birth. Moments later, we got to see little Waverly Love's beautiful face for the first time.

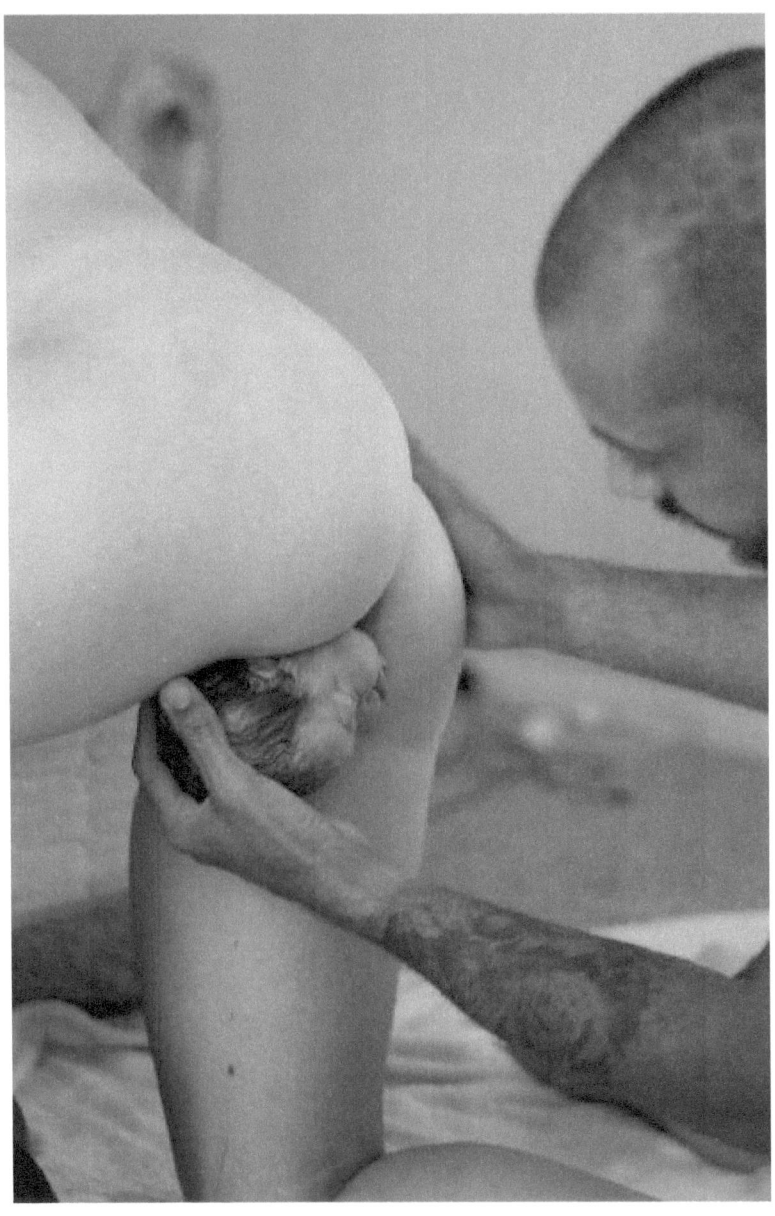

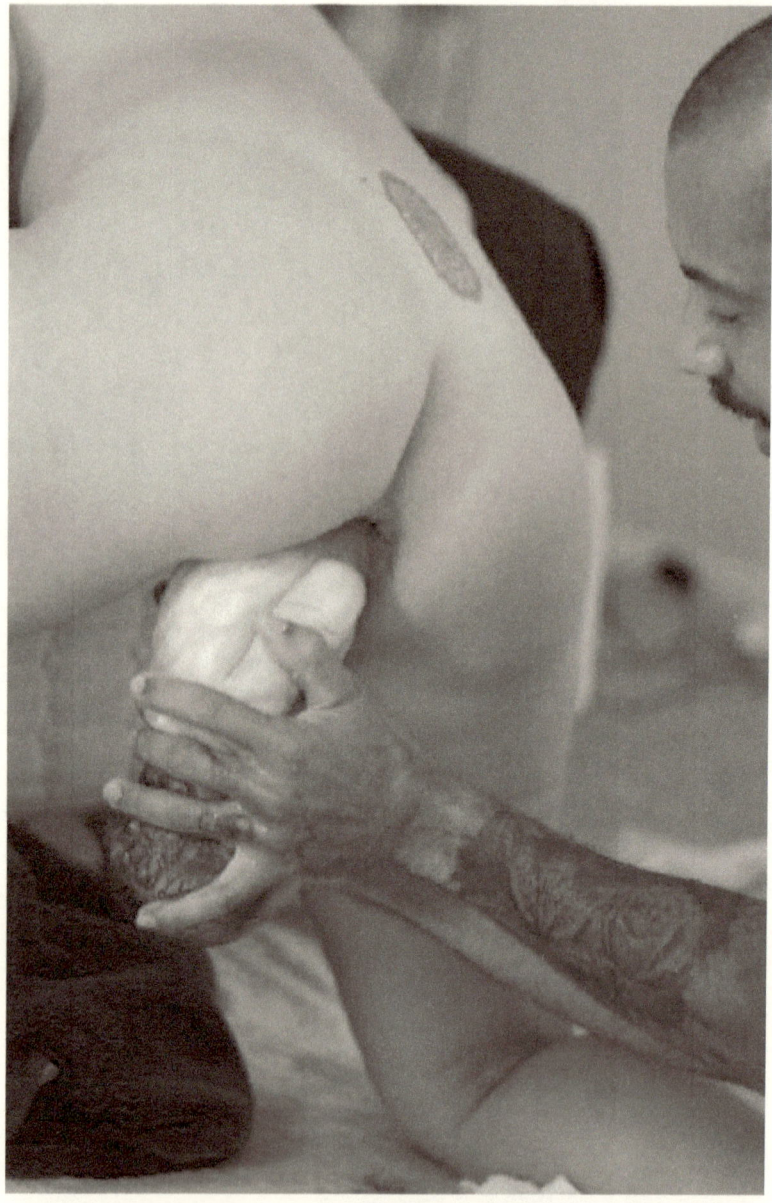

Her head was out! It took everything in me to stop the pushing while I waited for the next contraction. I got into a lunge position on the floor, still leaning over the bed. A couple of minutes later, the contraction came and Zackary helped to guide her shoulders out one at a time while my body pushed. Once the first shoulder was out, the rest of her perfect little body slid out into Zackary's arms at exactly 3pm. Instant relief! I turned around and plopped on the floor in exhaustion.

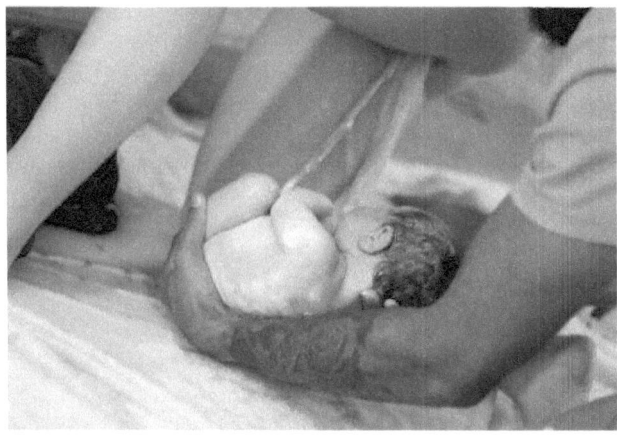

The first thing I said was, "Does she have a vagina?!" just to make sure the blood test was accurate. I heard Waverly's first little cry as Zackary laid her on my chest. She made a few gurgling sounds before falling asleep. She had also been working hard all day and was ready for a nap. She was covered in vernix and was perfect in every way.

We all breathed her in and I think I even saw some tears in the eyes around the room. Pure Bliss. Within minutes, Waverly started to look for my nipple and she latched on to nurse immediately.

I was very quickly reminded that just because the baby is out, doesn't mean birth is over. You still have work to do! The after pains started coming in strong as Waverly continued to nurse. The floor very quickly became uncomfortable and Zackary set up a space on our bed for me. He helped me get up and Waverly and I sunk into the bed.

At about 3:45 pm, I decided it was time to see if the placenta was ready. Zackary placed a table cloth and towels on the floor for me, as well as a bowl to catch the placenta. I handed Waverly to him and squatted over the bowl. It was very clear that the placenta had detached and was ready to come out. I gave a little tug on the cord and pushed. It easily slid out into the bowl–I immediately felt some relief from the after pains!

I climbed back into bed and Zackary handed Waverly back to me and placed the bowl nearby so she could continue to receive all the cord blood.

Waverly nursed and slept for a while longer until I wanted to get up and rinse off in the shower. Around 5 pm, we decided it was time to cut the cord and do her measurements. My mother-in-law had crocheted a beautiful cord tie that we used to tie off the umbilical cord. Zackary and Kingston cut the cord together.

We used a luggage scale and a ring sling to weigh her: 7lbs exactly! She measured 20.5 inches long.

I took a few minutes to rinse off in the shower while Zackary cuddled in bed with our baby girl. Beth and Addison helped to clean up and keep the other kids occupied. I could not have asked for more love and support.

The day was everything I could have imagined and then some.

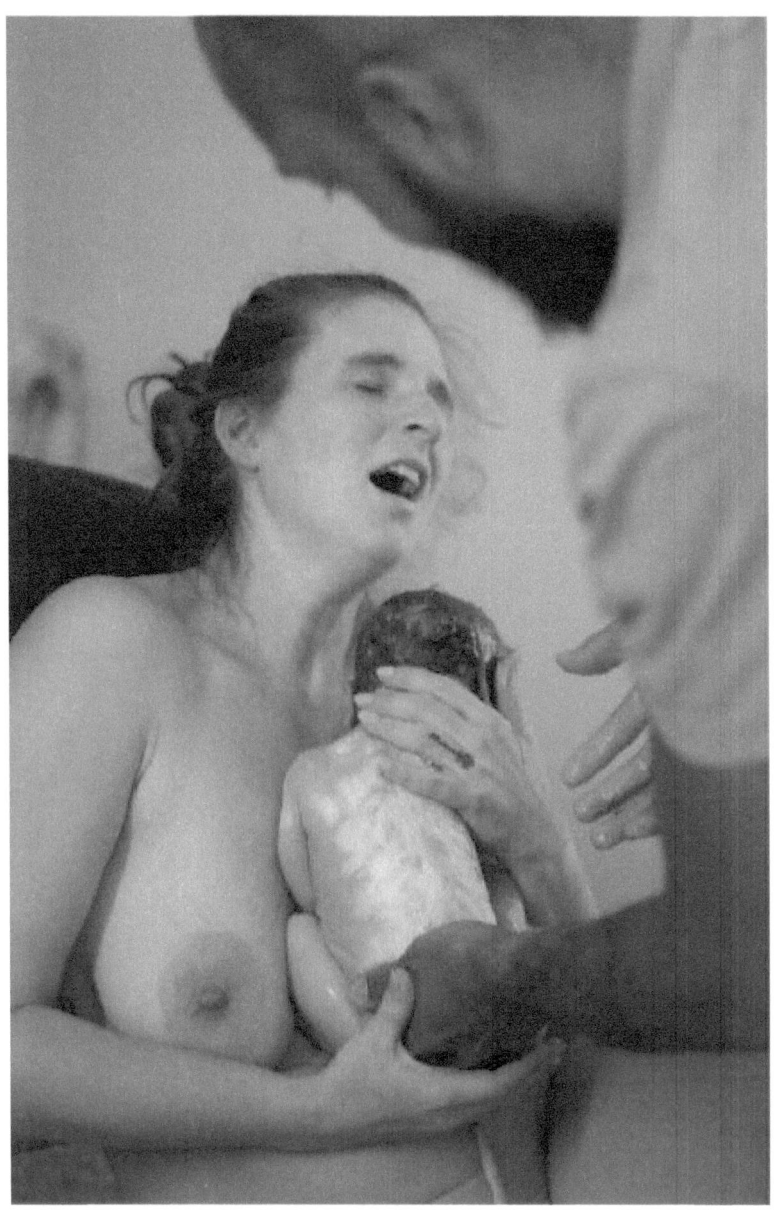

Worth it All – The Birth Of Agatha Wren Sue

By Brooke Collier

THERE IS SO MUCH wrapped up in this birth for me, sisters. I wrote it all down just a week after she was born, all the details and all the facts, even as I was still unsure how to make meaning of or peace with aspects of it. But I've been very nervous to share this one more widely, hence the delay.

Agatha is 3.5 months old at the time that I'm sitting down to write this "public" version of her birth story. I ask that if you venture to read/see this precious (and lengthy) story, that you hold it gently, with compassion, withholding judgment and suspending fear.

The weeks leading up to when Agatha would be born were incredibly challenging physically and psychologically and I was very impatient. I had never gone this far past my EDD, and so at 41 weeks and some days I even took Midwife's Brew (which I don't recommend per se, and which is one of those things I said I'd never do!).

At 41+5 I started experiencing pain above my pubic bone and in my lower back that was debilitating, leaving me unable to stand up straight or walk without crying! I was hormonal and emotional, and basically bedridden. I had two nights of contractions, and she was engaged in my pelvis.

I shed so many tears that week and would daily lay in the bathtub just sobbing and begging Jesus to "deliver me!" I journaled a lot and also tried to deal with whatever fears, mental blocks and emotions came up, letting them all go so that I could be ready to meet my baby. I was bedridden for a few days straight, forcing Tim to take time off work to watch the kids.

I could not comprehend how I would deal with labor when I was in constant pain as a baseline going into it. How would I do the labor dance? How would I get into different positions to work with contractions or to push her out? I was utterly weak and felt completely unable. I didn't want to labor to start! But I was also desperate to experience contractions so I could get her OUT.

I was so blessed during this week to have several friends reaching out to me regularly to say they were praying for me, to share an encouraging word or meme, a worship song, a scripture verse. They held me up and I clung to them for dear life.

Thursday, July 23, 2020

I thought perhaps I had a bladder and/or Kidney infection so saw my PCP at noon-time to have a urine test and lab culture done. I thought if the pain could be explained by an infection then it could be alleviated with antibiotics. But when the test came back negative, I knew that the only way to get OUT of pain was to have a baby.

I would have to go through the fire, cos the fire was not going to get extinguished.

Later in the afternoon I had a midwife friend come by to check me and do a membrane sweep, because psychologically I needed it to start soon. (This is another one of those things I said I'd never do, but my idealism was flying out the window).

She found I was 95% effaced, 4 cm dilated, with a vaginal vault that felt "squishy", and baby was at -2 station, but came down to -1 when I laughed. :) There wasn't much left to sweep cos my body had already done so much, but she worked it a little more.

The only time I felt better during these days was when I was in the bathtub. So though I had not been planning a water birth (nor have I ever had one or even been drawn to the idea of having one!), I began to think that maybe a water birth would be important in helping to alleviate just enough of my baseline pain to allow me relax my tight muscles and to do what birth required of me.

So, we reached out to my friend and doula-tographer, Annica, to borrow a birth pool and liner she had offered for us on-lend.

We got a hose and adapter from another friend, and set up the birth pool in Agatha's nursery (which adjoins our bedroom) that night, even filling it partway with lukewarm water, thinking that would make it quicker to top off with hot water whenever labor commenced.

I went to bed almost expecting to go into labor that night. I didn't. Just had a few contractions in the night, per usual, which stopped by morning.

Friday, July 24, 2020

I had been trying to stay off social media in preparation for her birth, not wanting to soak up all the negative energy and fear running rampant in those spaces about coronavirus, racism, politics, and more (what a scary, stressful year to birth a baby!). But on this morning I suddenly felt like I wanted to post on FB, to share about what I was going through and ask for prayers. I wrote a long and very honest post about how much I was struggling. This was at about 7:30 am.

The day went on like the others with me stuck in bed, crying and hurting and trying to rest. I watched some stand-up comedy (which became a favorite distraction of mine in the last weeks of pregnancy) and reviewed bits of my freebirth books.

It was about 4:20 pm when I recorded/timed what I though might be my first real contraction. I was laying on my side watching a comedian on my laptop when it happened. It felt like a strong menstrual cramp. For the next two hours, as I alternated between laying on my left side and my right side, I breathed through them, holding very still, and timed them.

They were 45 seconds to a minute or more long but spaced very erratically at 3-7 minutes apart. I was texting back and forth with friend and birth attendant Heather about them, asking her to help me discern if this was really labor.

Tim popped in at about this time and I told him what was going on. He said, "Why don't I just fill up the birth pool?" He also asked if he could ask Laura to come over and help with kids' bedtimes, and I said sure.

He finished filling the tub with hot water, and then he took the kids out for a walk. Unbeknownst to me, while on that walk he gave a heads up to Annica and Heather to be on high alert because he suspected that once labor got going it would go fast.

Meanwhile, I decided at about 6 pm to sit up and see what happened. I knew that if it was false labor, they'd likely cease when I changed position. So I first got on my hand and knees, then sat on the edge of the bed. The contractions became very weak, super short, and then just stopped. I sighed. Fake. It was a false start.

I texted Tim and Heather at about 6:40 pm and told them so. I said I was embarrassed and annoyed now that birth tub was all filled up for nothing and what a waste.

Heather suggested that I just get in it anyway, since it was already full and would probably feel so good for all my aches and pains. I thought that was a great idea so I put on a sports bra that was NOT the one I wanted to wear for my birth (because I wasn't having a baby today!), got in the water, and started playing a worship song she sent me a link to on YouTube.

The water felt AMAZING, bringing such relief.

And then, within a minute or two I was gripped by a very hard contraction that made me cuss.

Tim came back from the walk, having handed off the kids to the just-arrived Laura, to check in with me. Soon after he came in the room I had another contraction like that. He said he took one look at my belly and seeing the incredibly tightened uterus and hearing my vocalizations, he began texting Annica and Heather "come now" (but I didn't know that).

He stayed with me as the contractions continued to come, close and long and hard. I felt myself pooping and lamented that I'd failed to obtain a fishnet! So he had to get creative in scooping it out.

I also told him I had the wrong bra on for the birth, so he fetched the right one and helped me switch them out. Vanity! Soon the contractions started to have a pushy feeling to them, which I sort of couldn't believe. But it started to dawn on me that this baby was coming quite soon, but my birth team was not (because I still hadn't summoned them).

Tim asked if he could get the kids and I think I just mumbled, "I don't knoooow..." as a contraction started up again. I could feel baby descending as my body involuntarily pushed. Tim slipped out of the room— I didn't even notice — as I, on hands and knees, facing the window so I could look at the trees outside, tried to rest between contractions and center myself for her emergence.

The kids and Laura came up with Tim just as a very long contraction began.

Hazel breathlessly exclaimed, "It's happening! It's happening!" as she set to work taking photos on her new camera. I could swear that I groaned "fuuuuuuck" and then "help me, Jesus" as my body pushed without ceasing all the way past crowning and until her entire head was born, but my family tells me I was quiet!

I reached down to stroke the top of her head and talk to her, asking Tim and the kids if they could see her face, which they could. Her eyes were open. She was not in her sac of amniotic fluid but I have no idea when it broke, cos I didn't notice it!

Unlike with my other babies' births, there was a pause at this point. Instead of being entirely born in one contraction, I had to wait for another one to push out her shoulders and body. That pause felt so long! It was physically stretching, of course, and also mentally challenging. I had to remind myself that a pause like this well within the range of normal, and not a reason to be concerned.

That 2.5-minute pause, however, actually allowed me to slow down and catch up with this wild ride, allowed me to get centered and to connect to my baby. I remember narrating her restitution aloud for the my family and feeling her wiggle and maneuver inside of me to negotiate the pelvis. It was incredible to be so present.

During the pause my kids were also saying hilarious things, which are captured on the video footage Tim and Laura were recording.

Walter said, "Mom, when you're done having the baby, I'll give you this quarter." Maeve said, "Why are you having a baby right now?"

Finally, the next contraction came and she was born up to her waist/hips only! I thought that was rather unexpected. I asked Tim whether both arms were in and at that same moment felt that one was still tucked inside me at her wrist, so getting into something more like a runner's lunge, I gently pulled it free.

I did not want to wait for another contraction for her legs to be born, so I tried gently tugging to see if she'd come the rest of the way out without a contraction.

It worked! She kicked off the top of my uterus and out she came (about 7:20 pm).

I guided her to the front of me where I could see her through the water. I let there be a short pause here, just taking in her face and tiny self before slowly, gently lifting her out of the water.

It was so special to have this moment also be slowed down a bit, but I knew I couldn't let it be quite as slow as I wanted it to be because her color was not good. She was very pale, even beneath her thick vernix, and her lips quite blue. She startled slightly and grimaced when she first cleared the surface of the water, but then she went floppy.

I pulled her to my chest and smiled over her and took her in, but I also sensed that she needed some help. I started with rubbing her very vernix-covered back vigorously, as well as the bottoms of her feet.

I talked to her about how happy I was that she was here at last and that I loved her. I reached down to feel her cord to make sure it was pulsing. It was, but it was also thinner and whiter than I would have expected. I asked her if she needed some help and then used my mouth to suction her nose and mouth, spitting out the mucous into the birth pool.

And then I gave her breath, covering her nose and mouth with mine and puffing air into her from my cheeks, gentle and small.

I sort of did all of these things in varying order, instinctually (not at all textbook, even though I have been trained in neonatal resuscitation) and though she would peek an eye open or make a tiny grunt once or twice, I wasn't seeing her tone or color improve enough.

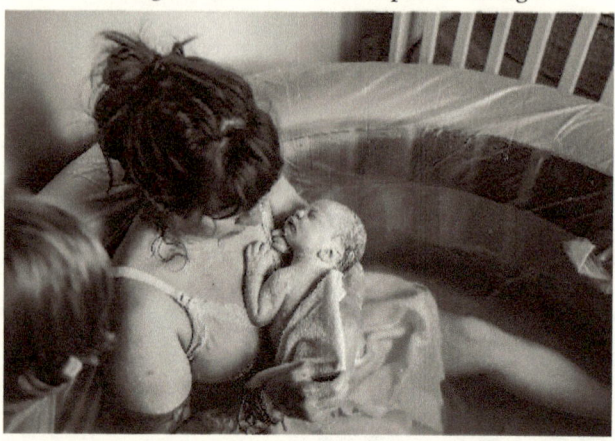

Though I felt calm, present, clear and very purposeful, I asked Tim how many minutes had passed and he—who had wisely set a stopwatch to keep track—replied it had been about 2.5 minutes. I instructed him calmly to call 911, thinking that if she did not come around quickly, I would want to know help was en route. He promptly dialed 911 from the adjacent room.

Meanwhile, I kept giving her breaths and changing her position and simulating her. Of course! Isn't this just the way it goes?!

Within 30 second of him getting 911 on the phone, she let out a cry, grimace, movement.

When Tim came back in the room I told him she was okay and that we didn't need EMS after all, but they had already been dispatched. It took some doing to get them to abandon their mission, since their protocol is to come in and check things over no matter what, but I really didn't want a bunch of uniformed men in my birth space when I knew we were fine, and I knew they would probably try to cut her cord and do things to her that weren't truly necessary.

Finally they agreed to leave our driveway once Tim told them a midwife was on her way to check on us (which wasn't actually exactly true, but you do what you gotta do).

Even after that first breath and cry, she was still slow-ish in coming around. She seemed to be almost half-asleep, but she was breathing and pink color was coming. Now that she is a week old, I see how she sleeps and how slowly and lazily she wakes up form deep sleep and I wonder if her nature played a roll in her slow-to-come-around status.

However, personality cannot account for her color and tone, so I have no regrets about assisting her in finding her first breath.

Once she was ok, the euphoria could kick in! I looked up to see my kids and Laura surrounding me, smiling, and Annica had also just slipped in, followed by Heather a couple minutes later. Tim finished up his phone call with the dispatcher and then also joined the smiling, amazed faces surrounding the birth pool.

I made eye contact with Tim and said, "We did it!" He cried, just as much about joy over meeting her as relief of the tension he'd held as he watched everything transpire.

I felt amazing. All the pain I'd carried in my body the days leading up to my birth was totally gone, which was such a relief. I had caught my own baby, my kids had witnessed it, and it happened in the daylight (which the birth photographer in me loved)!

My baby was beautiful and perfectly whole, putting to rest all those vague fears I'd had that "something would be wrong" with her because I'm 40 years old (and hadn't had a single ultrasound to check on her). We just sat in the tub and basked for a while, the kids reaching out in turn to touch her "slimy" head. There was no blood in the pool at all. I put Agatha to my breast and she did what I call "nipple-noodling" where she's not latching on, but just exploring.

Eventually, Heather and Tim helped me get out of the pool while still holding her to my chest. We didn't want to cut the cord because we had planned a cord burning for after her placenta was born. We hobbled over to the bedroom and got me situated on incontinence and chux pads on our bed, removed my wet bra and drying me off beforehand.

And then began the waiting for the placenta. I had a separation gush of blood, but was lacking any cramping/contractions to help expel it.

I wanted to try to keep a quiet, birth-like environment for the birth of the placenta to see if that would help it to come sooner than the 2 hours that I'd waiting at each of my previous births, so we sent the kids downstairs with Laura to bake a cake and watch a show on Netflix. I tried getting in squat and lunge positions both on the floor and on the bed to let the placenta be born, but none of it was working.

We had arranged beforehand to hire a midwife friend to come by to do a newborn exam and help us with navigate paperwork for filing for a birth certificate.

When Tim called her to let her know baby was born and to schedule her visit, it turned out the only time she could come in the next 24 hours was about an hour after Agatha was born. I would have preferred for her to come the following day, because I liked the non-directive and agenda-free energy we had going, but she wasn't able to do that so I consented to her coming right away.

When she arrived, my baby was still at my breast but fussing and crying quite a lot and had yet to latch on successfully as the midwife tried to talk through the paperwork with us. I started to feel very overwhelmed. Heather spoke up and asked me if it was all feeling like too much and I said it was and asked the midwife and Tim to go get started on that paperwork in the other room so I could work on settling in and calming Agatha. A while later, they returned to the room and she did an abbreviated newborn exam.

She then asked if I wanted help with my placenta, which still hadn't come out. Because I was feeling so impatient about it, I said something like, "Sure! I caught my own baby, I don't need to prove anything with my placenta!"

What transpired ended up being far more intense and prolonged than I expected, and every muscle in my body was tensing up with the discomfort and the energetic pressure of the whole situation and it wasn't working; the placenta was not budging.

Heather reminded me that my placenta had come out while squatted over a toilet after Maeve's birth and so perhaps we could try that again. So we got me and Agatha to the dark bathroom, put a chux pad under the toilet seat, and I sat down to try to relax my bottom.

I finally got in the zone and found the right way to push and out it slid (what a relief). I had to do it all without contractions/cramping though! I'm sure that makes it harder! I wish I had used the Angelica tincture I had on hand. It took a bit over two hours.

Now that the placenta was out and had been looked over for completeness, we got us both back to bed, placed the placenta in a bowl, and got out the things for a cord burning. The kids and Laura were summoned back into the room and the midwife took her leave.

Tim prayed over Agatha and thanked God for the placenta and the work it did to help her grow. The beeswax candles were lit, and each of oldest children held one over the handcrafted wooden box.

I held and nursed Agatha as we waited the 15-20 minutes it takes for the cord to burn through. It slowed everything down again, brought the energy of the space back to sacred and mindful bliss. Everything felt right with the world. My work was done, our baby girl was now completely separated, her own being, and our family was complete and in unity.

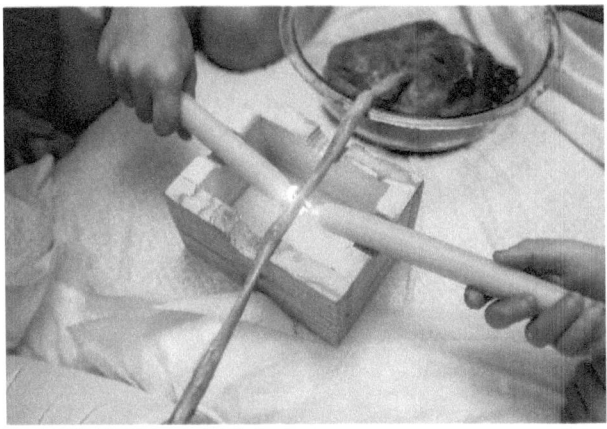

Tim and the kids each took a turn holding her after her cord was severed. All that was left after that was to wrap up some odds and ends of birth laundry, birth trash, a placenta smoothie, a diaper for Agatha, etc. Then our birth team took their leave (about 11:30 pm).

It took a while to get the kids to go to bed, but eventually, everyone settled into their respective beds. I didn't sleep. I was too overjoyed and hyper-vigilant over this tiny new human on my chest to get much sleep at all. Besides, she was fussy that first night. But it didn't matter. She was and is worth it all.

Learn more about Brooke's Christian birthing course, called 'EMBRACE', and see more pictures and video of her birth with Agatha on her website:

https://www.sisterbirth.com/

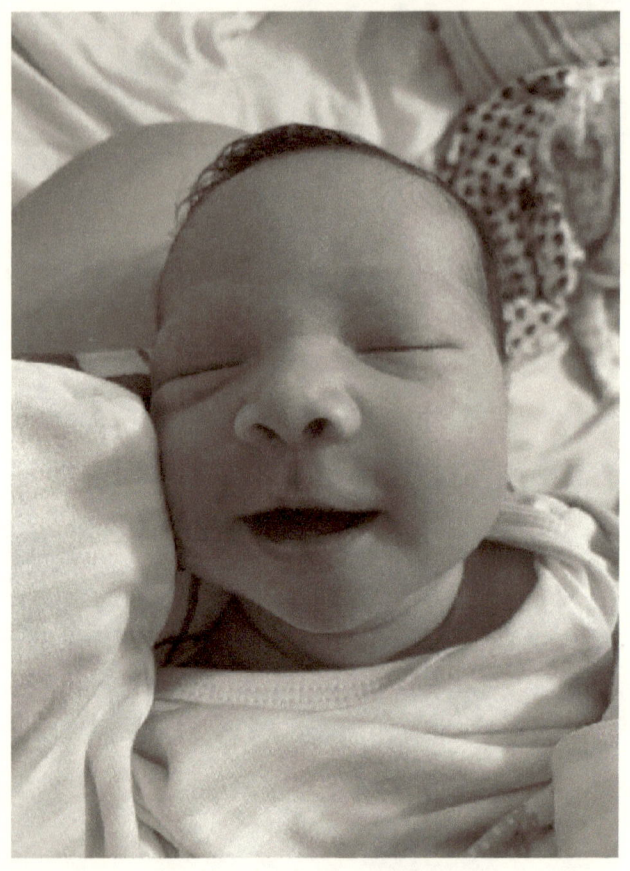

Baby Jazmine's Birth Story

By Heather Conley Williams

So MY DUE DATE o my due date based on conception was June 15th, 2020, but I told everyone it was June 14th because I didn't want to admit the due date was my ex's birthday. Plus, I didn't think it mattered, like what are the chances she would be born on that date?!

Anyways, I had been having contractions for a few days prior, on and off all day, but nothing consistent or really strong so I didn't time them.

They seemed to get more intense and closer together at night when I laid down, so I would have to walk around to get through them or lean over the peanut ball. I got through that night (13th) and waited for morning to ask my fiancé fill up the birth pool.

I stayed in the pool for a couple hours during the day but decided to get out and walk around to see if things would pick up a bit (I didn't want to stall labor). They still weren't consistent or as strong as before, so I stayed out of the pool until I knew it was time. That night (6/14) around 9 pm, they began to pick back up and seemed really close together.

I waited an hour or so and finally gave in and wanted to go into the pool to help with the pain because I knew I didn't want to be in pain all night again. I hadn't slept in two days and knew the water would help.

So, my family got the pool ready for me, again, and I hopped in about 10 pm. Contractions were about 6 mins apart, 1 min long. My mom waited outside the tent (with her husband) and timed contractions for me…but around 1 or 2 am I asked her to stay with me inside the tent because I was falling asleep in between contractions and didn't want to drown in the pool.

Within a couple hours, they became 5 mins apart, then 4 mins, then 3 mins, then 2 mins. Every hour I was getting closer! Thank God.

At exactly 3 am, I felt a POP! And my water broke.

I almost thought it was the baby, so my mom went to go get my fiancé (an EMT), who was trying to put our kids back to sleep. When he came in, I was feeling the FER *(fetal ejection reflex)*, but I didn't think it was time to push yet. I did a small push, and of course I pooped a little. My fiancé hopped in and cleaned it up for me real quick.

After a few more contractions, I started to push with them and with two big pushes she torpedoed out into the water where my man caught her. Born at 3:18 am, June 15th. 7 1/2 lbs, 21 inches long.

It was so surreal and happened so perfect, I am beyond thankful to God.

I did get a 2nd degree tear, but it's been healing nicely (using Manuka honey and seaweed).

This was my third baby. First was a C-section in 2017 and second was a hospital VBAC in 2018, both with epidurals at 4cm, so to do this all natural was such a blessing.

I highly recommend using the birth pool for pain management (the pool straps too), as well as blowing raspberries when you exhale during the contractions, it made all the difference for me.

Thank you to everyone for all your stories and advice, it gave me all the strength to have this home birth unassisted!

We are Warriors

By Savannah Haines

FOREST WOLF WALKER
Born at 3:48 am 4th August, 2020.
HBAC

First, a bit of history. My firstborn was delivered by EMC. I realise now the system doesn't always have it right, and they may also be the ones to cause an issue. Intentionally or not, it happened and my little girl ended up having hypoxic ischemic encephalopathy (HIE) and now has four limb Cerebral palsy. She's amazing all the same. This experience triggered me to want a home birth even more.

So, fast forward 11 months later, and I find I'm pregnant again, intentionally. I'd informed my local doctor and got juggled between two different midwives. They read my history and straight away told me I'd be high risk and I would have my baby on a delivery ward.

They didn't make me feel as though I had a choice. But I knew by then that I did. I stuck to my guns and geared myself up with a lot of information regarding their reasoning, etc. I wanted a home birth and was happy to have a midwife present, but even happier to have a freebirth.

I know how having someone - a stranger more so in my safe space (home) - could potentially ruin my process of birth. So I decided not to go back and do the urine checks and blood pressure at home. (That's mostly all they do at midwife appointments).

I did get harassed with letters, but my intuition by now was strong and I trusted my body, so I ignored them. With COVID they told me I couldn't have a midwife, so I was set to freebirth. I no longer wanted or needed their services.

This pregnancy I did it! Completely alone. I allowed myself to flow and trust my body. It began with a slow two days. I felt as though I just had trapped wind whilst slowly losing my mucus plug over those days. I'd planned on water birthing and had set up a beautiful birthing space with affirmations on the walls and fairy lights. On the 3rd of August, I'd told my partner the pool needed filling.

And thank goodness I did. I spent the night riding my surges in the water whilst mentally remaining calm. I felt the need to poo, so I went upstairs to the toilet. My waters broke whilst on the toilet, and that's when I realized it was go-time as my surges became more powerful.

I couldn't remain as calm. This was around 3.20 am on the 4th of August. I'd had the bloody show just before. I went back into the pool and by then I was on all fours not really in this world, my body was experiencing labour and I'd never experienced it.

I had to fight a lot of intrusive thoughts about what's ifs, etc., and I had my partner calmly reassuring me. I felt something had changed, and I needed my mum, who thankfully was watching my daughter upstairs who slept through my roars. As my mum reached my side, I told my partner to be ready for the baby's entrance. It was so intense. My body was pushing with every ounce of me.

There was another change in intensity and my body just pushed. I remember thinking if this goes on any longer, I'm not going to survive. It was such a quick transition and release on earthside just over 20 minutes after. I didn't really have time to process anything, just hearing the words 'you did it', he's here' was surreal. He was caught in the pool by his daddy. His nanna watched it all unfold. It happened so fast. I learned it was called precipitous labor.

I took the baby from him and sucked on my son's face as he was crying, but I just felt a need to do so for my peace of mind. I was all of a sudden nervous about the water he'd 'torpedoed' through.

As I took him, I realised the cord was really short. I got out of the pool onto the sofa.

We delayed cord cutting, but not for as long as I'd initially wanted as I needed the toilet, but it had stopped pulsing so I guess that's optimal. I birthed placenta on the bathroom floor at around 7:50 am. I checked for any big clots, but all seemed fine.

I used Affterease tincture after I birthed my placenta to help with blood loss, although I did feel fine. It helped massively.

Soaking up our new life as a family of four.

I recommend the book 'Homebirth on Your Own Terms' by Heather Baker.

I felt empowered towards a bullying system that had no consideration to me as an individual. I proved them all wrong.

We are not statistics.

We are capable. We are strong.

We are warriors.

Advice for a Summer Birth

From the women who wrote the stories in this collection.

Get yourself an outdoor set-up for postpartum! I bought myself a lovely camping rocking chair and a screened-in portable tent so that I felt like I could sit outside with baby during my postpartum lying-in and benefit from the fresh air and sunshine.

STAY HYDRATED! Drink SO MUCH water.

Embrace the sunshine, breath the fresh air, get a good water bottle!

I recommend staying well hydrated and keeping cool.

Rest while you can!

Whatever you're worried about happening, learn about how it's caused, ways to prevent it, or how to deal with it if it was to happen. But know how very unlikely it is.

Make homemade ice pops/smoothies.

Our lake and the ocean were my best friends

Stay hydrated, keep cool, eat lots of protein. You got this mama!

Tips on Beating the Heat While Pregnant

I'VE BEEN PREGNANT THROUGH the entire summer in four out of six of my births. I gave birth to another child at the beginning of the summer. I have a bit of experience when it comes to summer pregnancies! In four of those pregnancies I was pregnant in Utah (which is a bit of a desert with nice hot summers), and the houses we lived in had no AC, only swamp coolers!

Staying hydrated is obviously a huge thing, but it's easier said than done. You don't feel like drinking very much because you know you'll have to pee constantly, and you're also either nauseated or you get full quickly. Gulping down a glass of water was so unappealing to me, I had to trick my brain into drinking more by doing one of the following:

- Adding fresh fruit or cucumbers to my water (berries, melon, apples, mint, and citrus fruits are all especially good!)

- Drinking with a straw - for some reason this made drinking water so much easier and better!

- Using a water enhancer or flavor pack. My favorite brand is Stur, a stevia-sweetened more natural water flavor enhancer.

- Making an herbal infusion - Another way to flavor water AND get extra nutrients! Mint, Red Raspberry, Hibiscus, Ginger, etc. are all safe options for drinking during pregnancy. You'd have to drink upwards of six or more cups per day in order to cause any issues with any of these infusions. Plenty of other herbs would be safe too! Simply put the herbs in a tall mason jar with either warm or cold water and set on a windowsill or countertop. It'll be ready in 12-24 hours! Add sugar, stevia drops, or honey with ice and use a straw to get the best enjoyment out of it!

- Popsicles, smoothies, and yes, even soups are all fantastic sources of liquid intake. Even eating a nice, juicy watermelon counts as hydrating yourself!

Okay, now that you're hydrated, make sure you also stay cool! Swimming, taking cool showers or baths, and resting in the shade are all great ways to keep your body temperature down. If you live in a place where it's very hot in the summer, make sure you take frequent breaks indoors where possible.

Holistic Advice for Common Pregnancy Symptoms

IF YOU'RE READING THIS book, it's pretty likely that you lean towards natural solutions in many, if not most, things that come up in your life. And that includes pregnancy and the various discomforts women can experience in that sacred time.

Having had six babies, I have a lot of experience treating common pregnancy symptoms naturally. I am by no means an expert, and no advice given in this book is substitution for speaking with a wise woman, herbalist, midwife, or doctor as you prefer.

Take these ideas below as suggestions, and know that they are certainly not a comprehensive list. There are several books out there that cover herbs for pregnancy, various diets and supplements for pregnancy, and more. This is simply based on my own personal experience, and I'll do my best to direct you to other resources that I know exist.

HEARTBURN

Some women down entire bottles of tums, but I reach for the **almond milk.** That's right! Unsweetened almond milk is one of the best treatments I've found for heartburn. It is high in calcium, which is one of the components in Tums that helps reduce the acidity of your stomach acid, so it really makes sense that almond milk would work. I find that half a glass, or even sometimes just a swallow or two, can reduce or eliminate heartburn very quickly.

Another option, especially if you'd rather chew something than drink or if you don't like almond milk, is **papaya enzymes**. These come in a chalky, sweet, white-colored tablet at your local natural foods store or online. They're quite pleasant and harmless, so you can munch on them during, after, or between any meal and get relief! I found these to be effective, but not as effective for me as almond milk. Give them a try!

My third tip for heartburn is the most difficult to accomplish, but by far the most effective. During my sixth pregnancy I discovered a book called **"Powerfully Pregnant", by Donna Young, N.D.** In it she describes, in detail, a diet for pregnant women that she claimed eliminated the "normal" symptoms most women often have in pregnancy, and even shortened and improved birth outcomes for the women she served as a midwife!

I was intrigued, and so I bought the book. I have zero regrets. It was a fantastic read, and honestly, every time I followed her dietary recommendations exactly, I felt AMAZING. I lost excessive weight in my early pregnancy due to eating so healthy, I had ZERO morning sickness, and NO HEARTBURN. Plus my aches and pains went way down too.

So, if you're serious about not dealing with any of these symptoms, you'll want to consider following her diet. In short, it included no grains, no dairy, no sugars (except sometimes honey, and stevia), no tomatoes or citrus, etc. It's not for the faint of heart, but if you want results and you want to be at the peak of health during your pregnancy, definitely look into following her recommendations.

Sciatica/SPD/Any Ache or Pain

I already mentioned the book, Powerfully Pregnant, and it's my top recommendation here as well. But for those who need a simple, quick, perhaps more palatable solution, try the following:

I mix a teaspoon of turmeric with a quarter teaspoon of black pepper. They interact when mixed together and the black pepper "activates" anti-inflammatory properties in the turmeric. I add this to a cup of almond milk, warm or cold is fine (you can use any kind of milk you like, or make a tea). Then I add honey or maple syrup to taste. Within 15 minutes of drinking this mixture, I'm often in a lot less pain. It's absolutely fine to drink multiple glasses a day.

"I want to share with you what totally cured me of [SPD]. Mine was so bad with my last pregnancy. I literally couldn't not walk anymore. Exercises only made it worse. I couldn't roll over in bed, put on my shoes or socks, husband had to help dress me, sometimes I couldn't even wipe myself on the toilet. It was pure torture. I mentioned it in a freebirth group I was in at the time and one of the ladies told me about **Liquid Dulse Iodine** and how it helped her tremendously. So I did some research and decided to get some.

I went from being unable to walk at all to all my symptoms completely disappeared in about 1 week. It's super cheap, easy to take and totally safe. Spd is caused by your body releasing too much of the hormone Relaxin, which is the hormone that causes your body to loosen up your joints for labor. However, too much causes your hip and pelvic joints to shift too much, get stuck, and pop snap, etc.

You can't walk, roll over in bed, etc. It can be quite debilitating. The liquid dulse iodine regulates and balances the hormone. I ordered more this pregnancy because I'm starting to get SPD symptoms already this pregnancy at only 18 weeks! No way I'm going through that again! So I thought I would share. I didn't need chiro, specific exercises, or anything else for SPD. This took it away 100%. It's about $15.

Dosage: it will take at least 1 mg of the iodine to feel some relief. Start there for a few days and up dosage as needed. That's about 8 drops 2-3 times a day.If you want a stronger product so you can take fewer drops daily, you can take Lugol's iodine. It is 2.5mg per drop. But I suggest working your way up with this one first and then switching to Lugol's if that's what you want to do. Here's a great article on dosage safety if you are interested."

Link to the recommended Iodine to start with: https://amzn.to/3ty BtFD

Link to the Lugol's supplement you can take if you want a more concentrated dose: https://amzn.to/3BW8I8O

Iodine is safe to use in pregnancy, in moderation. Consult with someone who knows more than me if you have an concerns! Again, not medical advice, just an amazing suggestion.

Nausea or "Morning Sickness"

Before this one, I have to give a disclaimer. I don't get severe morning sickness. I don't even throw up. I DO get nauseated in early pregnancy, or at least I DID before I discovered Donna White's diet, as mentioned above. Once I started her diet, my early pregnancy nausea was gone by 7 weeks. That's right. 7 weeks! Normally it lasts until about week 13 for me. If you have hypermesis gravidum and throw up constantly, you can absolutely try these recommendations, but also, don't be afraid to get medication or IV help if you're having severe symptoms.

Aside from the common ideas of eating when you first wake up, eating frequently, getting enough protein and electrolytes, here's my list of nausea-prevention must-haves:

2, you can make suckers with sugar or honey, you can juice it, buy the ginger chews, etc. It's so versatile!

Next is **pressure points**. You'll want to look this up on your own since I won't go into detail, but there are some great pressure points for nausea. I know of one on the ear lobe that's pretty helpful.

The diet in the book "Powerfully Pregnant" is getting mentioned here again because I feel I can't talk about it enough. It was life-changing.

And last, but not least, **peppermint essential oil**. Diffuse it, dab a tiny bit on your chest or wrist (watch out, it's a "hot" oil and can burn a bit if you don't dilute it). I prefer DoTerra or Butterfly Express oils.

I wish I could just sit in a room with you and answer all your questions about the dozens of other symptoms women experience in pregnancy! This very short list only covers the ones that bothered me the most in my own pregnancies, but if you ever have questions, I am available to answer those in my email (authorbreemoore@gmail.com) or as a pregnancy consultant on my website: www.daydreamdoula.com.

Link to original Iodine Facebook post:

https://www.facebook.com/groups/19041103996/posts/10157679577503997

Link to gelatin:

https://amzn.to/3lbzgfK

How to Talk to Your Husband or Partner About Freebirth

from "Birth Becomes Hers" by Bree Moore

GETTING YOUR BIRTH PARTNER on board is one of the most-asked questions in freebirth circles. I remember when I first brought the idea to my husband before the birth of our third baby. I had been interviewing midwives but didn't feel great about any of them.

We'd had a home birth before, but with a midwife. I knew he was already comfortable with home birth, which was a big help, but he was TERRIFIED of the idea of an unassisted birth. When I first told him I was considering it, my super-supportive baby-catching husband stared at me with wide eyes and said, "But what if you DIED?"

"What if I died? How likely is that to happen?" Was my reply. He didn't know, and together we researched until we found a statistic for maternal mortality in birth in the United States. I think the biggest shock for him was seeing that all the countries higher than us were third-world countries without access to medical care. And that a lot of European countries were WAY ahead of us with low maternal mortality rates, and they tend to value midwifery care models for the majority of women.

He didn't agree right then. He was, frankly, overwhelmed, so I let it go. I let the seed get planted, and then I watered it occasionally. I read everything I could get my hands on, every freebirth story, researched every emergency and how to deal with it. We would be sitting together doing our separate thing after the older two kids were in bed and I would just show him a quick statistic, or ask him how he would react if the baby were breech.

I talked to him as if we were having an unassisted birth, I stopped looking for midwives. Essentially, I acted as if he had already said yes and gave him time and space to figure his own emotions out.

One night, I was about halfway through my pregnancy, I asked him what he thought about it and he said that he trusted me. He was still afraid, but he trusted me to be prepared with the knowledge and tools needed.

He also asked me to help educate him, which was incredibly humble of him. He asked me to tell him exactly what he would need to do to help me. And he wanted a Doula, another person there just to be an additional set of hands in case he was busy helping me and we needed something fetched or someone to be with the kids.

There are resources throughout this book, websites, podcasts, and books that you can use to persuade your partner to come with you on this freebirth journey.

When you've already decided you want a freebirth, it can be hurtful when he initially says no, especially if he acts like you're crazy or starts spouting his fears. Take a deep breath and ask him why he feels that way. You might be surprised by the answer. Just listen, don't respond.

Communication 101: Too many people hear what the other has to say and then jump down their throat with a response without validating the other person's opinion. Instead, listen carefully and repeat back what they say as calmly as you can manage.

For example:

You: I want to birth this baby at home without a midwife. No doctor, no hospital.
Him: No way. That's crazy. We're not doing that.
You: Why do you feel that way? What is your biggest fear?

Hopefully, he responds with at least one reason. "The baby could die. You could die. What if you bleed everywhere? What if you tear?" Those are a few of the most common ones. He might not give you much insight and just repeat his refusal. If that happens, you could use this line:

Do you have any evidence that supports the hospital being the safest place for me to give birth?

Most likely he doesn't. He might bring up a relative he knows that almost died or whose baby had complications. The best thing to do in this situation is to ask, "Do you know how likely it is that

X complication will occur?" Again, he probably doesn't. Don't make him feel ignorant, just gently help him come to a realization of his own ignorance. You could ask him if he would watch a documentary with you, or if he'd be open to seeing statistics about that specific complication.

Sometimes it's better to end the conversation there, as frustrating as it is for you, and to address it another time. Even then, you might respond to one fear he has and another one will come up. Be patient as you work with him. This might mean that you have to compromise for a little while, like attending prenatal visits with a care provider you don't intend to birth with. Or, especially if your partner isn't very involved with the details of your pregnancy, you could start your own prenatal care and begin to act as if your plan to birth unassisted is going to come to fruition.

I have to add that I fully recognize that not all relationships are based on the mutual respect and understanding needed to work through fears and objections in this way. Sometimes partners are toxic, abusive, or manipulative, and even bringing up the subject could be dangerous to you physically or emotionally. If this is the case for you, please evaluate why you are in this relationship and whether it is even safe for you to stay. You might need to consider getting help to leave and finding another place to birth your baby.

"If the marriage is strong before the birth, it is likely that a newfound tenderness occurs after the birth. Lovers observe each other in new ways and new revelations are made. Husbands and wives usually experience a greater bonding. The yearning to become visible in your beloved's eyes will be felt the moment a new addition arrives in your family. It's magical, mystical, and divine.

The visibility that is most meaningful is the shared event that takes place inside the family bubble, an historical moment best experienced in private. It is an ordinary, yet extraordinary life event between two lovers."

For a more comprehensive presentation of this topic, please refer to the book "Unassisted Homebirth: An Act of Love".

That isn't to say that all partners who say "no" to freebirth are abusive. It is far more likely that he is afraid. He's afraid of the "what if", the terrifying unknown. If you've had a previous birth inside the medical model that he witnessed, he may have experienced second-hand trauma that he never dealt with. He may be afraid that the same thing will happen again, or that it could be worse.

On the other hand, if nothing went "wrong" in his eyes during a hospital or midwife-led experience in the past, he may think it's illogical for you to want a different experience. This was the camp my husband fell into. We'd had a wonderful experience with a midwife at home before, so why would I want anything different? At the time all

I could tell him was that it felt right and that none of the midwives I interviewed seem to have my interests truly at heart. For so many men, living in the logical side of their brains, *feeling* something is right isn't an entirely valid reason to make a critical life decision.

In the end, if your partner doesn't commit to your vision of a birth without assistance, you have three choices:

Compromise

It's not ideal. Some would argue it's completely dis-empowering to give up your autonomy and ignore your intuition. But there are situations where it may be the best option. I can't tell you what those situations are. That is for you alone to decide, and the situations vary so widely it wouldn't be fair to assign certain situations to the category of compromise. Just know that it is a valid path to take and that you can still have a wonderful, even autonomous birth experience.

Try to find out where your partner's comfort level is, and try to stretch it and help him grow. Maybe he just doesn't want to be the only one there. Your compromise could be to have a Doula, midwife, or traditional birth attendant on call as someone with more knowledge about birth.

Maybe homebirth midwives aren't widely available in your area or even legal, or he'd rather you not birth at home. Your compromise could be to birth at a birth center, preferably free-standing, but if that's not available then a more naturally-minded hospital would be your next step.

If he is very fear-driven or being heavily influenced by the fears of friends, coworkers, or family, he may insist that you give birth at the hospital, and if there are no hospitals known for being supportive of natural options, you may find yourself in a rather tight spot, trying to find an obstetrician that supports autonomous birth but is still covered by insurance because hospital birth is expensive. That alone might be a point that persuades your loved one to support your birth at home if you mention that the only care provider or hospital you'll give birth with is out-of-network.

If there's one thing that speaks well to men in the absence of all other reasoning, it's money. Freebirth is free. You can give birth with just yourself and a towel, no other equipment needed. There are things that make it a little nicer, cleaner, more convenient, but nothing you truly need beyond yourself. You actually don't even need your partner, but you may want him there. Remind him of this, of your love for him and for the child you've created together, then give it time. A compromise early in your pregnancy might soften his heart enough that he agrees later on.

It's up to you how far you're willing to take the compromise, but you'll get further convincing him of your desires the more you pour on love and respect in every conversation with him about where to give birth and with whom.

My Body, My Birth

Or, in other words, "No uterus, no opinion". This baby is growing inside YOUR body. What happens during pregnancy and birth has physical and emotional ramifications for you that can last throughout the rest of your life. Is that something you're willing to compromise in the face of someone else's fear?

This isn't just about you, it's about your baby and your family. Standing your ground in where and how you give birth can lead to new levels of respect and love in your marriage once you're on the other side of the experience. Emilee Saldaya of the Freebirth Society Podcast is one of the biggest advocates of making sure your partner understands and respects that birth is your domain, and therefore your decision. She says, "Never let your partner's fear of birth ruin your right to birth freely."

Remember that your husband can't stop labor once it has started. He has no power in the face of Mother Nature. The most he can do is call 911, and even then you will give birth, and you can give birth in the way you see fit or you can give in to his fear, the emergency personnels' fears, and do whatever they say regardless of your own confidence and intuition. The choice is ultimately yours.

I encourage using the utmost respect as you express this to your partner. It can be very inflammatory in a relationship and your partner could feel disrespected, disregarded, shutout, and angry.

Using your autonomy in this way will bring up all sorts of emotion, so be prepared. Your partner might seem to agree, or at least not fight you on it, and then lose his cool when it comes time for you to give birth. He might also get angry and it could be a source of stress and contention the rest of your pregnancy, creating an toxic environment for labor.

He is your partner; you wouldn't be with him unless you loved him, and he's the other parent for your baby, so consider that he feels concern for the baby, concern for you, and that he's doing the best he can to protect both of you with his current knowledge and understanding.

Having this attitude might seem inflammatory, but consider the reality of birth. It's absolutely your domain, your birthright. No one can give birth for you, though in the hospital they often try. Birth is YOURS, and if you step fully into that it will cause shockwaves going forward and backward in your genealogical line, healing mistreatment women have undergone at the hands of men (and other women) essentially since the beginning of time. This is you in all your divine, feminine strength.

If you do tell him it's your body, your decision and go on to attempt freebirth, there are a few things that could happen:
1. He could call 911 while you're in labor without your consent, leading strangers to barge in and insist you go to the hospital while you're in the throes of labor

2. He could stand around paralyzed, spouting fear and being generally unhelpful

3. He could jump into action and actually end up participating exactly the way you hoped.

What it really comes down to is, are you willing to risk that he might call 911 and end up disrupting your entire birth experience? If not, consider this as a truly last resort.

Uninvite Him

Just what it sounds like. Whether you tell him to his face or not, you have the power to uninvite him from your birth. It IS your body, and it IS ultimately your decision. Make plans to birth at a friend's house, hotel room, or just not tell him when you're in labor and try to birth quietly in a distant part of the house if he's home. This option relies on the belief that "it's easier to ask forgiveness than permission". It also depends on finding a space to birth, or him either being a heavy sleeper, frequent traveler, or at work when you go into labor, so it's definitely not foolproof.

I caution the use of this option on two counts: first, your relationship might never recover once he finds out. And second, it's REALLY nice to have a second pair of hands helping when you're in labor! Yes, women can and do give birth completely by themselves, sometimes even outside in the wild. Personally, however, I appreciate having my husband give me hip squeezes, gather birth or postpartum supplies, hold the baby while I birth the placenta, and bring water or food as needed.

You could invite a supportive female attendant, friend, or family member to be with you during this time instead of your partner, but you should make it clear whether your partner is allowed in the room.

AN AWESOME RESOURCE

While writing this book, I was introduced to a midwife by the name of Mike Harris. You read that right, and yes, Mike Harris is a man. He's been a midwife in the UK for over 20 years, and he supports a woman's autonomous right to give birth where and with whom she pleases. He's known for his award-winning book, "Men, Love & Birth: the book about being present at birth your pregnant lover wants you to read". He has a website with articles specifically geared towards men and what their role is in birth, as well as an online course called "Birthing for Blokes". We love our men, but they don't always listen to us as well as...well, other men. Which is why I interviewed my husband in my book Birth Becomes Hers.

Ruska

Ruska: the time and process of leaves changing colors.
Concept from the Finnish language and culture

My First Freebirth

by Bree Moore

THIS STORY IS AN excerpt from my full journey from hospital to freebirth from my book BIRTH BECOMES HERS. In that book, I talk in detail about my first two births, an unmedicated hospital birth and a home water birth with a midwife, and all the decisions that led me to this experience. I also include my second and third freebirths. If you'd like to read about my fourth freebirth (and sixth birth), see "Birth of Ivy Arabella" in the last section of this book.

After my second baby was born at home with a midwife and we got pregnant for the third time, we moved. Naturally, I started looking for another home birth midwife. I Interviewed a couple, picked one, and had our first prenatal at 14 weeks. We couldn't find the baby's heart rate with her Doppler. She told us to get an ultrasound, and we did. The ultrasound showed a healthy baby boy.

The second prenatal, things went a bit downhill. The midwife told me she wanted to order lab work and talked about the testing she preferred. If my baby happened to be breech we would have to transfer, if I went over 42 weeks we would have to transfer. I didn't like it. I told her I would refuse most, if not all the testing. She asked me why I wanted a midwife and told me that I was endangering her reputation with the hospital if we ended up transferring and she didn't have those test results. As much as I could see her point, I was completely turned off by her fear.

Surprisingly, she suggested I look into unassisted birth, something I had never considered or even heard of.

I looked into it and never looked back.

I told my husband I wanted an unassisted birth and he was very opposed to the idea, at first. He'd come a long way to accepting home birth, but not having a midwife there was a big trip for him. He asked what would happen if I died, or started bleeding, if baby was breech, etc. I'm a big researcher. I started pulling up studies about the likelihood of those things happened and asked him to read them. Being my partner in all things, he did, and he gradually came around. I fired my midwife and we started doing my own prenatal care.

I read Laura Shanley's "Unassisted Childbirth" book and everything I could find online. We went the whole nine yards: blood pressure, bought our own doppler, weight checks. I think I was trying to mimic mainstream prenatal care so my husband would be more at ease. I know better now!

We didn't tell anyone our plans. I wanted to see it through, first. Most family and friends knew we had a home birth with a midwife before, so when they asked about this time I just said we were having a home birth. In the beginning I gave them the name of the midwife I planned to hire. Later on I just didn't share that our plans had changed.

I was in my third trimester when I went to visit my parents in Virginia. I felt likesharing, so I told them about our plans to birth unassisted. They had lots of questions. They mostly wanted to make sure that I wasn't going without a midwife because we couldn't afford it, and offered to pay for one. I declined, saying that having an unassisted birth felt right. My parents were respectful and didn't try to pressure me into anything. They just asked about my plans in case there was an emergency and left it at that.

I was truly tested with this baby! She waited long after her siblings to be born. I still wonder if her estimated due date was off, since I never had a period between her and her sister. As 42 weeks passed my mother in law asked when "they" would be inducing me. I said "they" wouldn't and that we would keep checking on the baby and as long as everything was well we would still birth at home.

We lived next door to her, in the basement of her mother's house, and she didn't know our plans to have an unassisted birth. My husband's grandmother didn't either, though she was supportive of us giving birth in her home with a midwife. "That's how I was born," she said, laughing. This incredible woman had nine kids. Her mother had eleven, including a set of twins and a set of triplets all born at home. I was so grateful that she supported my plans to birth at home.

My oldest son (almost 3) had a fever on the 13th of September. My husband cancelled his appointments for the next day, just feeling he needed to stayhome. Hewas startingto getanxioustoletthepregnancy go much longer, so we did our own little "stress test" at home by checking my blood pressure and checking baby's heart rate with a

Doppler. Baby's kicks were strong and we felt confident waiting a few more days, at least.

We had been having sex regularly several times a week even at this point, which just goes to show that babies come when they are ready. I wanted to avoid all other induction methods, however natural. This time there would be no induction massages, just trust in my body, my baby, and birth.

Anyway, early the next morning at 42 weeks + 3 days, I felt twingy and cranky. About 10 am I couldn't handle having the kids around. We put my daughter down for a nap and sent my son to my mother in law's house next door. We started a card game to pass time. We flirted and really felt some chemistry. I'd wanted to try having sex in labor, so we messed around a bit until we heard my husband's older brother upstairs visiting with Grandma. Awkward! We snuggled and kissed some more, then I started feeling kind of nauseated so we got dressed and went back to the card game.

I started breathing hard through contractions. I didn't want a water birth this time, but I did have a friend who was going to support me during this birth, more for my husband's peace of mind than anything. I called her and asked her to stay upstairs for a while. She did our dishes and made me a bagel.

Contractions were strengthening now. Desperation and a strong longing to be done with labor filled me. I started voicing my fears. I told him at one point I didn't want to have this baby anymore. A bit late for that! My husband was an incredible comfort during this time, which we soon recognized was transition.

I had taught my husband counterpressure and Rebozo during this pregnancy, and he used both to help me cope. I find his touch very relaxing when I'm in labor. I had beautiful Celtic music playing. My husband was using the Rebozo on my behind while I rested on all fours, "shaking the apple tree" or "motorcycle" is what the move is called. It felt SO GOOD. Labor was really intense. I kind of worried about grandma hearing me and felt my space invaded a bit by that. Luckily, my husband's brother had gone home by now.

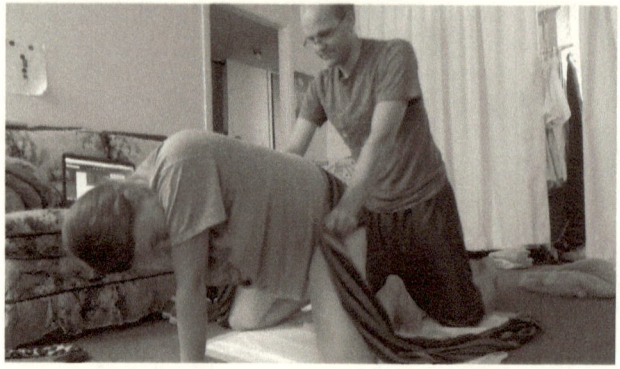

I invited my doula downstairs to help us. She got me coconut water and took a few pictures since my husband was the one massaging and giving me counterpressure. I used mantras like "easy" to get through transition, checked myself and felt the water sac bulging. Breaking my water felt intuitive. I gave the bag of waters a pinch during a contraction and it burst right away. The pressure increased INSANELY. I slowed things down, though, visualizing my baby sliding out of me.

At one point I felt a cervical lip in place, kind of holding baby up. Following my intuition and my body's cues, I used my fingers to pull the cervical lip aside. It was a VERY intense sensation, but it didn't hurt at all because I could feel how hard to pull to get it out of the way. At that point, I knew I was complete and kept my hand inside me to feel my baby come down the birth canal. COOLEST FEELING EVER. Really helped me control my pushing so I didn't tear.

Baby crowned with a major ring of fire just like my other ones, and then the head was out.

My husband mentioned there was a cord around her neck and quietly slipped it off. He knew just what to do in the moment! The rest of her

slid out into his hands, all 9 lbs 7 oz of her! She was HUGE to me. And yes, I said HER. The ultrasound was wrong (surprise) and our baby boy was actually a girl. She was born after 9 hours of labor, sweet and slow, my longest but easiest labor so far.

Her placenta was stickier than my first two, taking almost two hours to come. Afterbirth contractions were so painful I was convinced I was having another baby until the placenta came out, fully intact and without excessive bleeding. I used a mirror the next day to check for tearing and to my absolute shock and thrill found NONE. My biggest baby and no tearing! I finally had a nice, easy recovery with no stitches.

Took us three days to name our sweet surprise girl. There was never any flack from my husband's mother or grandmother about the unassisted birth. My mother-in-law was shocked, but I think just relieved everything went well.

At about three weeks old, our new baby got a viral infection, most likely from a visiting relative, and ended up in the hospital. I stayed with her the entire time. She contracted spinal meningitis and was life flighted to Primary Children's Hospital, but I never felt panicked. I just felt calm.

I believe her coming "late" helped her to fight the illness and cope with the medical treatment she was subjected to. I advocated for her, refusing care I believed was unnecessary. They pumped her full of antibiotics, unfortunately, afraid that it was a bacterial infection. The results came back on day five that it was viral and I pushed for them to let us go home that day. They did, luckily.

There was never any flack from my husband's mother or grandmother about the unassisted birth. My mother-in-law was shocked, but I think just relieved everything went well.

My Unassisted Home Birth

By Bonnita Nel

Pretoria South Africa
April 2, 2021

I was in prodromal labor for about 3 weeks. Lower back pain. Diarrhea and one night of vomiting. Surge of energy, etc.

I went in on March 24th as I thought my water broke. The doctor checked confirmed my cervix was 100% effaced but not yet dilated. He said baby would come before that Sunday if he can predict which would have been March 28th.

My 40 weeks due date was 31st of March. That day came went. When I reach the 40 week mark, I had this unbelievable calm feeling like it was okay to be waiting. I was ready to wait.

I laughed and told my dad, maybe it's the calm before the storm.

On Thursday the 1st, I had a discharge at around 10 at night. Again, I informed my husband and my dad what was happening and I said, "I have this feeling it is time."

We all laughed again.

But I said, "I'm seriously thinking it's time! It's a different feeling I can't explain."

We decided to just check on all the cameras again and plug them to charge. My two girls, 7 and 5, asked if they could sleep with us, after explaining that I think baba is on his way and they were over hearing that for the last 3 weeks.

I said okay but if anything happens during the night we would put them back in their bed, they agreed. We all went to bed at around 00:30 (after midnight).

April 2nd, at 40 weeks 2 days, I went to go peepee at 2:40am. Got into bed again just to hear our puppy starting to whine to go outside. As I got up again, I felt water running down onto the bed. That could NOT be urine!

I got up put the light on and checked. It looked like normal fluid, so I took our husky pup outside, and as I passed I boiled the kettle. I went to the toilet to check, and my underwear was soaked. I took it off and cleaned myself with a cloth.

Heard puppy whining to come back in, and as I reached the door I felt another gush of water. I ran onto the grass and stood there for about 2 minutes thinking it was indeed amniotic fluid, and maybe I should wake up hubby just incase.

I went to the bed at 3am, and as I leaned over to wake him a huge gush of fluid was falling onto the floor. He was so sleepy, and I said, "Love, its time please move the girls to their room."

I stood in the same place to prevent him from slipping while carrying the girls. I phoned my dad who lives in the flat at the back of the house.

Hub came back, and I said, "Let me clean."

He said, "No, its fine. I can unlock the doors for your dad."

I put on a gown and a linen saver between the legs, and we went to make coffee. We were all chilling outside for an hour and a half, and at 4:30 we decided to all go to the room and nap as nothing was happening.

We got into bed, and my dad made a bed on our couch in the room. I couldn't sleep after that and at 5am, I started feeling slight bits of period like pains. I opened the contraction timer on my phone and started checking.

They were 4 minutes apart, and the app said its time to go to the hospital I smiled and thought, "No, not me!"

At 6am, I got up took a bath and sat a bit in the warm water. I was so calm. I listened to some affirmations, and at 7am I went to lay down again, still feeling regular surges. At 8am, I woke my hub because I could feel it was getting stronger.

We got up made coffee, and I went outside fluid gushed out again. I swayed my hips side to side, and by 8:30am my dad joined us.

I started to feel the surges getting stronger by 9am. I said to hubby, "I am going to get into the water."

I ran a bath put in on maximum heat and got in, put my earphones on, and listened to the same affirmations.

By 9:30am I was boiling. The bath was way too hot, and I got out to take a cold shower. I stood in the shower for 10 minutes and then went to sit on the stair leading up to the bath. My dad came to check on me.

At 9:45am, I called hubby as I felt a very strong surge. He came, and I said, "I need you to be here because I'm starting with active labor now."

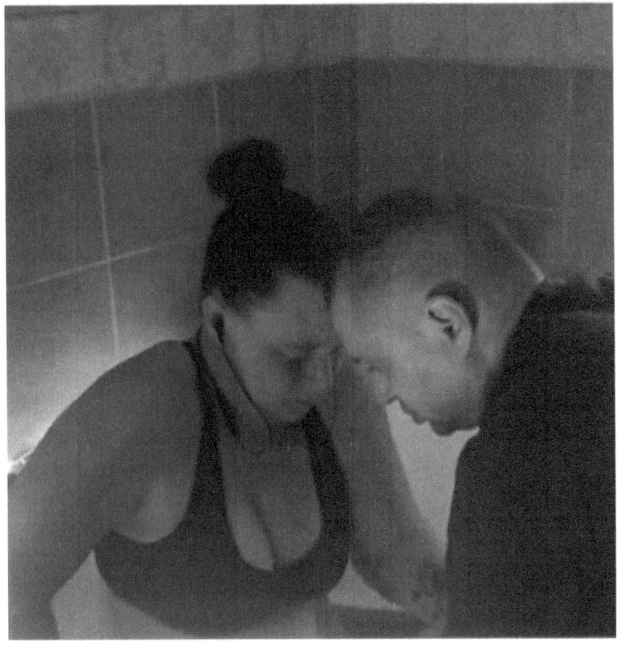

He sat quietly in front of me, and 9:50am I put out my hand and said, "It's time love. They will be coming every second minute."

He held onto my hand as every one of them came and went. My dad started taking video clips and photos. At 10:10am, I decided to get back into the bath. By now it wasn't so hot. The time went, and I had my earphones on and listening to a mantra song that only lasted six minutes, so I had to tell hubby to replay it every time it was almost done.

By 10:50am the surges had reach their highest, and I was getting tired emotionally. I reached down to feel and could feel my son's head and what I thought was 9cm of dilation. After 5 minutes, I felt again but it felt the same.

I decided to change position from lying on my back in the water at a 45 degrees angle onto my knees, and I opened as far apart as I could.

My husband stood with his knees on the stair in front of the bath, still not knowing how far the process is because I had said nothing to anyone.

As I changed position, I knew the surges would be massive because of the gravity, but that was fine because I needed my son to be born. I held onto my husband, and I could feel my son's head descending into my vagina.

I gave out a yell, to which my dad ran back in with the camera. I took a big breathe, and as I was holding his head, my husband also reached in and held his head.

I said with the next contraction, "His body will come out, just hold onto him!"

And so it happened!

I was so relieved and proud of myself and my family. Everyone played their roles excellently.

Our boy was born at 11:05am. While bonding with my boy still in the bath, I breastfed him while waiting for the placenta. Hubby ran a new set of water. The placenta detached at 12:24pm, and hubby cut the cord at 12:40. I gave him his son, and he did the weighing and measurements. 3.8kg and 36 cm h/c and he measured 51cm. I went to the other bathroom, took a bath, and went to drink a lovely cup of coffee outside in the afternoon sun.

A great thank you to Unassisted Births in South Africa group on Facebook for the lovely and encouraging ladies who were on my journey with me.

Truly Biological Birth

By Anna Shaw

My husband, Zach, and I consciously conceived our baby in January 2020. Two years prior, I had already decided that I would have a wild, autonomous pregnancy and birth. I was introduced to these ideologies from a classmate of my Zach's when he was in chiropractic school. She told me to check out the Free Birth Society podcast to learn more about it, which I did that evening.

Each time I listened I felt this veil of lies strip away and the deep-rooted knowledge of my ancestors reawakened in my bones. I felt it so deeply and I instantly became consumed by the physiological birthing world - podcasts, books, and wise women's Instagram accounts. It all translated as common sense to me.

I was already aware of corruption in Western medicine, but it was heartbreaking to peel back the layers of the obstetrical field: how they have stripped away women's trust and ancestral knowledge of pregnancy and birth, instilling fear into this already vulnerable population. Terrible.

I had first decided that I was going to opt out of ultrasounds after I read about all the harmful effects and risk they posed. I continued my research on standard obstetrical procedures after hearing women say they opted out of these as well. I sat, connected with Earth, and asked myself what felt right to me while running it through a primal lens as I do everything else.

My primal, ancient wisdom rang loud. I wanted the complete sovereignty of my entire journey into motherhood, of my body, and of my baby in my womb. I turned inward, tuned into my body, and listened. I decided that I would only consult an obstetrician if something started to feel off.

I knew to eat well, take high quality, necessary supplements and I continued to rid our house and products of toxins. I spent a lot of time outside and received Upper Cervical Chiropractic adjustments. Zach's chiropractic office is the only doctor's office I stepped foot into.

I completed Freebirth Society's Complete Guide to Freebirth course. I had a fetoscope, but that was more of a hobby than "procedure" to me, only using it on occasion. I weighed myself a handful of times out of curiosity and honestly laughed when I had gained 50 pounds.

I felt comfort in knowing that extra weight was my baby, my placenta, and my body doing what it needed to grow a healthy and strong baby. I dealt with food aversions in the beginning of my pregnancy, which cleared up with milk thistle capsules. The one and only time that I had a concern was this awful pain when bearing down to go to the bathroom, which turned out to be round ligament pain three months in.

This cleared up after Zach used a specific chiropractic technique, which allowed the major ligaments in the pelvis to relax by stretching them away from the bone. It didn't return for the rest of my pregnancy. I had never been so connected and in love with my body before. I felt one with the universe and with our creator – a goddess carrying life within her. A goddess indeed, with no one coming between her and her baby. Just this wondrous dyad for nine months.

I first thought I'd like to birth at home with a midwife when I was in high school. From trying to breastfeed my crying newborn sister when I was three years old, to asking my mother if it's hard to poop sometimes to prepare us for birth at the age of seven, I have long had a deep-rooted trust birth and have always felt connected to motherhood. Knowing my mother birthed my three sisters and me naturally (unmedicated and vaginally) established this as well.

However, listening to podcasts and reading women's stories online, I learned that many birth workers don't trust the physiology of birth and end up sabotaging the process in one way or another.

So, I thought, "Why risk it?"

My trust in the Divine Feminine and my body grew steadfast after learning about the hormonal blueprint of birth through completing the Complete Guide to Freebirth course and reading various books. I acknowledged birth as a life event, not a medical one.

I sat and wondered what how our ancestors birthed before hospitals. If it wasn't a natural human function, our species would long be extinct. I was eager to enter the birthing portal and did so with the absence of any fear.

I entered that portal at 8:40 a.m. on October 11th, 2020. Zach and I opened our eyes to each other in tandem. He kissed me good morning as I got up to go to the bathroom. Before I got there, my waters released, an ounce or so dribbled onto the floor. I told Zach and he shot up and asked how I knew.

I chuckled and replied, "Because there's liquid on the floor and I didn't pee!"

I had my first intense sensation a few hours later. Zach made breakfast as I started to prepare our home and clean in case this was the real deal. He left shortly after to run the last errands. I called him about five hours later to tell him it's time to come home because my sensations were becoming more intense and frequent.

I FaceTimed my family in Ohio to tell them it's time to head down to North Carolina. I wanted them present after the birth and my mother would stay with us to help for a couple weeks.

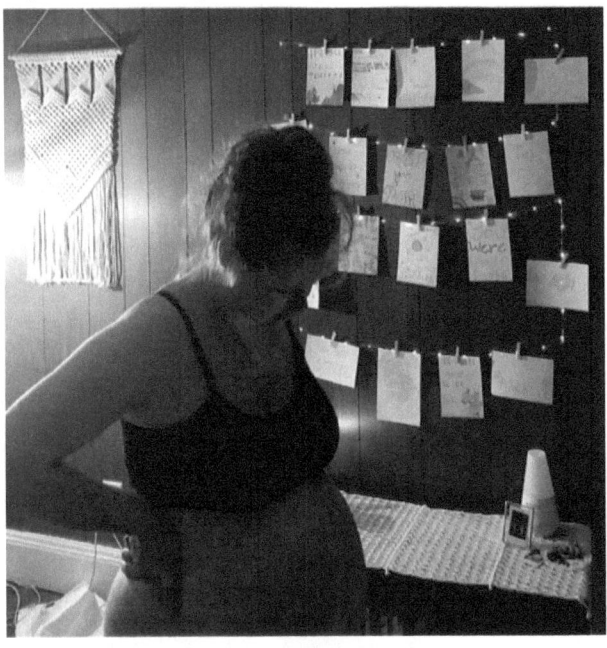

I started rolling on my yoga ball in our living room in front of a small birthing alter I prepared as Zach made a homemade Pedialyte drink. He popped his head in to tell me that he forgot the magnesium. I had him contact my younger sister to get it because I didn't want him leaving again.

Zach was hanging sheets over our curtains in the living room to provide more darkness when my sister arrived with the magnesium and asked for my permission to enter and give me a hug. She did so and gave me some words of affirmation before leaving. Zach started to prepare the birthing pool shortly after and helped me into it when it was prepared.

While in the tub, I moved back in forth between being on my knees and lounging while holding Zach's hand. At some point, he left to cut up strawberries and mangoes and made himself coffee. I remained in the water for quite some time, eventually getting out to labor next to the tub.

Zach put down towels and absorbent bed pads to cover the floor. By his account, this was all from 8:45 p.m. to 4 a.m., then returned to the living room. I never wanted to know or have any sense of time or educated analysis.

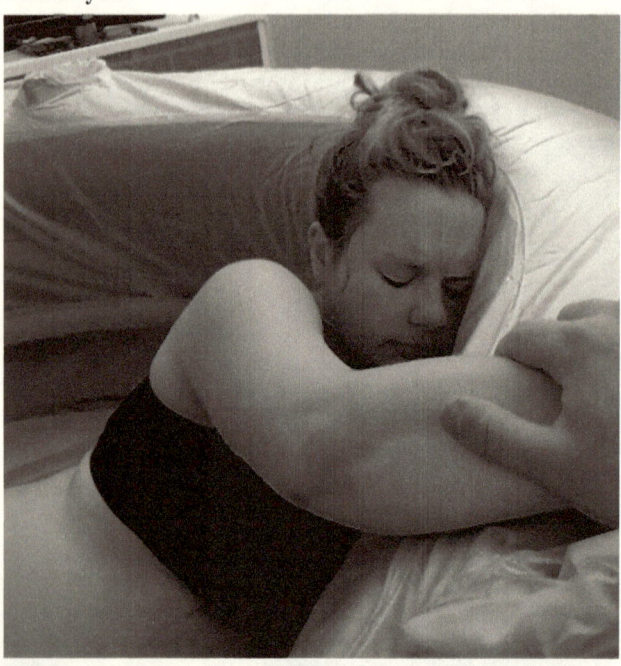

Here I rolled on the yoga ball and got on my hands and knees on the couch but spent most of the time sitting on the floor with my back against the couch with my arms draped over Zach's knees. At this point we were both exhausted and dozed off here and there for minutes at a time. With each sensation I was shaken from my dream. I was disappointed when I could see the sun rising in a crack of the windows and curtains. Around 8 a.m. I decided to get back into the pool. I felt like baby was starting to descend further an hour or so later. Hours passed and sensations slowed down a bit.

I asked Zach to get in the pool so that it was easier for him to provide hip pressure. We remained here for around four hours and then went to our bedroom. I told him to go ahead of me to close the blinds and turn the clock around. He also laid bed pads down on the bed and floor. I was absolutely exhausted at this point and desired sleep. I laid on my left side and slept in between strong sensations while Zach held my hand and eventually laid behind me.

Between 1 and 2 p.m., I decided to get on my hands and knees. This started on the bed—first with my hands on the bed then on the headboard. After this was no longer comfortable, I moved to have my knees on the floor with my arms up on the foot of the bed, kneeling on folded towels. I moved back and forth between this position and standing at the side of the bed leaning over it, swaying back and forth. I didn't have much of an appetite throughout the process and I was feeling so worn down. Finally, it clicked that I needed to eat something to give my body energy to get my baby Earthside.

I asked Zach to get me a banana as I remained on my hands and knees on the bed. He peeled it, so that I could hold it by the skin with one end while eating the other end, but instead I removed the entire peel, tossed it aside, and ate it a little bit at a time: smashed in the palm of my hand. I love this part of my birth story because it always reminds me of how I was so tuned into my limbic system, deep in this primal space, eating a banana like a primate. Feeling how much energy this gave me I then asked him for more of the hydration drink, so he made a second batch.

It was at this point that every time it hit my lips it electrified me, surging through me, bringing on a strong sensation each time. It felt so good that I began taking long chugs of it through my straw. The two of these, combined with resting, really got things moving.

My knees started to hurt from being on them for hours, so Zach tried to think of things I could kneel on to comfort me. First, we tried the knee chest table knee pad, a piece of chiropractic equipment. This worked for a few sensations until I felt that I needed my knees further apart because of the pad not being wide enough. Zach wrapped a towel around the pad to help cushion the sides, but this did not work. He had the idea to use a couch cushion from the basement couch.

He wrapped one in a towel, and this would end up being what I birthed on. During strong sensations, I swayed forward and backward while Zach applied inward pressure on my hips. He helped coach me through my breath. The slivers of light through the blinds started to fade. Zach brought beeswax candles I made into our room placing one on the nightstand and one on the dresser. The candles, paired with the salt lamp, provided just enough, minimal light.

A few hours had passed when Zach told me he was starting to see something, which turned out to be baby's head as it descended further. He continued to provide hip pressure, while it seemed like the head stayed in this position for many intense sensations, which I later connected as the ring of fire. Baby's head came closer to emerging and then went back up. I stopped to take a break and some deep breaths to recenter myself. I told baby that I trust them and that I was so excited to meet them.

With the next strong sensation, I started to push as my body told me to. I remember feeling like an egg cracking open. I like to think of it as a butterfly emerging from its cocoon. I put my left foot flat on the floor to be in a lunge position. Shortly after, the entire head was fully visible along with a shoulder. I instinctively stood up as baby fully emerged.

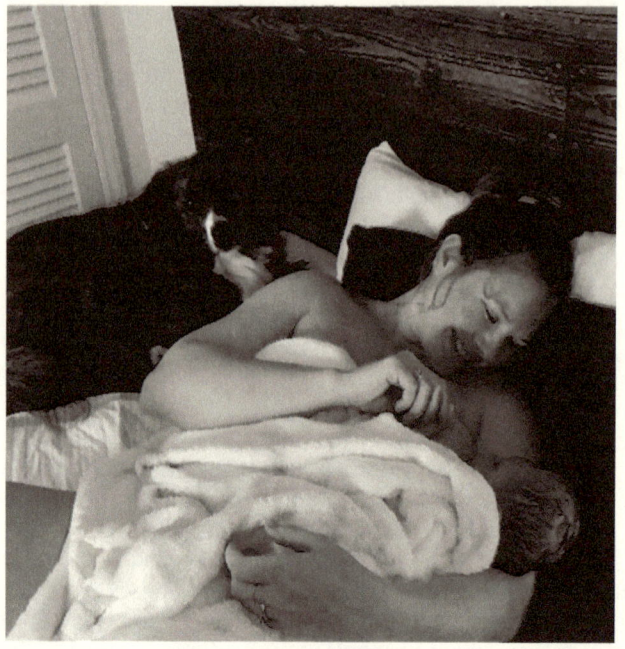

Zach caught the slippery baby and fluid released in vast quantity. I bent over as he handed the baby to me through my legs. I placed baby up to my chest and with a big smile said, "Hi, I'm your mama" while gazing at the most perfect face and Zach wrapped us in a towel. I smelled the head, examined the fingers and toes. I felt as if I was hovering over the ground, so high on pure oxytocin. I scanned the body and while I was looking at the cutest little toes, Zach asked me the sex of the baby. I lifted the towel, looked, and said, "Girl. It's our Sylvia!" Sylvia Jade entered the world at approximately 8:54 p.m. on October 12th in the same spot my waters released. She is named after my maternal grandmother who passed away the week before we conceived.

Zach laid the bed pads to cover the bed so we could all lay down. Shortly after, I had another strong sensation, knowing the placenta was coming. A few minutes later, another. The umbilical cord was short, and it was painful to hold Sylvia to my chest while riding these waves. I remembered how our friend I mentioned at the beginning of this story also birthed her baby with a short cord. I told Zach to call her so that we could remember what she did, which was to sit on the toilet. Zach helped me to the bathroom and after getting there we remembered we'd need a bowl to place in it. He ran to the kitchen, put the bowl in the toilet and I sat down holding Sylvia and offered her my breast.

She lightly suckled as I thanked my placenta for completing its job and a moment later, I birthed it. After handing Sylvia to Zach, I realized the bowl was too big to get out of the toilet with the seat down. I held a towel between my legs and waddled to the kitchen for a smaller bowl. (I'm not sure why I didn't just have him do this!) When I returned to the bathroom, I picked up my placenta, put it in the other bowl then washed my hands. The three of us returned to our bedroom. Sylvia laid completely naked on my chest, still attached to the placenta which laid in a bowl next to us. Zach cuddled up next to us on the other side and our dog by our feet. Zach told me that he remained by my side the whole time. What felt like minutes was hours. We laid there, holding each other in the still, dimly lit sacred space. It was unearthly, dreamy, perfect, and it remained that way into my fourth trimester.

I absolutely loved birthing in the Autumn because it allowed for the windows to be open in our bedroom for fresh air to fill the room. Our backyard of that house was filled with tall trees. With each breeze I'd breathe in the crisp, fresh air, my baby's sweet skin, and watch the shower of falling leaves.

My birth was transformational yet felt so simple and natural. I listened to my body, did what I felt it wanted and didn't question it. I will choose this way of pregnancy and birth every time. I can only hope that my story will inspire and encourage more women to question the routine obstetric model. I dream of a world where women and men all trust the biological blueprint of birth.

My 23-minute Birth

By Amanda Turner

I HAD AN INCREDIBLY difficult and painful pregnancy, and it ended up being my longest one too. Both of my previous pregnancies went to 39 weeks and 3 days. This one went to 41 weeks and 2 days.

I started having contractions at 37 weeks that really made me think that the baby was coming early. They were 40 seconds long every 2 minutes for 10 hours. They were uncomfortable but not intense, but I was quite drained from them.

They got less noticeable and further apart after I finally fell asleep. Even though I had had enough of this pregnancy, I was relieved that it wasn't leading up to active labour.

I went for a scan the next day just to make sure everything was okay. Baby was already very low down, we could only see her jaw but she was facing the wrong way (facing up instead of facing my back). Everything else was good. But the lady who did the scan was sure I would be having my baby the next day because I was still having contractions while I was there.

During the next four weeks I had prodromal labour, and every few days I would have new signs of being in labour. I had a few days when it really seemed like it was time, but still baby didn't arrive. In the meantime, I did Spinning Babies exercises to rotate baby.

Once I hit 40 weeks, I became quite frustrated and started to doubt myself and felt like the baby would never come. I chatted to a wonderful person and midwife, Vanessa Louise de Beer, who encouraged me and gave me wonderful suggestions of things to do to get things going.

The day before she was born, I was still having light contractions but they weren't anything noteworthy. I also finally acknowledged that she would arrive when she and my body were ready and the timing was right. I also finally admitted to myself my fears and worked through them.

The night of the 14th of September was uneventful, and I managed to get some sleep, I was a bit restless but didn't think anything of it.

I woke up at about 3:15am on the 15th to pee. And all of a sudden, whilst still on the toilet, I had two strong contractions about two minutes apart that I had to breath and focus to work through. Then I sat crossed legged on my bed looking at Facebook and timing contractions. With every contraction I felt some water run down onto the towel I was sitting on.

By 4:00am, I woke my husband, Don, because I had shifted and quite a bit more water came out and I realized only at the moment things were actually going to progress and baby would be there that day.

It was a whirlwind after that. Don started getting the birthing stuff ready, and I told him he better let my sister know that she could come if she didn't mind coming so early. He let her know at 4:16am. Then I could feel baby coming down.

I told Don I had to shift positions and went onto hands and knees with a bit of difficulty. Don left the room and the next contraction I felt a burn down below and felt a bit of fear rise up, so I said out loud to my body, 'No, I'm not ready' and 'Calm down'. Next contraction, I breathed to calm down more and said 'No, not yet'.

I called Don saying she was coming, and then with the third contraction, I braced myself and her head just came out. She just hung out there, and I could feel her wriggling. It was such a weird feeling.

Don didn't think I meant she was coming that moment, and when he got back he just saw her head hanging there! The next contraction her body came out, and luckily Don was quick enough to get to me and catch her at 4:23am. Unfortunately, we didn't manage to get any video, and I only managed to get a few photos because it all happened so quick.

I also didn't get to have her in the water like I planned, and my sister didn't even have a chance to leave her house before I gave birth. Baby looked rather purple and didn't make any noise so I tried to suck over her nose and mouth but nothing came out, then started to rub her with a towel then she made a small noise and pooped all over me. After nine minutes, I birthed the placenta.

It wasn't quite what I had planned, but I'm grateful it was fast and that I didn't have any negativity or trauma to deal with this time around.

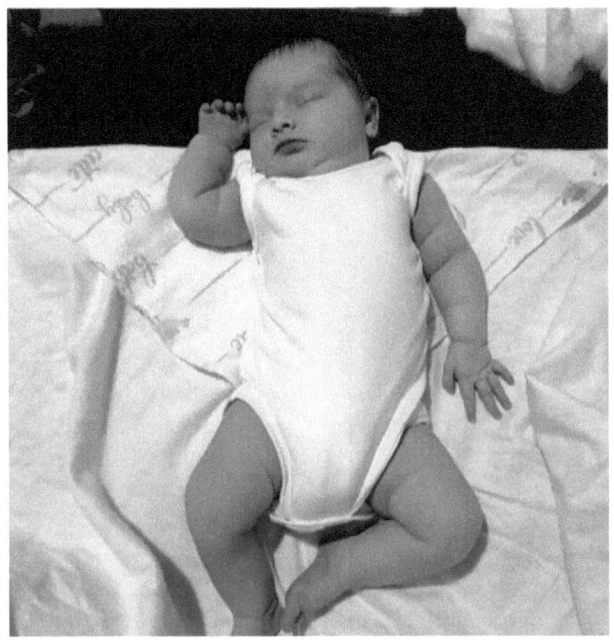

The Birth of Ledger Wolf

By Laycie Sharpe

In February of 2020 I took a test. It was positive. My initial reaction was fear, hesitation and doubt, not because I didn't want more children or because I was scared of child birth, but because five months prior my mother was diagnosed with stage four pancreatic cancer and was told she had six months to live.

My first thoughts were, "Will my mom still be here in October?" and "I can't possibly take care of two kids and mourn my mother at the same time!"

The thought of giving birth without her crushed me, and I was in a dark head space for weeks, but I pulled myself out of that and refused to let those thoughts back in.

My mother accidently gave birth to me in her friend's bathroom 27 years ago and went on to have three more home births, all of which I witnessed. It was a huge influence on my views of birth.

Fast forward to Wednesday September 30th, I had strong contractions, lost my mucus plug and threw up my dinner. I thought "Maybe this is it."

Later that night, everything fizzled out, and I was disappointed. Saturday, October 3rd came around, and I was miserable, grumpy and nauseous all day long. I was having mild contractions all day and seeing mucus every time I used the bathroom. I went to bed around 11 p.m. and could not get comfortable, but I finally drifted off to sleep.

At 1:30 a.m. Sunday October 4th, I was dreaming and awoke to a pop and warmth between my legs. I ran to the bathroom, where there was a big gush of my waters into the toilet. I noticed the light brown color of the waters and decided not to mention that to my husband because he is a worrier.

I woke him up telling him my water had broken, but to sleep until things got more serious. Not even ten minutes later I was calling for him to go pick up my mom because my contractions were strong and back to back, and I wanted nothing more than to have my mommy by my side.

My three year old son was asleep in bed, and I labored for about an hour in the bathroom, moving from the shower to laying on the cold floor back and forth.

My dog never left my side.

Around 2:30 a.m., my mom and husband walked through the door, and as soon as I saw my mom I felt a sense of calm over me. She held my hand, caressed my forehead and whispered words of encouragement.

My husband didn't waste a minute setting up the pool in the kitchen and getting the supplies ready. I got in the pool around 3:30 a.m., and things were really getting serious. I held my hand on my bum with each contraction and could feel the pressure from his head and knew he was coming soon. I kept repeating things in my head such as "relax," "surrender," and "open up."

His head descended quickly. The contractions did all the work. I did not intentionally push at any point.

My three-year-old son woke up, and I told everyone baby was coming soon. They didn't think it would be within minutes.

The next few contractions brought out the animal in me, and I let out low deep noises I didn't know I could make. His head was born, and I felt so much relief. The next contraction pushed his shoulders out. I could see the excitement and joy in my mom's face, and I could not contain my own excitement.

I could tell baby was caught up on something, and that's when my husband said the cord was wrapped around his shoulder and arm. My mom unwrapped the cord, and he was born!

My husband handed our baby to me. I rubbed his back and sucked his mouth and nose, and he immediately made small sounds and wiggled around. It was the most amazing, emotional experience of my life!

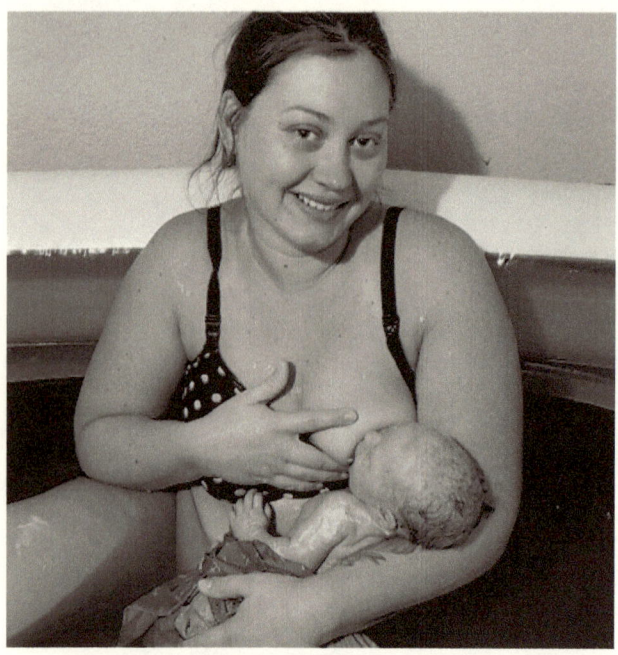

In Denial

By Misty Wiser

Last night, at 9:56pm, I gave birth to our first fully freebirthed baby!!

I was 37 weeks and 6 days. I was convinced that it was "prodromal" labor until I hit transition, since my surges were anywhere from 2-9 minutes apart. My other births that weren't induced were born at 40 weeks!

The night before, I had surges all night every five minutes. I thought that this was it! Then, in the morning, they fizzled.

They picked back up again during the day and stayed irregular. I told myself it could still be weeks. Around dinner time I retreated to my room, turned on my Hypnobirthing and essential oils diffuser, and rode the surges on my yoga ball.

I felt so much pressure. It hurt in a way I'd never felt before. When I had my husband check me, he told me that my water bag was bulging. I believed him. It hurt!

He was such a wonderful support system. Any time I started breathing erratic, he would just gently remind me about my Hypnobirthing breathing. It kept me very grounded and very focused.

There was a point that I just needed to get in the bath. It felt so good. After getting in, my water broke, and I immediately hit transition. I went to needing to push in about 5-10 minutes. ER (fetal ejection reflex) kicked in, and he was born after about two surges. So thankful for Heather Baker's book (Home Birth On Your Own Terms). My husband used it to check me and the placenta. It was so helpful!

I can't imagine birthing any other way!

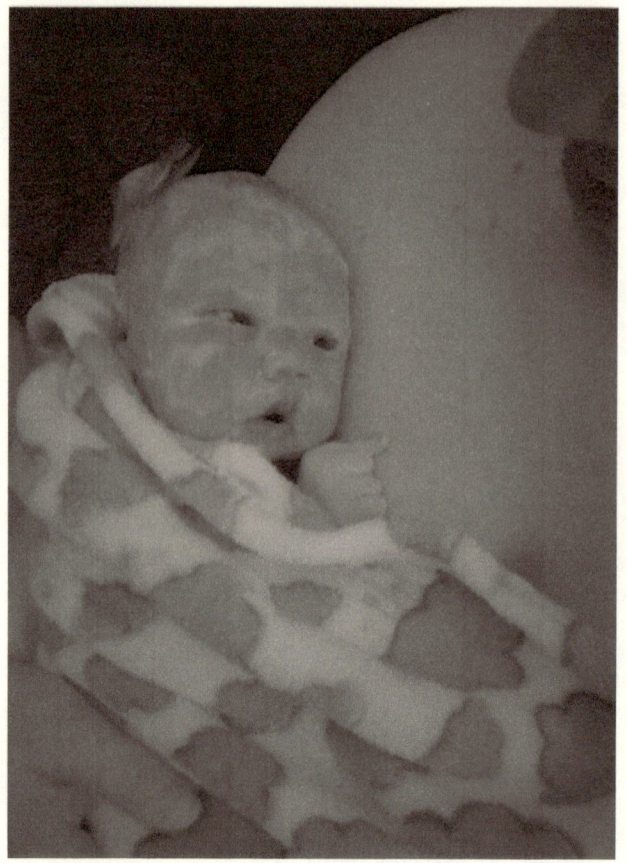

The Incredibly Long Birth of Theodore Ignatius

By Pamela Hersh

I WAS OVER AT my mom's on Thursday, just hanging out like I often do. I was having prodomal labor all day, with contractions every 5-15 minutes, and I decided to run a bunch of errands and later dye my sisters hair. Things fizzled out by the end of the day.

The next day I had some more prodomal labor, contractions about 10 minutes apart, my aunt came in from out of town to spend the day. My husband, siblings, and cousins swam in the lake while I chatted and relaxed with my aunt and vented about my hostile mother-in-law, a vent I desperately needed to have.

On Saturday I had contractions every 3-5 minutes that were getting more intense. They started at about 3:30pm, and by 8:30pm I was sure this was it and called my mom at work and told her there was no rush.

She arrived about 9:30pm with BBQ wings for me. I was certain that this was it, I would have a baby tonight. I asked my husband what time he thought our baby would be born, and he said 11:43pm. Well, he was wrong.

Things slowed down, and we went to bed. I slept for a few hours and woke up, and about an hour after I woke up, contractions started again. This started the ridiculous pattern. I would have hard labor for about four hours, get to an almost pushing stage, and as soon as I started to get tired it would stop completely. Then I would sleep for 3-4 hours, and then an hour after waking it would start again.

On Tuesday my water gushed, and continued to leak for days, continuing this same pattern. I walked, I climbed stairs, I bounced on the ball, I took a shower, I sat in the birth pool. I talked to my baby, I fondled baby socks. I prayed, I listened to music.

Nothing.

I did the side lying release, and the Walchers maneuver from Spinning Babies. After the Walchers maneuver, I could feel baby descend. Throughout it all, I sang along to the music from every genre you can imagine, I chatted, I laughed, I cried. I had a few really disgusting farts that made my husband pull his shirt over his nose, and I laughed for the next 15 minutes.

One of the times I got to an almost pushing stage, I pooped on the floor and that made me laugh too.

On Saturday, things stopped completely. No more pattern, no more contractions. Nothing. I had been able to almost will contractions to start and now nothing I did brought them back on.

I worked through all the possible mental blocks, that my mother-in-law might somehow stop by while I was in labor, that I wasn't wearing my wedding ring because of swelling (I prefer to wear my ring to have sex, I like to feel married, it only makes sense that if I had to feel married to conceive this baby I had to feel married to birth this baby).

I gave over control to my body, I went to go see all of my siblings, and still nothing. I had no mental blocks. My body just kept stalling. The second I would think, "I'm to tired to keep doing this," everything would stop.

I sent my mom home, and thought, "I guess we're done then. This baby will never be born." I told my husband he could go back to work on Monday. And then I didn't sleep well. Contractions woke me through the night. I got up at 5-ish, and I went to the bathroom and there was blood.

Finally!

I told my husband. "Never mind, baby will most definitely be here today!"

At 6:30am my contractions got more intense. I sat in the pool, and I showered and things didn't slow down. Contractions were almost unbearable, and I was so tired from the nine days of on and off labor. I was having trouble coping.

The only thing that seemed to help was looking into my husband's eyes while he gripped my wrists, and I tried to breathe/moan deeply. I was all over the place. In the pool, in the shower, on my hands and knees, in the bathroom, the bedroom, the living room, everywhere.

My mom followed us around with a receiving blanket and her phone for pictures, otherwise she stayed out of the way and let us do our thing. Thirty hours of hard labor, contractions were so intense and so painful. I got to a point where I couldn't cope unless I was pushing, and I was so tired. At this point, I'd been awake for 30 hours. I pushed for six hours. I could feel his head just inside. I ended up in the bathroom on my knees against a chair pillow I'd received for Christmas a few years ago.

My husband kept telling me I was so close and I was doing so good. He and my mom made sure I had water and juice and some smoothie thing that completely got rid of the swelling in my feet and ankles.

I had just enough time to take a sip of something between contractions. I just wanted to be done. I told my mom that I better get a steak for Sunday dinner next week, and as soon as this baby was out I needed some Sonic. I wanted the Ham and cheesy hash browns I'd missed the previous week.

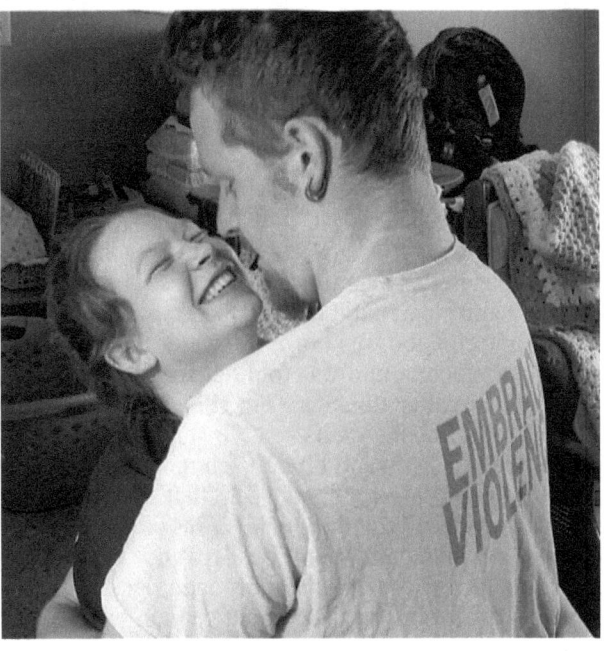

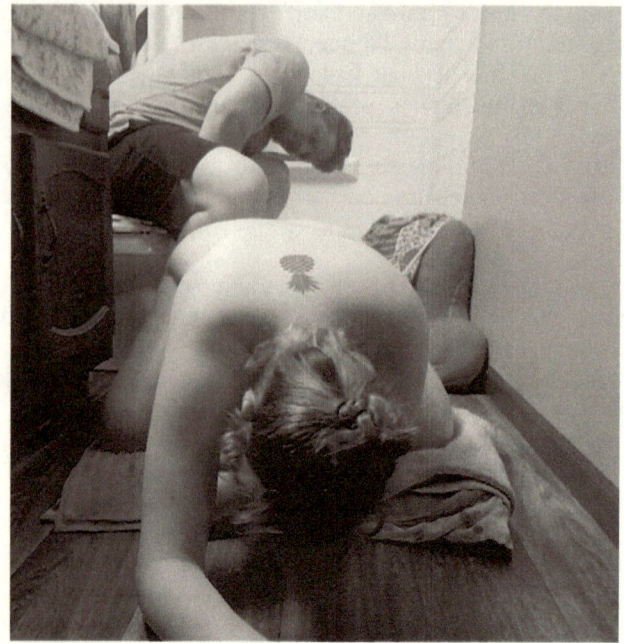

My husband could see the baby's head stretching me, and it burned, but I liked this part better than the contractions. The rest of my water exploded, clean and clear, and I had stopped talking.

30 minutes before babe was born, the water that was leaking had turned dark with meconium. I was told not to give up, we needed to get baby out. I remember thinking, "I'm goings as fast as I can, babe will be here as soon as babe wants."

Finally the head was out, and I barely felt it.

My mom said two things, "Oh my gosh, that's beautiful!" and, "Oh poor baby," because of all the dirty fluid on his face.

I had to take a minute, and then I pushed, and my husband caught the baby and laid him on the ground between my legs. My mom gasped and mouthed at my husband asking about gender.

Babe was blue and needed to have nose and mouth suctioned. My husband and mom took turns helping me rub babe's back.

When babe started to make noises, we looked and saw that we had a boy! I continued to try to rub him, but I felt like jelly. I was so week and so tired. I'd been awake for more than 36 hours at this point.

My husband helped get us out of the meconium and blood-stained mess and into the clean bath tub. I sat in a couple inches of water until I was ready to cut the cord. I passed babe off to my husband and sat in the bathtub with water pouring over me while I rinsed off and my husband bonded with him.

My mom held babe while my husband lifted me out of the tub and onto the toilet to birth the placenta, which came out 45 minutes to an hour after birth. I tried to fart, and it just sorta fell out.

My husband then helped me get my bottom half dressed, and then helped me into bed so I could cuddle my perfect pink squishy baby.

My brother brought us Sonic, and I decided I wanted to call people about two hours after he was born. I slept with my beautiful boy on my chest.

He was born at 6:10pm after 36 hours of nonstop hard labor.

Theodore Ignatius

September 1, 2020

Freebirth of Elijah Sage

by Lauren Tousa

OCTOBER 23RD, 2020

I had been having prodromal labor that was on and off the last few weeks. Nothing too strong, mostly a lot of vaginal/cervical pressure. I had been preparing for months. I was really worried about a few things because they had been problems for me with my previous births. I had dealt with hemorrhaging to the point of almost needing a blood transfusion.

I had my two older kids at home as well but had midwives there for both of them. I couldn't find a midwife that was in the area and I had precipitous labor with baby #2, so I wasn't sure how long I would be in labor and if the midwife would actually even show up on time. I felt like I needed to be prepared for doing this on my own. The more I thought about it and the more I read and educated myself, the more accustomed I became to the idea of not having a midwife. It felt right, but I also felt so alone in my choice.

I didn't really tell anyone because I didn't think I would be very supported. Just choosing to have my kids at home at all made me a target. I had many people tell me I would die, it was too dangerous, and that I just couldn't handle doing it.

But I proved them wrong and had my oldest at home with a midwife and I caught him myself in the bathroom. My second child I had a water birth that was very quick and intense, also with a midwife present. Now with the third one, I wanted to have water as an option so I bought a kiddie pool online.

This was all in the middle of Covid so more people were having home births and birth pool prices skyrocketed. Anyways, I found a pool and got a fetoscope and measuring tape to measure my belly. I got a blood pressure cuff to monitor my BP. That was all that I felt like I needed to monitor for myself as far as "medically/physically". To me, birth is deeply spiritual and getting in the right headspace and making sure my mind was as healthy as my physical body was so important.

I read EVERYTHING I could find about postpartum hemorrhage and how to treat it. I acquired all the herbs/remedies needed to combat it. I joined Facebook groups and online forums where I could talk to other women who had free birthed before. I read books and tried to fill my headspace with positivity. I pushed out the negative and constantly recited to myself how healthy I was and how my pregnancy and birth would be normal and healthy and safe. Creating that space is so important. We manifest our thoughts.

Contrary to what most will advise about reading everything bad that could happen(which is to avoid reading it), I dove right in. I went through every possible worst case scenario and how to handle it if it arose. I made a list of the top 10 biggest problems and if they warranted going to a hospital or not.

I made print outs and wrote down detailed instructions on how to handle any situation that may come up. This was for my husband in case I couldn't tell him what to do for some reason. I hung them up on the wall in my "birth space". They were next to all of my mantra pictures. I like to draw my own mantras and decorate my birth space with live plants and beautiful things. I also use sage and crystals to cleanse the space for months and weeks before birth. All of this preparation, which was an immense amount of effort, was so worth it.

When the day finally arrived, I knew it was the day. But I'm always in denial in early labor. I think this is because I've experienced prodromal labor so much that I don't want to get too excited about it and then have my hopes dashed by it not happening. It was the day after my "guess date".

I was really certain about the date, but babies come when they're ready and my second child had been very "late". I wasn't expecting labor to start the day after my "guess date". It started getting more intense and I was trying to get as much done as I could before it was full blown. I was trying to make lunch for the older kids, I wanted to have the dishes done and clean more and was trying to do it all.

My husband realized that it was the real deal while I was walking around, still in denial. I finally went back to my birth room and tried to do some cat/cow stretches. I also laid on my back and tried to feel my cervix, which I never seemed able to do before. It was always too high up. I could barely touch it now. However, every time I touched my cervix, it sent me into a HUGE surge. So strong that I would have to flip over as fast as I could, back on my hands and knees, just to get through it.

My husband kept asking if he should set up the birth tub and I kept saying no I didn't want to just in case labor stopped. He ignored me and did it any ways, thank god. Because by the time it was mostly full, I was ready to be getting in the water. We had some friends come over to help watch our other kids. I remember all the kids, there was my two (2 and 3 at the time) and two more (1 and 3) who were all around me while I was naked in the birth pool. They were splashing water and laughing and having a great time. It became a little overwhelming for me though and I asked them to leave. The adults then tried to keep all the kids outside, but it was cold so they came inside periodically.

I remember being in the pool and feeling so tired. I asked my husband to get me something to eat. I wanted fruit and water, which is odd for me because in labor I get extremely nauseous and typically don't want to eat. He got me a pear that I ate in like 10 seconds.

I took a big gulp of water and wanted another pear but got distracted by a huge surge. They were coming fast and strong now. I knew if I stayed in the water, it would draw out the process a bit more. The problem was that the pool wasn't quite deep enough and the surges were becoming extremely intense. I felt like I needed to get out and use gravity to help my baby move down.

So my husband helped me stand up. Helped me walk into the bathroom and then I sat on the toilet. I had read a story about a woman who had become constipated before birth and when she had a bowel movement she was able to release and give birth quickly after. For some reason I thought of this and that's why I sat on the toilet. The urge to push was overwhelming. I had a large bowel movement and my water broke. It relieved a huge amount of pressure that I was feeling.

Almost as soon as that relief was felt, the surges became so close together and so strong that I felt powerless and almost lost confidence. I thought I would throw up and took a drop of peppermint essential oil. That immediately took away all nausea. I then looked at myself in the mirror and repeated some of my mantras to myself. "You are a queen" "you can do this, you are doing this" and called on the strength of all my foremothers and all women in the world. Then I pushed. I growled and moaned and yelled deep guttural noises.

At this point, my daughter (2) walked into the bathroom and seemed very scared. I wasn't able to offer much reassurance because I was beyond speech but tried to say "Everything's ok". We had watched hours of birth videos and talked about how "mommy might get very loud but that it's ok and I will be alright." But it got very animalistic and raw and primal. It was a little more intense than she was expecting and both my kids seemed concerned about me.

It was pure instinct that I was running on. I stood up and reached down with my hand and felt my baby's head finally emerging from my cervix. The surges kept coming and I pushed with each one. It was uncontrollable, I couldn't stop myself from pushing. I had kept my hand there the whole time and could feel his head slowly descending. Once his head was down at the vaginal opening I was feeling the ring of fire real hard. It was so intense and I was struggling with feelings of inadequacy.

At that point, I fully realized that I needed to push this head out and even if I ripped, I would be able to heal but it's not something I could be too worried about in the moment. I tried to apply counter pressure and explain to my husband to do it, but it was too difficult to explain and after three surges that were back to back, I had finally pushed out his head.

With my other two, once their heads were out, the rest of their bodies just kind of shot out. With him, I had to slowly push the rest of him out and it took another couple minutes that felt like an eternity and a blink at the same time.

Birth is just a timeless place. It's a conundrum of feeling infinity and nothing at the same time. I pushed him out in a squat and grabbed him with my hands. I sat back down on the floor of the bathroom. Covered in blood, feces, and vernix, I declared "it's a boy, we did it". I felt so much relief.

He looked a little pale and it took him a second to make much sound. I think he may have gotten some fluid in his lungs, but I had read about what to do in this situation. I rubbed his back and helped him "get started". After a short while, he seemed to be a normal color and his heart and respiratory rates were normal as far as I could tell.

Then I stood up and immediately took Angelica root to quickly birth my placenta because I noticed I was bleeding quite a bit already. This helped me get my placenta out within a few minutes of taking. As soon as it was out, I started my whole process of what to do in case of hemorrhage. I used everything I had. Wombstringe, tinctures, massage, to name a few. It would slow down for while but it wasn't stopping. I was soaking giant pads within minutes and starting to feel a little light headed.

I massaged my uterus to make sure I didn't get clots and to help my uterus contract down. I was starting to feel a little desperate and in a last ditch effort I picked up the placenta and started taking bites out of it. It was covered in blood and still warm. Absolutely the most primal thing I have ever experienced. But after taking a few bites, my bleeding basically stopped. It slowed way down to just a small amount and eventually stopped.

We did a burning ceremony with the kids to cauterize the umbilical cord. This was very special and intimate. I recommend this over cutting the cord. We waited until it was white and limp and then did the burn. I was hemorrhaging throughout all of that but managing it with the herbs. I waited to eat the placenta after it was separated. He didn't have any issues with breastfeeding and I've never had issues with milk. He latched the first try and hasn't stopped since.

We weighed him and he was 8.5 lbs, a full pound heavier than both of my other kids.

I have never felt such pride in myself or felt so capable. All insecurities that I felt about myself completely subsided and were replaced with feels of being able to do anything. I felt like I was on top of the world. I wanted to tell everyone. Unfortunately, most people think that free birthing is "irresponsible" instead of being happy for you, so I didn't talk about it much.

My biggest wish is that all women could know the feeling of free birthing and taking back that right. There's nothing more oppressing than having a natural right taken away from you and being told that you are too inadequate to do it.

As women we need to stick together and bring each other up and support each other. The most badass thing you can do is birth your own baby and feel that power. Time to take back birth.

Advice for an Autumn Birth

From the women who wrote the stories in this collection.

Breath! Controlling your breathing can make contractions so much more manageable and helps you to relax.

Trust in your body and baby. It is incredibly important because it helps minimize fear.

Take advantage of the long warm summer days. Bask in the sunshine and swim as often as possible. Strengthen your mind and body connection for your autumn birth.

Take plenty of evening walks while the weather is nice.

It's a lovely season not too hot and not too cold it's just in between. Don't overdress baby as they tend to still get too hot easily.

Trust your intuition always and keep these two mantras with you: The only way out is through and each surge brings me closer to my baby. And have a nice pair of warm, fuzzy socks!

Not just for autumn; don't be afraid to eat your placenta to stop a postpartum hemorrhage; it works.

Unpacking Pain-free Birth

ORGASMIC BIRTH. SUPERNATURAL BIRTH. Pain-free birth. There are a multitude of terms used to describe the experience of going through pregnancy, and even labor, without sensations one would describe as "painful."

I believe that pain-free birth is possible. I've read hundreds of first-hand accounts by women who have experienced it. I've studied the concept of pain-free and even pleasurable birth through courses, audio tracks, books, articles, and more from dozens of sources.

Ever since I got pregnant with my very first child, I have strived to have this experience. And every time - six times - I have come through the same struggle, the same pain-filled experience.

Wonderful, life-changing, but not painless. Not orgasmic. Not supernatural. And not for any lack of trying.

In the name of eliminating my fears, I have prayed and received blessings. Gone to energy healers and mentors. Taken classes in self-hypnosis (really, just full-body and mind relaxation). I have focused on nutrition, on exercise, on meditation. I spoke affirmations and prayed some more. In six pregnancies, I took just about every supplement recommended for an easier birth, changed my diet and my mindset, set up vision boards and read the scriptures.

Ultimately, all of it made for a beautiful journey, but a journey tainted with an undercurrent of disatisfaction when, at the end, I felt every labor pain.

Don't get me wrong. I'm immensely grateful that my births have been "normal," even boring! I'm grateful all of my babies have been healthy, my labors have been short (under nine hours each time).

My fourth labor came closest to this pain-free ideal. A three-hour labor at 40 weeks exactly, an 8lb baby (my smallest) that flew out of me in just a few pushes. But still not pain-free.

I tell you this, not to discourage you, but to give you a balanced perspective. Maybe there's something I neglected to do. Maybe I didn't pray hard enough, have enough faith, or root out all of my fears. But as an experienced (four times!) freebirther, having had six unmedicated births and having studied my heart out, I firmly believe that some women are meant to have pain free experiences, and others are not.

I would encourage you to approach pain-free or pleasurable birth as you are called to explore it. Nourish your body and your baby. Move however you feel comfortable. Take the supplements you innately know you need. Pray if you pray. Meditate if you meditate. Read books and articles and birth stories, listen to the podcasts.

Prepare in every way to have that incredible experience that I KNOW is possible! I've seen the videos, read the stories. Women can have painless, pleasurable, orgasmic, transcendent birth experiences.

Be prepared to accept any outcome. That's the best piece of advice I can give you. Be prepared for a long, painfree birth. A short painless one. A long, strenuous birth. A short, easy one. Be mentally prepared to accept whatever journey you go on with your baby to bring them here. And you'll have a good experience, one way or the other. Whatever happens.

All of my birth experiences have been good. I can say that, despite the pain. They were peaceful, most of them in my home with just me and my husband and our chosen support (usually a family friend or hired doula or photographer).

That experience alone has been a miracle every time. No complications that we couldn't handle ourselves. Good births. Beautiful births. And as you prepare for your freebirth experience, you can have that too. Even if you transfer, even if there is trauma and difficulty that we often don't want to think about, much less talk about.

If you are prepared, you will not fear.

Above all, know that no matter whether you feel pain or not, you are not broken. You have not failed. You experienced what millions of women have experienced and have passed through the same milestones.

You have gone from maiden to mother.

A NOTE ON FAITH AND BETRAYAL:

I felt betrayed by God every time I didn't have my supernatural childbirth experience. As a faithful Christian who had studied and prayed and knew that God had the power to grant me a pain-free birth, who had declared it in prayer with her husband at her side, it hurt when I didn't receive what I saw other people receiving.

I still battle these thoughts, sometimes, when I consider having another baby and going through this experience again. Will I get my pain-free birth that I've worked so hard to have?

It's very likely I won't. Something in my body or brain or spirit just doesn't seem to let go of the pattern of labor pain that I go through each time. And it's hard not to blame God for withholding a blessing I've "earned" until I realize that it's not something to earn.

The Atonement of my Savior Jesus Christ covers all of my experiences, from my joy to my sorrow. And in my sorrow, and especially the sorrow that has accompanied my child-bearing, I have learned what it is like to suffer for the sake of another child of God, and that has brought me closer to him.

If I had to experience pain in my (so far) six births in order to come to this understanding and testimony of Christ and His Atonement for me, then I would do it again. If having a pain-free birth would in some way have hindered my spiritual growth, then I would not choose it. And God in His wisdom has blessed me with a different experience.

But, to speak frankly, it does suck. And every time I pray and seek for a pain-free experience and don't have one, I have to go through this process of acceptance. Thy will be done, Lord.

I'm still here. Still believing, still faithful. My faith has been rendered stronger, like coal that undergoes the pressure and heat to become a diamond.

Whatever your beliefs, birth is a process that we go through as women to bring us closer to intuition, to Spirit, to self and to all others that have existed now and before, all those who will exist. It is meant to refine us, in our bodies, hearts, and minds.

Striving for a painless birth or a supernatural birth is never bad if you approach it with a balanced perspective.

Remember, whatever happens, you've got this. And it's worth it.

My Favorite Books, Blogs, and Podcasts about Birth

I've gathered my top favorite media resources for unassisted and autonomous birth. It was so hard to narrow it down to the ones I'd recommend the most!
If you think an important resource is missing, please email me at authorbreemoore@gmail.com and I'll add your suggestion to this list!

BOOKS
Birth Becomes Hers by Bree Moore
Unassisted Childbirth by Laura Kaplan Shanley
Home Birth on Your Own Terms by Heather Barker
Unhindered Childbirth by Sarah M. Haydock
Mother's Intuition: How Belief Shapes Birth by Kim Wildner
Orgasmic Childbirth by Debra Pascali-Bonaro

BLOGS/PODCASTS
Evidence Based Birth:
https://evidencebasedbirth.com/
Unassisted Childbirth by Laura Shanley:
https://unassistedchildbirth.com/
Freebirth Society:
https://www.freebirthsociety.com/
Indie Birth:
https://indiebirth.org/

DOCUMENTARIES
Orgasmic Childbirth
Why Not Home?
The Business of Being Born
Birth As We Know It
Microbirth

Apricity

Apricity: The warmth of the sun in winter.
From the Latin aprīcitās/aprīcus ("warmed by the sun")

Birth of Ivy Arabella

By Bree Moore

THIS BABY'S STORY STARTED nearly a year ago. In November of 2019, we found out we were pregnant for the 6th time. Feelings of overwhelm washed over me with that positive pregnancy test. I wasn't ready. I had five kids, and my youngest was only 10 months old.

After 7 years of back to back pregnancies, I had some extra weight, I knew I had nutrient deficiencies, and I was *tired*. We do our best to embrace each baby as they come, however, so I prayed for a change of heart and the strength to manage, and we announced the pregnancy at Thanksgiving that year.

A week later, I fell down the stairs and had some bleeding.

Two weeks later, at 9 weeks gestation, I completed my first ever miscarriage. I had mixed feelings. I had just started to feel excited about the baby, but I still had a strong sense of overwhelm. I felt guilty for feeling relieved that the pregnancy had ended. At the same time, I had the impression that we hadn't "lost" this baby, but that she had decided to come at a later time.

Four months later, in March 2020, we prayed and felt strongly that we should get pregnant. This time, it felt exciting and joyful. This time, I didn't feel overwhelmed. It felt right. It was time. We got pregnant the first time we tried and oh the joy! My impressions were strong that this spirit inside of me was the same one we had lost the previous year.

I still had some weight to lose, I still felt a bit depleted, but I immediately improved my diet and started taking specific supplements. My nausea vanished by week 7, though it usually lasts until week 13. Initially, I worried this meant I was miscarrying again, but truly it was just my body finally receiving what it needed (and none of what it didn't need) in those early weeks. I lost 10 pounds in a healthy way and felt better than ever using the protocols outlined in "Powerfully Pregnant" By Donna White, a midwife.

I didn't continue the diet as well as I had hoped from the beginning, but I continued to use the recommended supplements and moderate my eating so my weight didn't get out of control. I was hoping to have a smaller baby than my last - he had been 10+ lbs! So I did my best to be healthy, but also to have a healthy mindset towards my growing body.

There was never a question whether this would be another unassisted pregnancy and birth. I did pray, just to check in with God and make sure that I wasn't missing any inspiration for this baby, but didn't feel anything was different with this pregnancy that required assistance. So, we proceeded with our 4th wild and free pregnancy, the only assistance being an ultrasound at 20 weeks with a birth center ultrasound technician. We found out we were having a healthy baby girl.

The pregnancy, technically my 7th, proceeded without issue beyond the normal pregnancy complaints. As things advanced, the veins in my legs grew (but weren't painful), I had constipation that was resolved by the regular use of magnesium, and back and sciatica pain that was resolved by the use of the mommastrong.com program.

As long as I was consistent with the stretches and deep muscle release routines in the program, I didn't need to see a chiropractor until my final few weeks of pregnancy, which was a huge blessing. I highly recommend this program for any woman who has had or will have a baby! It's not your typical exercise program but rather focuses on strengthening and stabilizing your pelvic floor and core through breath, postural awareness, and etc.

37 weeks rolled by. I thought I might go early, but I've found in my six births that this is largely wishful thinking, not intuition, on my part. All but one of my pregnancies have gone over my "due date" by at least a week. As much as I wanted my baby to come early and free me from the discomforts of that final month, it was beautiful to realize that this baby would be due, and most likely come, the same week I had miscarried the previous year.

Physically, I gathered the supplies I would need. I bought a used birth pool, having felt strongly that this needed to be a water birth, despite my past three freebirths being on land. This baby sent me clear messages that she wanted to be born in the water. I bought twinkly lights and a beautiful mountain tapestry and made up the guest room in our basement to be my birth space.

My birth kit had almost everything, but I ordered a couple more umbilical clamps, postpartum supplies like pads and diapers, and an herbal spray. I noticed I was out of Angelica tincture, but I figured I wouldn't need it since I had Shepherd's Purse. Boy, I wish I had refilled it now! But everything turned out alright in the end, as you'll see.

Mentally and emotionally, I prepared for a spiritual birth experience and hoped for a pain-free one. I prayed and read books and scriptures and visualized the birth going hundreds of ways. I hoped it would be fast, I hoped it would be slow, I hoped my doula would get there in time, I hoped that I would birth alone at night before anyone realized what was happening. My mind was filled with birth visions and ideas. Interestingly enough, the night before she was born I had no dreams of birth or pregnancy at all, but a peaceful, full nights' sleep.

I started helping my body prepare for this birth by taking the 5W birth preparation supplement around 35 weeks. I figured after so many pregnancies in such a short time my uterus could use something to help it strengthen. As a result, I had Braxton Hicks on and off throughout these weeks, which was unusual for me. It really put me in the "Maybe this baby will come early" mindset, but this baby had other plans. Patterns are fun, and I've had enough births to have a pretty good idea of when my babies come. My average is 41 weeks, with only one baby coming on her due date and another one coming past 42 weeks, so I was pretty confident that this baby would follow suit, even with the Braxton Hicks and my wishful thinking. And I was right!

Sunday, December 13th, 2020
41 weeks +1 day pregnant

Contractions started 10 minutes apart around lunchtime. I tried not to focus on them, but they did feel different, starting lower down and in front, more of a concentrated sensation than the Braxton Hicks had been. I didn't feel like eating much lunch, but I told myself that if I was going to be in labor, I probably wanted something to eat. So I had a quesadilla with chicken. I made myself two, but I could only eat one.

My husband set the kids up with some calm Sunday TV downstairs, and I stayed upstairs and focused. He came back up to talk to me, and I asked him for a blessing. We're Christian, and in our church a "blessing" is a special kind of prayer of comfort and healing. My husband prayed over me and over my labor, asking God that I would have strength for what was to come and praying that my back especially would find relief. As soon as he finished with the blessing, my back felt so much better! It has given me problems ever since my fourth birth, which I've managed with a number of things, but until the blessing was over I didn't realize how much the contractions were straining it. I definitely felt God's presence in this labor.

After about an hour, the contractions were still going. I told my husband I was going to take a nap. I laid down and turned on some hypnosis tracks from the Christian Hypnobirthing app. It was very relaxing, but I couldn't quite fall asleep. I drifted in and out, realizing that the contractions were keeping me from falling fully asleep.

When I got up about an hour and half later, the contractions were feeling more random in timing, possibly because I'd lain down, but once I got up and moving they got closer together, from seven minutes to five minutes. I told my husband it might be baby day and said he should plan on not going into work the next day, and then I messaged my doula and the birth photographer who would be filming. It still didn't feel like "it", but I was playing it safe updating everyone just in case.

Most Sundays, my husband and I take our kids to his moms where his siblings gather with their kids. It's a very enjoyable time that I look forward to, and they live just around the corner from us so it's really close and convenient. Well, this week I wasn't sure I wanted to go with the contractions I was having. I hate having everyone "know" I'm in labor and much prefer to just bomb drop everyone with a baby after the fact rather than sending out updates while I'm in labor.

It was getting close to 5 pm and the contractions were still 5 minutes apart. My husband and I decided to tell his mom that I might be in labor and ask her to take the kids and feed them the dinner we had made. We asked her not to tell anyone we might be in labor. We did send pajamas with the kids just in case and told grandma to bring them back around 8:30, which would be their bedtime. I told myself I wanted to have a baby in my arms before then!

I told my doula and birth photographer where I was at and they both decided to head over. I was worried it would be too soon, but it turned out perfect. While my husband took the kids over, I made my way downstairs to my birthing space set up in the guest bedroom. I turned on the twinkle lights I'd bought, a lovely silver Christmas star set above the moon and mountain scenery tapestry I'd hung up, and an amethyst crystal set above the mantle of our (non-functional) fireplace. I put out birthing supplies and pulled out the pool, though I left the setting up of the pool to my husband.

My birth photographer arrived. We chatted, with me occasionally pausing for contractions. I love having photos and videos of my births, but I don't love the "watched" feeling that sometimes comes with it. Fortunately, this time it wasn't so bad. I hardly noticed when she would pull out her camera. My husband and doula arrived next in quick succession, and the contractions began to intensify and get closer. This was getting very real! We started filling the pool. My doula rubbed my back during contractions and it felt so good. I loved having someone there to do that while my husband worked on the pool.

When the pool was about half full, the hot water stopped flowing. We started boiling pots on the stove. I got into the pool, even though it was only half full, and it felt really nice. It didn't do much for the pain, exactly, but it helped me relax more fully in between contractions.

I'd really hoped and prayed for a pain-free, or at least somewhat "comfortable" delivery, using hypnosis tracks and scripture to prepare my mind and body. I've done this with my past three deliveries, and each one has been an incredible experience, spiritual and beautiful, but very grueling and hard work and definitely not pain free. This birth was no exception, but I'm learning that while God doesn't always give us what we want, he gives us what we need.

He took my back pain during contractions and made them more manageable. He gave me incredible strength of mind and body to maneuver through the labor pains. He gave me a curious mind that reads everything about birth to prepare, so I knew what things to try when my baby wasn't descending so well. He gave me a husband who did everything in his power to provide the things I felt I needed to have this birth experience as it needed to be. In short, God gave me everything I needed.

I had a worship playlist going in the background with a vibrant, upbeat, and hopeful lineup of various artists. When "You Say," by Lauren Daigle came on during a contraction, I cried. These words filled me up to the brim and helped me strengthen my resolve through the rest of my labor:

"You say I am loved
When I can't feel a thing
You say I am strong
When I think I am weak
You say I am held
When I am falling short
When I don't belong
Oh You say I am Yours
And I believe, oh I believe
What You say of me
I believe"

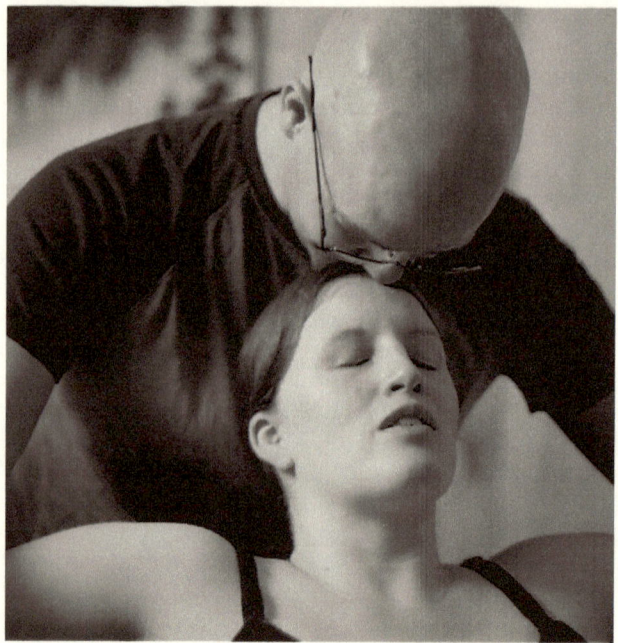

Time became a nonessential, abstract thing. The only thing that mattered was getting through the next wave as it crashed down on me. I tried breathing patterns, movement, standing, kneeling, sitting, lunging. I was moving all over the pool, not really in the same position for any of my contractions.

I thought my husband might get in the pool with me, but there was no room! He held my hand, touched my head, was there as a witness for me. And he kept filling the pool with hot water, which felt amazing.

My doula poured it over my back after each contraction and kept reminding me to completely release the contractions as they ended, which was super helpful because I found myself wanting to hold onto them, to make them last longer and work harder so I could have my baby sooner.

My doula said at one point, "You're being so gentle with your body," and I realized that I wasn't being very gentle, making it work when the contractions were done, so I started to release and fall away from the contraction and let it be what it was, nothing more, nothing less.

In my mind, I fought a war between negative and positive, hope and despair. I entered transition. I could feel my baby's amniotic sac bulge out of my cervix during a contraction. I felt like I was about 9cm, though I wasn't measuring. Almost open. I let about ten more contractions go by and felt more open, so I decided to break my water. A little pressure with my fingernails during a contraction and it popped! Baby engaged and pushing pretty much started at that point.

I definitely pooped a few times as baby descended. Unfortunately, it wasn't the solid kind and that was a bit gross, but it was pretty diluted in the water and I didn't worry about it, especially as we took some cool water out and replaced it with boiling hot water.

My pushing phase usually lasts about thirty minutes after my water breaks. This time, it took an hour. An entire, excruciating hour. I wanted to run away.

Contractions rocked through my pelvis and uterus and I distinctly remember wanting to stand up and flee from them. But I stayed and pushed through and reminded myself that my baby was coming.

Outloud I spoke that I didn't know I could do it, that it was taking a long time and I was done. My husband and doula and birth photographer comforted me, told me I was doing amazing, that my baby would be here soon. Not soon enough for me, but what could I do? The only way out was through.

I roared. I kept my voice deep and loud and focused my energy downward. I prayed during and between contractions. God, deliver me from this. Give me strength for this. The music stopped at one point, and I asked that it stay off. It was distracting me now.

The pool started deflating, it had a hole somewhere in it (we'd bought it used), and they had to keep filling it with air. They apologized for the noise of the pump, but honestly, it sort of helped me focus, in a way.

I could feel my baby's head inside, still caught up on my tailbone. She wasn't coming down, coming around, and I thought something was wrong with her position.

Either that or this baby was going to be bigger than my last, something I definitely feared. I remembered God's promises of strength and started different things to get her out.

My doula wrapped a rebozo around her shoulders, and I pulled on it during a few contractions, arching backward and squatting to open myself up more. I got out of the pool and went to the bathroom, not because I needed to go, but because I needed to be alone.

The contractions on the toilet were excruciating, but ultimately I left the bathroom and went back to the pool for the warmth.

I moved into lunging on opposite sides next. My doula suggested spinning babies moves. None of them felt right except the Miles circuit, but I didn't have the mental energy to get myself out of the pool to try it out.

After one contraction I put myself in a modified Miles Circuit position, butt sticking out of the water into the air, my head down just above the level of the water.

I'm not sure it did anything, and I couldn't stand to stay in it during a contraction. I literally flipped myself from one position to the next, the water giving me a sort of weightless mobility I wouldn't normally have at 41 weeks pregnant!

I followed my intuition, moving from one position to the next, and still that baby head wouldn't move.

Until it did. Slowly, over the course of several contractions, I felt progress being made and my baby came down.

I visualized her head filling that space in my pelvis. I imagined her crowning, slowly. I forced myself to let the pressure of contractions and the force of her head open me wider. I tried not to make it go any faster than my body was willing to go.

She crowned. I breathed and held her head and pressed against my skin, hoping to prevent tearing. Her head, to my vast relief, came out.

I felt a thick, ropey cord wrapped around her neck and swiftly unwound it. Her body turned slightly, and another contraction came on and I let her shoulders out. She gushed into the water, finally outside. Finally here.

I brought her up slowly, leaning back, keeping her in the water. My husband reached over my shoulder from behind to help me bring her out, and I told him to wait. I wanted to bring her up slowly, to remember this part, and give her an easier transition into the world of air and light. Just a moment, a pause, a breath, and then I brought her out of the water myself.

She was here! I was exhausted and exultant. We watched her eyes open, admiring her cheesy vernix-covered skin. Her head was molded on one side, showing how she had tried to come down the birth canal with a tilted head. No wonder I had to work so hard to push her out!

She seemed so small and petite, I thought for sure she was one of my smallest babies. She was slow to catch on to the concept of breathing, but her tone and movement were good, and she still had oxygen through the umbilical cord. I flipped her over on my arm and rubbed and patted her. I told her to join us, that it was safe.

She started to make little choking breathing sounds like there was some mucus or something in her passageway. I asked for the bulb syringe, but my husband couldn't find it, so I gently sucked at her mouth, spitting out afterward. That seemed to loosen things up and her breathing got a bit better. Then suddenly, a cry! We all laughed and the room filled with relief.

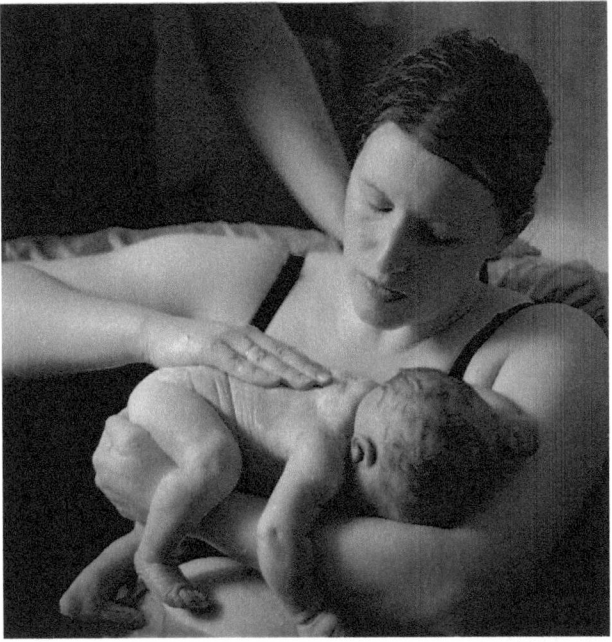

About ten minutes later, my mother-in-law walked in upstairs with the kids. Perfect timing. She was born right at their bedtime! We invited them to come downstairs and see their new baby. They were fascinated with the pool and the baby and everything going on. We thanked their grandma, and she had to leave to get somewhere so we bid her farewell and my husband turned on a movie for the kids while I got out of the pool to wait for the placenta.

We snuggled on the bed. We chatted and laughed about the experience I'd just had. The kids ran in and out, distracted by the movie but wanting to be close to their new sister. My husband went to put my (now) second-oldest to bed - he was exhausted! When my husband came back, we cut the baby's cord so I could try to get the placenta out in a more upright position. I squatted over a pot. Placenta didn't budge. My bleeding was great, I felt great, but the placenta didn't want to come yet. It had been over an hour since the birth. My past few births the placenta had taken 2-3 hours to come out, so I wasn't worried yet.

We weighed our daughter - 9lbs 5oz! I couldn't believe it because she seemed so tiny. She was 20.5 inches long.

My husband got the other kids to bed, but only after they insisted on each having a turn holding their sister. The photographer let them practice taking pictures of her with her camera. They loved it, and my 3yo insisted she wasn't tired - she wanted to keep taking pictures! But my husband ushered them upstairs and got them in bed somehow.

I ate the rest of an orange I'd started eating during labor, then tried again with the placenta once the kids had been down for a while. It still wouldn't come out. Four hours after the birth. I knew of women who had freebirthed and their placenta took 12+ hours and everything was fine, but I was still feeling eager to move past this part, and I wanted to be wise and aware of any issues that might arise.

I consulted Heather Baker, author of "Home Birth on Your Own Terms" (my copy was upstairs and my husband was still gone putting kids down at that point). She asked if I'd peed since the birth, and I hadn't. I had tried the "peppermint oil in the toilet trick" already, but as soon as she said that I realized that my urethra was possibly swollen, or blocked by something.

My doula and birth photographer decided it was time for them to go home. I agreed, hoping more privacy would help my placenta come more readily. They were both the best support I could ask for, and I was so glad they were there for all of it. I wish we'd caught the footage of my placenta's birth! But they needed to get home, and I understood that.

They left, and I got out my mirror to check "down there" to see what was going on. Maybe I could see my placenta coming out, which would help me know if I could give the cord some traction. I could also check for tearing.

I checked for tearing first. I was pretty sure I could only see a minor, first-degree tear. I felt peace that it would heal on its own. I tried to feel up the cord a ways, but I wasn't sure what I was feeling. This entire time, I kept letting our baby latch and nurse, and I could feel my uterus contracting regularly, and my bleeding was minimal. I also felt really good, not dizzy or loopy or cold at all. My body was fine, the placenta just wasn't coming out! I talked to it. I prayed.

Eventually, I felt tired and wanted to sleep. It was nearing 1 am at this point. I asked my husband for another blessing. He prayed over me, rebuking anything that might be causing my placenta to be stuck and not come. When he finished, I consulted Heather's book (my husband had gotten it for me), and I read the part about what tinctures help the placenta come. I knew all about them, having studied them over the course of my three previous freebirths, but I also knew I didn't have the tincture that would be best to use to get the placenta out.

Angelica tincture is best for use before the placenta comes, and Shepherd's Purse or Wombstringe is best after the placenta comes. I only had Shepherd's Purse, but in Heather's book she mentioned that it could be used if it was all that was available. I chose to give it a try. 3 dropperfuls of tincture in water, 3 minutes apart, and then I decided that I would let myself sleep and the next time the baby woke to nurse, I would get up and try again to urinate and get the placenta out.

We slept for about two hours. When our baby woke again, she actually only stirred and fell right back to sleep without nursing, acting like a little baby alarm clock for me to get up and get that placenta moving. I went to the bathroom and tried the peppermint trick. No pee, no placenta. I coughed. I stood and pulled gently on the cord. Nothing. My husband came to the door to be with me and encourage me as I squatted on a towel.

I reached two fingers up inside, following the cord, another suggestion from Heather the midwife. I could feel my placenta bulging out from my cervix. It was right there! I think my bladder and the placenta basically choked each other out, both too squished to move on their own. I pushed on the top of my uterus and felt the placenta move slightly. It was all squished up in there and just needed more help.

So with one hand down on the cord and one on my fundus, I pushed and pulled at the same time, and my placenta came out with a great woosh and plop. And then pee GUSHED EVERYWHERE. I couldn't stop it. I laughed and exclaimed and apologized to my husband as pee just splashed all over the floor. My husband said, "I don't care. I'll clean up your pee. I'm just glad it's out and you're okay!"

I was glad too. I praised God's goodness and just immediately felt so, so much better. My bleeding was hardly anything, too, so I knew I'd been right to wait patiently. I imagine that if I'd waited even longer, my placenta still would have come out on its own, as my uterus was contracting and slowly pushing it out of my cervix, but I'm glad I got it out when I did. I headed back to bed, ate a small snack, and snuggled my baby.

Finally, her birth story was complete. Ivy Arabella, our sixth beautiful babe, such an incredible experience.

"Arabella" means "yielding to prayer" in Hebrew. This lesson was present for me in every aspect of this pregnancy, birth, and even in postpartum. God was with me, and I'm grateful for the lessons I learned in this birth experience. It wasn't easy, but as always, it was worth it. God is so good!

A Thanksgiving Freebirth

By Jamie Lewis

I WAS 41+1 WEEKS pregnant and woke up at 2:30 am with some discomfort. It wasn't abnormal by that point, I'd had plenty of discomfort and false alarms leading up to that morning. My baby's head had been lodged up close to my hip for the last several weeks, and I was sure that is what was holding up labor.

I'd often done some spinning babies stretches to encourage better positioning, and had managed to move the head down into my pelvis several times, but whenever I laid down that head would migrate right back up to my hip.

As I debated what to do that morning, I went through my stretch routine because I could feel the head up in the normal spot. Within minutes I could feel the head back down in my pelvis, but I wasn't sure what to do next. If I laid back down I was pretty sure the head would move, but it wasn't even 3 am and I wasn't ready to be up for the day. I decided to build myself a chair of pillows in bed so I could rest without going completely vertical.

Once I was situated, I went from feeling uncomfortable to experiencing strong, regular surges. I started timing them, trying to sleep in between but not quite comfortable enough to do so. I tried not to get excited as the surges became more uncomfortable, but at 41 weeks I was emotionally and physically over it. My hip had given me so much pain during this pregnancy, and more than once I'd gotten completely stuck in bed or on the ground, almost always ending in sobbing while my husband gingerly assisted me in getting upright again.

This was my 3rd baby, 3rd pregnancy, 3rd birth. I knew better than to assume anything. On the other hand, it was all new. This was our first time going unassisted. No prenatal visits, no midwife, no doula. This time I was completely relying on my own instincts, and it was as exhilarating as it was nerve-wracking.

I waited a couple of hours before deciding to get up and move to my birth ball. The contractions had become too obvious to relax through, and I wanted to get in a better position to help my baby descend down. As I swayed in the darkness, the contractions continued to build and grow in intensity.

They were closer together, lasting longer, and I began to grow hopeful that my two other children would be waking up to a new sibling. I closed my eyes, set aside my contraction timer, and let my body do what it needed.

My husband Mike snuck out at some point to greet the kids, and as they stirred in the living area, my contractions began to fade. I stayed in our room for a while longer, wrapped in a blanket and swaying on my ball, but the contractions slipped away and my focus left. I decided to go make breakfast and coffee and go about the morning as normal. Maybe things would pick up as I occupied my mind.

I had a couple of very strong, catch my breath contractions as I made breakfast. Then nothing. The kids, who were 2 and 1 at the time, were oblivious to anything out of the ordinary. I sat on my birth ball and watched them and my husband play quietly together. I snapped a picture of them with their blocks, thinking that soon they'd be joined by their new sibling.

As the day progressed and my contractions continued to subside, my husband decided to get the kids out of the house and let me have some quiet space. It was Thanksgiving day, and we had family in town. He took the kids to Grammy's house and left me to work through what I was beginning to doubt was labor.

I moseyed around the house in their absence, waiting for anything to give me new hope that I was in fact still in labor. Only the occasional contraction kept me just slightly uncomfortable, and they were no closer than 45 minutes apart.

I managed to nap before they got home, and once they were back and napping, Mike suggested watching a movie. We sat down, but before the opening credits were done I realized I couldn't make it through a movie. My mind was in labor, even if my body wasn't. I began the climb downstairs and immediately was hit with a contraction that froze me in place. I made my way down the rest of the steps just in time for another to course through me, and another when I reached our bedroom. However, they dissipated again and I was left waiting.

At this point, we had to decide what to do about Thanksgiving. I didn't want to miss the dinner we'd planned on attending if I wasn't going to have a baby, but I also wasn't sure I wanted to feign normalcy if contractions did pick up during the meal. We decided that Mike would take the kids, and I would again just relax and let my body do what it needed. He packed everyone up, asked if I was sure I was ok staying home, and took the kids.

About 1/2 hour after they left, I was hit with a big contraction. I got on my birth ball and swayed, closing my eyes and trying to not think about what my body was or wasn't doing. The contractions started coming faster again, and this time they didn't go away. I called my husband and told him that I thought it would be good to have him back home, and he said he'd leave the kids with grandma and grandpa.

As we talked, the contractions continued to build and eventually got to the point where I had to set the phone down and vocalize through them. He let me know he was hurrying home, and I hung up.

I started to panic at this point. The contractions were now so strong and close together, and my other babies had been all night labors. I was scared that I didn't have the energy. Scared that the contractions would be too much. I texted a friend and she assured me that I could do it, and offered encouragement.

I had the passing notion that perhaps this was transition, but dismissed it since my contractions were really only just getting strong. As soon as my husband got home he set to work on my birth pool while I tried to find the most comfortable position. He got the hose and hooked it up to the water heater, then started adding ice to offset the heat.

He quickly realized we did not have enough to make the water tolerable, and so told me he'd be "right back". A few moments later he was back, arms full of bags of ice and a neighbor warily standing at our door with more bags. I could hear him thank the neighbor and shut the door, then resume his task of making the pool just right.

Meanwhile, I'd knelt in front of a chair in our room, trying to relax my body during each contraction. I could see my husband going to and fro in my peripheral, and it offered me so much peace. I wasn't afraid anymore, and at one point he tripped over the bed and I managed a full laugh at his expense. He asked if he could do some counter pressure on my back, which sounded perfect.

The next contraction he pushed on my lower back and it was exactly what I needed. I was excited that we'd found something that helped the pain, and as the next contraction surged I motioned him to do the same again.

It. Was. Awful. I couldn't talk, so I smacked his hand, and vigorously shook my head. He stepped back and waited, and as soon as it ended I apologized for hitting him and said it had made it worse. So we decided to try a double hip squeeze. The contraction started, and I again had to smack him and shake my head. We both laughed after the contraction, I apologized again and he went back to filling the pool.

Shortly after I was feeling pushy, and moved to the bathroom in our room. I didn't want my water breaking on the bed. I knelt by the toilet and began to vocalize loudly. Mike asked if I wanted to try the water, and I didn't, but I decided to at least see how it felt. It was cold!

"Mike it's freezing!" He looked so defeated and immediately ran to the kitchen to start boiling water, as we were now out of hot water. I returned to the bathroom and howled my way through the next contractions.

At some point, I noticed our bathroom window was slightly open, and I could see The neighbors house. I hollered at Mike to come shut it so they couldn't hear me. He continued running back and forth from me to the kitchen to the pool, and I continued yelling through contractions.

By now my urge to push couldn't be ignored, so I began to bear down. My biggest concern with going unassisted had been not knowing when to push, so I tried to hold back. But the relief I experienced from that push was all I needed to go 100%.

Prior to labor, I'd asked my husband to remind me to breathe my baby out. I didn't want to tear and I wanted to be as serene and peaceful as I could. So as I pushed and yelled with all my might, I silently willed him to not say a word. He had given up on the pool, and stood behind me, waiting. My waters broke, and within a handful of contractions, I could feel a head.

I gleefully informed him that the baby was close, then gripped the toilet with one hand and the sink with the other as I bore down and pushed with all I had. The baby's head was born with that contraction, and my husband exclaimed behind me "Those cheeks!"

At this point he came in and knelt next to me. I reached over to him for support, and something inside of me knew that I needed to readjust my position to birth the rest of my baby. I stood up partially, one knee on the ground and one pushing my body up, and immediately felt the baby's body squirm and adjust inside of me.

I looked at Mike and said, "This baby just moved and it is the weirdest thing I've ever felt!" Then the next contraction came, and he moved behind me to help catch our baby. I reached down in front and together we welcomed our baby earthside, exclaiming together "It's a boy!"

I sat back against the tub and held my baby up as he began to cry the most beautiful newborn cry, and I looked at my husband in awe, "I did it! We did it!!" He was so happy, and the look on his face was one that I'll never forget. He was so proud, and joyful, and in love. It was such a romantic moment, being together with this new tiny person and knowing we'd done this together.

I asked him to get a picture of us, then we moved to the bed. As soon as the cord had stopped pulsing we tied and cut it, then he held our baby while I birthed the placenta. Once I'd showered off and climbed into our chair, Mike called his mom and asked that she bring the kids to come meet their new brother.

It was so wonderful, sitting there snuggling my baby while my children came running in to meet him. We all snuggled on the chair for a bit while they oo'd and aw'd, then we weighed him. 9.6lbs. We hadn't solidified a name yet, but as we looked at his squishy wrinkled face we knew that he was our Miles Adam.

Mike and his mom got the kids to bed and then got the room cleaned up and the pool drained. We laughed about the poor unused pool, and he told us the story of how he'd run to our neighbors to ask for ice, and then mentioned it was for me who was giving birth after they'd already gotten it.

They were shocked, and suddenly frantic to get all the ice they owned over to our home, which is why he'd followed Mike to our doorstep with more ice. It was so funny, we still joke with our neighbors about it.

Once the cleanup was done and his mom had gone home, we climbed into bed and snuggled our new baby.

Everett's RV Birth

By Leah

Monday, January 6th, 2020

I woke up and it started just like any other day, my 2-year-old and 3-year-old needed breakfast, RV needed cleaning, my husband needed breakfast and coffee before work. Just the usual weekday routine, except that I had been having prodromal labor for the last 6 weeks and today was no better.

By lunchtime, I noticed the contractions were almost around 30-40 min apart but today they felt real! All day that day they stayed the same length apart but were noticeably stronger than any of the other previous days. That night, I woke up every 30 minutes with strong contractions that got me up and walking around and sitting on the exercise ball to ease them.

Tuesday, January 7th

After waking up all throughout the night with those pesky contractions, I was tired and exhausted but our normal weekday routine needed to be kept. After I got my husband off to work and the kids fed breakfast, I rotated between sitting on the ball, doing stretches, and resting on the couch. By lunchtime, my contractions were only 20 minutes apart but the pain wasn't unbearable so we ate lunch and the kids and I went for a nice 2-mile walk since it was so sunny and beautiful outside.

By dinner time, around 5:30 pm, my contractions were 15 minutes apart and were definitely getting stronger, and I did not feel like eating dinner so I skipped out. I got the kids to bed and then headed to the shower house to take a hot shower and relax. Since we live in an RV, we walk to a building that has shower rooms and a laundry room. After a very long hot shower, I went back and sat on the ball and watched TV with my husband for a few hours. At one point I started craving oatmeal so I fixed myself a bowl and scarfed it down. Note to self: labor does not stop pregnancy cravings!

The clock rolled around to 11 pm and my contractions were 5 minutes apart and too painful to sleep, so I sent my husband to bed and I stayed up. I didn't see much point in keeping my husband awake when I preferred to deal with pain in quiet and on my own. I always found it much easier to focus and relax this way.

While my sweetheart slept, I walked the floor and sat on the ball to relieve pain. The feeling of contractions is like no other feeling. It's like an ocean wave; it slowly builds up as it rolls along and then slowly fades out. Throughout each rolling pain, I closed my eyes and breathed in a soothing rhythmic fashion, moaning deeply on the breaths out to help relax my muscles.

Wednesday, January 8th

3 a.m. came around as my contractions got closer and were averaging 2-3 min apart. They were more difficult to handle and just like any labor, I needed to use the bathroom! Once I sat on the toilet, I had no idea that I would not be getting back up until my baby started coming out. I moaned and rocked back and forth with every earth-shaking contraction.

At this point, my husband could not stay asleep because I was being a bit loud but he stayed in bed and rested until I finally called him over.

I felt my body pushing and bearing down on its own. It was something I could not control. My uterine muscles had pulled up as far as it could go and were ready to push the baby out! It is such a strange feeling when your body is doing something that you have no control over. In a way, it made me feel helpless since I couldn't stop it.

After that first push, I told my husband to bring some towels and lay them on the floor in front of the toilet. I was in too much pain to move any farther than just off the toilet. He laid them on the floor and brought me a pillow to lean on which helped a lot! I only pushed maybe 4 or 5 times but it definitely felt like forever.

With each push that my body did, I leaned into the pillow and bit down on it, and tried my hardest not to scream. I went back and forth from hands and knees to sitting on my knees and using the door frame to hold onto. I could feel my baby making its way through the birth canal and it was such a new feeling both physically and emotionally.

I kept telling myself "just one step closer", "Just one push closer", "this pain is not for nothing, it will bring me my baby". Telling myself these things truly did help. Throughout this process, my husband was behind me rubbing my back and reassuring me it is all ok. I was shivering and cold and he made sure my blanket didn't fall off and didn't get messy even though at this point, my water had not broken yet.

I felt a burning fire! This was the ring of fire that everyone speaks about; my baby was crowning!! I reached down and felt my baby's head still inside the water sac and then seconds later it burst which relieved some pressure. I looked down and could see my baby's head coming through. I kept telling myself that I'm almost there and my baby is almost here.

My body pushed again and this time with an agonizing scream! I couldn't help but worry about the kids waking up but surprisingly enough they didn't. My baby's head came through and boy did that feel great! My husband was excited and was getting ready to catch the baby. With one more painful push, my body ejected the rest of our baby out in a slippery plop into the hands of my husband.

4:50 am and it was such sweet relief to feel empty. I looked back to see my husband holding our baby and smiling the biggest smile I had ever seen on him. He looked at me and said, "It's a boy!" He finally got his first boy and he couldn't be happier. He passed our slipper baby to me and I sat there on the floor with trembling muscles and my brand new precious baby.

I sent my husband next door to get our neighbor, who is an experienced free birther. She came over and they helped me get up and sit back on the toilet so we could clean up. Right as I sat down, the placenta just plopped right out with ease. We tied off the cord after it turned completely white and then cuddled up in bed to rest and rehydrate.

My husband and I are so thankful that we had decided to downsize and move into an RV. It gave us the opportunity to live closer to families who believe the same as we do, including beliefs in free birth, and I believe living small has brought our small family even closer together (not just physically closer haha). Birthing at home with just the two of us has also helped our faith and trust in Yahweh. He built our bodies to naturally know how to grow, birth, and nurture our precious babies.

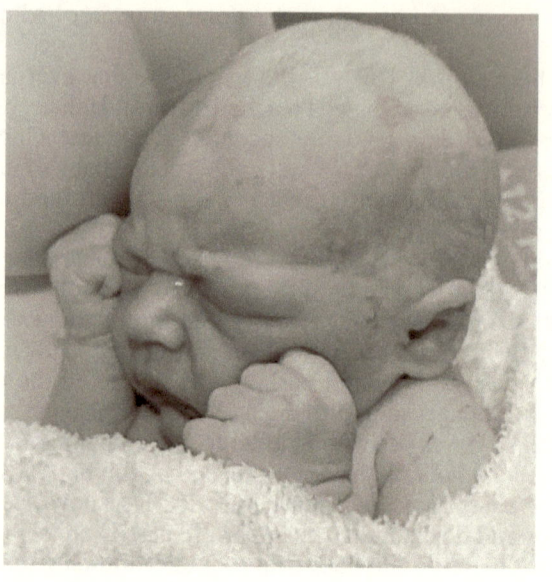

Born Free and Breech

submitted by Carissa Pople

HERE IS MY UNASSISTED complete breech baby story. It still seems so crazy! I hope it encourages and blesses you.

Let me start by saying that I didn't plan to have a breech baby, from home or otherwise. I tried to figure out her position for months and failed. Thankfully, because I would have been terrified!

This was my fourth pregnancy. My boys were all birth center births. But around 20 weeks with her, during my prayer time, I felt that I needed to not only have the homebirth we planned but go unassisted and fully trust the Lord with my body and my baby. I didn't think twice. I started reading about supernatural, pain free births, and that's exactly what I started praying for, along with no complications and a quick labor.

With my previous pregnancies, everything was the same. 37 weeks, start losing mucus plug. Around 38-39 weeks, cue prodromal labor, then have baby.

This little one gave me no signs of anything happening. No plug, no prodromal labor NOTHING! On Sunday I went to Walmart with my mom to walk around and see if we could get things moving, came home and felt some pelvic pressure. Woo-hoo! Finally something!

I had one or two contractions during the night. Monday morning, I woke up and felt completely exhausted, emotional and nauseous! I told my husband, "Please stay home, I think today is it and if not I just need some emotional support and SLEEP!"

Still no contractions, just alot of pressure and hormone drop. Monday night I woke up a few times with slightly stronger contractions, not painful just strong, still nothing major, but I could tell when I got up

Tuesday morning that oxytocin was in full swing, and I felt so peaceful and happy.

I kept noticing harder contractions all day and they seemed to be pretty consistent, but as a mom who dealt with her share of prodromal labor with the others, I didn't even think to time anything. I didn't want to end up disappointed. Around 4 p.m., after feeling a lot of pressure, I could tell she wasn't lining up fully, so I got on my knees, grabbed my yoga ball, and lay my arms across to sway my belly and stretch it a bit.

No sooner did I do that I heard a click sound and movement. I felt a trickle, followed by a gush of water. I called my mom and husband who were both an hour from me, and they started over. I noticed some light meconium but had just read an article and remembered what to look for, plus I had dealt with that with my oldest.

I tried setting up my birth space as best I could without alarming my boys, who were the only ones at home (ages 6, 4 and 3. By the way, they were amazing).

My mom and husband got here within minutes of each other, and around 5:30 she must have heard daddy's voice and knew we were good to go because things picked up. Still not in pain, but could feel the pressure of each contraction as they gained momentum and got closer.

Around 7:30 I knew it was time to start pushing even though FER for this labor was very different to me. I remember knowing it was time to start pushing but urges weren't there. She felt stuck, and I couldn't figure out why. I tried so many positions, and at this point, even though I couldn't feel pain of contractions, there was extreme pressure on my hips and pelvis and I couldn't seem to open them enough.

After like what seemed forever, I sat on my squatty potty (which I was using as a birth stool) and laid my head back for a minute to rest. I interally said, "God, I can't do this. She's not budging, and I have nothing to fix it."

Within seconds I felt this strength come over me and heard a respond inside, "You rest, I got this part!" And I sat up and roared my baby out! The need to push through and get her out was so strong it took over completely, and even though that was the hardest part, I knew I couldn't quit and I was almost there!

My mom and husband cheered me on at the end as they watched her BUTT and FEET pop out first. They didn't let on that anything was different, and I'm so thankful for their support.

I still can't believe she's here, and how she got here, but now I'm fully convinced I can do anything.

Born 2/23
7.14lbs
18 inches

Elizabeth Ariel Pople

Yacuruna Storm's Free birth Story

By Cindy Marie Andersen

YACURUNA STORM CAHUAYA ANDERSEN
"The Keeper of Water"

Born on Wednesday, December 13, 2017
Labor start 2:45 am
Birth at 5:23 am
2hrs and 22min of labor exactly from start to finish!
11lbs, 22inches

After weeks of prodromal labor, I was 7 days past due and had given up all hope that it would ever happen. I caved a bit and went to get evening primrose oil four days before his birth. I was breaking apart four capsules and putting them inside, up near my cervix, figuring it couldn't hurt to help things soften up down there. Still not sure if it even did anything, but I'm a doer, a fixer, and it helped my brain to chill out a bit.

On day three a creamy, white, good-sized glob of boogery stuff came out, but nothing else happened. I was so sad! But something was better than nothing. Then again, the day after that, more globby white stuff came out with minimal cramping, but when I got into the tub they stopped. I woke up the next day still pregnant! I was way past my due date then.

At that point, I was getting really annoyed. I was almost a week past my due date and baby was more than well-done. I just couldn't believe it anymore. I also did an unassisted pregnancy, I was 100% certain on my due date, having had on-point periods and keeping track of them very closely.

This was my 4th unassisted pregnancy. And I didn't care about all of that "there is no exact due date stuff" anymore. I was miserable! Having been in prodromal labor for at least a month was killing me. I was a single mom taking care of five other kids, running a business at the same time from home.

I worked really hard through pregnancy to build it up, and I had established it well enough by then that I could mostly chill out and roll with this. But what I still had on my plate with taking my kids to school and back, to dad's and back, dealing with their behavioral issues along with their dad's, groceries, homemade meals, cleaning, renters behavioral issues, etc. I was barely making it! In addition, being 41 years old, couldn't this baby just be born early? Nope! Haha!

That day mild contractions were on and off *eye roll*, but I was determined that night had to be the night.

I went to bed, boys asleep all around me, my daughter and her friend asleep just outside my door in case I went into labor. At 2:45am I started with contractions. I laid there and observed for about 15 min to make sure they were legit this time, and they were very strong and consistent seamed legit! It was time to go empty my tubes and check for any signs of mucous bloody show etc. Sure enough, there was bloody show mucus! As I was wiping, my water exploded right into the toilet! WOW! I was shocked! I had never started labor that way! My water would always break when it was push time with the others.

Leaking amniotic fluid with a towel between my legs, I snuck back to my nest to birth the baby.

Back in my nest, I pulled out the doggy bed where I planned on birthing my baby. It was already lined with chux pads. I stood to labor, breathing through every contraction. I was setting things up that I might need in between, but there wasn't much time available in between! Things were super intense from the start!

I got out my massage vibrator thing which I used to massage the sore areas when I'd contract in front of my belly, my sides, and my butt. It was the best idea ever! It felt so good! Where was this at all my other births? I was so tired I just wanted to sleep. After all that waiting it was finally happening and all I could do was wish it would hurry or stop so I could sleep, lol.

Not too long into it, Leonidas (5) woke up and he was so excited that it was happening! He was chatting to me, telling me to "push mommy, push!" Lol. Then my other two boys, Willow (3) and Mason (6) woke up as I was getting more and more vocal. Really loud! I couldn't help it! The other two joined in on the coaching, haha. They commented "Ewww!" on every drop that came out of me. "Ewww, mom is pooping. Ewww, mucus. Ewww, blood", etc. It all fell on chux pads, which I would remove as they became soiled. They would all tell me to push and it wasn't push time.

About 40 minutes into it, I tried to call baby's daddy a few times in Peru. He didn't answer. I tried, but it was too hard to keep calling, so I decided I'd record it for him instead.

I kept laboring with the boys so excited, talking to me and to each other. I didn't want them to wake anyone else up, so in between contractions I'd tell them to shhh the best I could, and that's all about I could get out until another one would come. Literally back to back! I started to feel freezing, a thing that can happen when one is in transition, so I asked Leonidas to put my socks on. He struggled and struggled, but it was too hard for him. I had only one sock on halfway, and I couldn't do anything about it, lol.

I could barely catch a breath in between contractions. When I tried to laugh, a hard contraction would come. I was laughing on the inside. I'd heard my son Bobo (9) wake up. He was in his bed playing on his phone at that point, so I called him over to please help me put my socks on, and he reluctantly did. My sweetest child. In our house, birth is treated like breath, always has, it's normal life. All my kids have been around birth and birthing. We bathe together, etc. To them, it's all normal. "Oh, mom's giving birth again."

I got my robe on and kept laboring. I felt up my vagina with my finger, and I could feel my baby's head right there, about an inch inside! He was so close! I was freezing, and contraction pain was brutal. It was taking an enormous amount of force to get this "little" one out!

All of a sudden I heard my renter's dog making noise. He was going to wake her up! Of all the people, I did not want her to wake up. So, of course, she did. A concern I had was the renters noticing I was in labor and calling the ambulance due to their ignorance and fear about birth. But as hard as I tried to get a place to rent to birth away from home, I could not get one. The funds were just not available.

So there I was, laboring with five unpredictable renters in my house. I guess everything happens for a reason. Whatever that reason was, I'm not sure yet. I heard this renter get up, my mother also woke up, the girls were up, everyone was now up because I was so darn loud! When my mother peeked in to see how I was doing, I told her "I'm fine, but will you take the boys?" They were so cute, and I hated to kick them out, but they were also very distracting and hard in that intense part of labor.

I also sent my daughter Trinity and son Bobo to call my renter. She had said if I needed any help to call her, and well, she was up.

I was in so much discomfort, I just needed a little bit of relief. I asked if she had some greens - she did not (this was a helpful thing in my other solo births). Since she was already in my room, I asked her if she could massage my upper butt with my magic wand massager. I don't think that's what she had in mind when offering to help, but it's what I needed! This woman is totally medical, fear-based beliefs about birth, etc., so it was just too funny. It felt so nice, but I was so freezing. My teeth were chattering, and I was shaking so badly I could not get a grip on it.

I asked the renter if she would fill the tub with hot water and she did. I wanted my feet to warm up. I walked past the kids and a friend to get into the bathroom, I closed the door behind me and my feet touched the water. It was sooo nice! I got completely in the water. Instantly, the freezing went away and the pain was immediately and instantly gone!

I had a few moments of a break when my baby's head started pummeling out of me. I reached down and I hesitated pushing. I had no other choice! Right away the next contraction came. I controlled my push and screamed as his emergence to the outer earth ripped me apart to the fullest I could be. I used my hands to wrap my vagina away from his emerging head. I was left quite wide open, beaten, bruised, and feeling battered, but not torn to shreds. If I tore I don't know. It felt like at least some good ski marks, like a rug burn down there. I didn't look, I used my ointment and frozen herb pads. It took a good bit to heal and pooping was not a fun party, but after some time it all healed back to perfect.

I was in the water with his head out of me, totally under the water, a now unplanned water birth! I was waiting for the next contraction to get the rest of him out when my renter came back in the bathroom! I forgot to lock the bathroom door! She'd brought towels. She started freaking out about his head being under the water and was trying to tell me what to do. Like in the movies, she told me "Quick, put your feet up here and push!" So now I have to be a teacher with baby's head between my legs. I said "No, I'm not putting my legs up there, and I'm not pushing. No, I'm not doing any of that! This is not a movie! The baby is fine, just relax, I have to wait for the next contraction."

It was so interesting how a grown woman who had birthed something like six babies herself didn't have the slightest clue how to really give birth. That's what happens when you're not allowed to *really* birth your own baby. Not her fault.

A few moments later the next contraction came and all 17.5 inches of his YUGE shoulders came out! One shoulder at a time, then the rest of the Giant! He came sliding out. Sweet relief! I let the renter grab him from between my legs and hand him to me.

He was floppy and not responding and it was a bit hard for me to want to focus after all I'd been through, and he was limp. I was exhausted. My renter was freaking out that he was limp and not immediately breathing. No relaxing for me now, I have to calm and teach her more about how he's totally fine and sometimes it takes a few minutes for them to react, breathe, etc. I felt for the cord and it was still pumping blood and oxygen to him very strong.

It took a few minutes, but he started reacting and pinking up a little bit at a time. It took him a total of 3 minutes to start to breathe, calculated from the recording. Again, I did not worry at all to give him mouth breaths because his cord was still pumping very strong. I knew he was getting the same life-giving oxygen he was getting for the past 9-months through his pulsing cord.

He ended up being a huge 11+ lbs and he'd just gotten pushed through a very tiny hole, I understood he was in a little shock!

The kids came in to see their baby brother and were grossed out about the red blood in the water. I told them it was just red color bath colors, a thing we regularly used so they would relax about it, but they didn't believe me, lol.

After a while, I decided I wanted to get the placenta out. I was getting strong after-birth contractions, I was so uncomfortable. I got up in a squat to see if it would just come out in the tub, but nothing. I could feel the placenta was up at the top. I decided to go to my bed to see if I could massage it a bit to dislodge it by getting up, engaging my ab muscles, and walking.

Getting out of the tub while holding a huge baby was a bit painful, so being that my renter was there, I asked her to lend me a hand to get out. She'd already seen all my naked lady bits, so... fine for me, not so much for her!

When I got to the bedroom, I felt to see if the cord was still pulsing in hopes it was not so I could cut it. I wanted to be free of the baby to work on the placenta. It was giving me so much pain with more huge contractions. I really wanted it out and to know I was done-done! Luckily it had stopped pulsing, so I let my renter, who had followed me into the room, cut the cord. She was so excited about having seen his birth, having "caught" him, "delivered" him as she tells it, lol. A *wee* bit of an exaggeration.

I was just happy to have him out, I let her have the honors! It was really cute and cool to see her joy in what was doing and for sure a super cool thing to be a part of. She took the baby to show him off to his brothers, sister and friend Katlynn. The cord was soo long, it reached all the way to my feet!

I got on the bed to massage the spot where my placenta was and immediately felt that it was gone from that spot. I stood up and felt inside there and could feel it right at the vagina entrance. Success! I could get it out now! Knowing it was totally detached from the uterus, I pulled gently on the cord and pushed with a very painful contraction and the giant placenta came out with sweet relief! Almost the size of a small baby! It was born into a dog bed, the place I had planned on birthing Yacu.

Seven days past due, 11 lbs of baby boy was out plus the placenta. The kids went to school, placenta was frozen for consuming later, and Mommy, Willow, and Yacu slept and relaxed all day. All was well, and it was done!

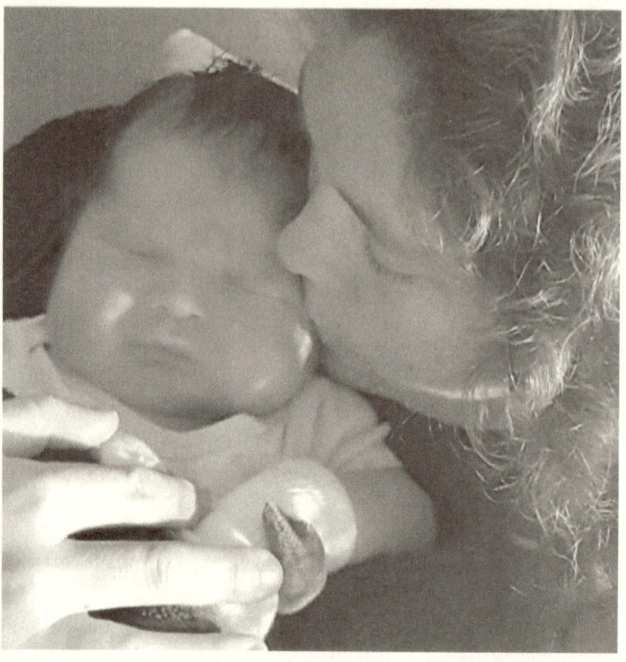

For links to supplies used during her birth and postpartum herbal pads recipe, visit her website:
https://www.wildmotherswisdom.com/

Lavender's Birth Journey

By Nicole Brown

THE BEGINNING WAS JUST like any other labor, I'd assume, where the mama wakes up hoping it'll be the day she and baby meet, but also pretty sure the baby has decided to stay in forever.

At 5am I had woken to a contraction that pulled me out of bed and had me hunched over trying to breathe. It ended, and I looked up to see the crescent moon shining so brightly through the fog outside the window... that's the moment I should've known.

Lavender's nickname would be 'Luna', which means moon, and this whole pregnancy I'd been attracted to the moon in a whole different way. I recognized it's beauty and strength and influence on all the things around it.

Things were calm, and Bellamy and I went downstairs to make coffee and oatmeal for everyone. Surges were coming now and again, but I just wanted to take care of everything and prepare the spaces (nesting in making sure everyone and everything was taken care of, I guess!).

By the time everyone was awake a couple hours later, things had slowed down and we were getting our minds prepared for the Christmas party we would be leaving for soon. But around 11am the surges came back strong to remind me I probably should stick around the house.

At some point after lunch and cleaning the house through the early stages of labor, I needed more space and privacy and moved upstairs to the room to navigate through the "waves". Tommy had taken over full control of the house and kids' needs and would come check on me, but it still didn't feel real. I wasn't in terrible pain and the contractions were pretty far apart now, but doubling in strength. The kids would come in the room and ask how we were doing, bring snacks and water and just be present with me, which was so amazing to experience.

At this point, I got a hold of my midwife to send her updates from the morning to ask if it was too soon to get into the pool. It didn't feel "real" yet, but it definitely felt strong enough when they did come. I checked charts that she had made and she let me know it was a good time to get in the water. Based on the charts, I was probably 7-8 cm dilated. Tommy came upstairs and filled the pool for me while I grabbed everything I would need, lit the candles and turned on the lights. It had just started getting dark outside and was exactly the time I wanted to be laboring.

Tommy set up the kids and spent more of his time upstairs with me rubbing my back and just being nearby. When he would need to check in on the littles, Mikey would come take his place and hold my hand and just be there through the surges. Emelia would check on me and bring anything I needed and ask questions about what was happening or what would happen. They were so curious and present, and able to speak when they felt scared or unsure and we could walk them through those moments together.

At some point, things had gotten much stronger in the water, and I asked Tommy not to leave. Labor was stronger, and I struggled with thinking I couldn't do it much longer, and as soon as I said that I knew we were almost there. Tommy read the affirmations to me and reminded me of all the beautiful things: that baby would be here soon, and that we were made for each other, and that baby knew exactly what to do.

I felt 'stuck' and asked Tommy to pray over us. It was the most beautiful prayer filled with the reassurance of God's goodness and direction over this entire pregnancy, reminding me that God has showed us so many times this would be our path, and He was right there present in the room with us.

After the prayer, I felt so much peace, a reminder to let go of fear and focus on this process. I knew birth would be extremely spiritual for me, and it definitely was. I had crossed over from this space of fear and pain into the place of peace and assurance. In between contractions, I would lay my head back and see white and flowy fog, my headspace was clear and calm, and I spoke to Tommy what would happen next.

I reached down and felt baby's head, crowning and almost there. I knew it wasn't time to push even though every previous doctor would've instructed me to do so because the baby was there!

I asked Tommy if he wanted to climb into the pool and help bring baby out of the water, and told him we would lift baby out slowly like planned and that it would be soon. In the back of my mind, I heard

Bellamy coughing downstairs and Tommy was gone, but the calm was still there. I knew he must've gone to check on her but there was no stopping baby anyway.

It was a mixture of FER (*fetal ejection reflex*) and knowing I would also need to push, and baby's head was born just as Tommy came back into the room and climbed in the pool. Her shoulders and body came next as we reached down to carry her out of the water slowly.

We brought her to my chest and she was absolutely perfect. No crying, just staring up at us and peaceful as can be. We rubbed her back and just absorbed the beauty and peace in the moment we had just birthed and carried our baby into this world. Our literal dreams had come true and it was happening in that moment.

Tommy wrapped baby and I to keep us warm and grabbed the kids. Shiloh had gone to sleep a little earlier, so Emme woke her up and everyone gathered around moments after Lavender had joined us in our home. All of us were so filled with love and so thankful she was here!

Tommy rocked Bellamy to sleep and then we all gathered around Lavender for the kids to burn the cord together. We talked about the placenta and the kids asked questions and wanted to see up close. We grabbed two beeswax candles and Emelia and Shiloh got to hold the candles to burn the cord. After a while, we decided to cut the rest of the way, so Mikey got to cut the cord and complete the process.

Everyone got to hold and cuddle Lavender before they went off to sleep for the night and it was literally the most amazing day we have ever had. A memory that will forever include each of our children in such a beautiful way. We experienced strength, compassion, and curiosity in our children that I'm so thankful for, they experienced the same in Tommy and I in a journey that was entirely new for us.

Lavender means healing and calming, and her middle name means calm as well. We had a few names we loved but this journey began long before we ever knew we would be welcoming another baby into this world. From the mental and physical preparation to the spiritual preparation.

It was all a journey filled with peace and faith as we continued to trust that each sign and answered prayer were exactly what we needed.

Lavender is our 'sea turtle', chosen because of their intuition, peace, strength, endurance, and the story of their journey. I've known her for days, yet my heart has been ready for her for years.

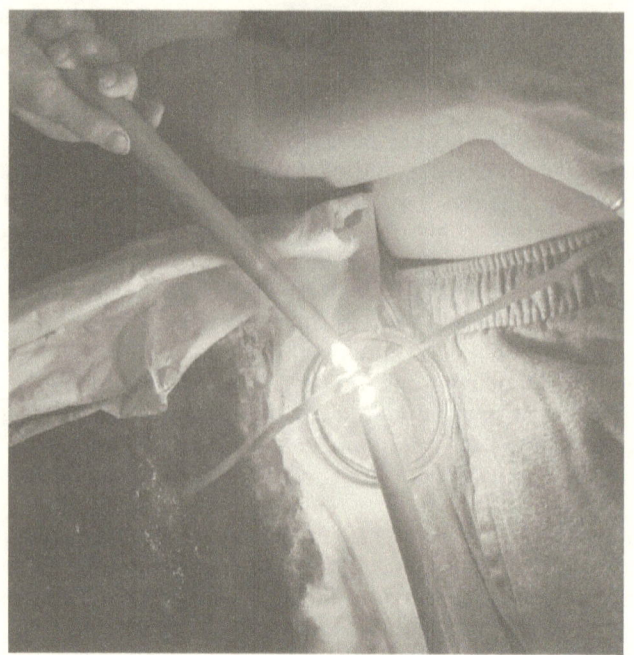

Burning the cord

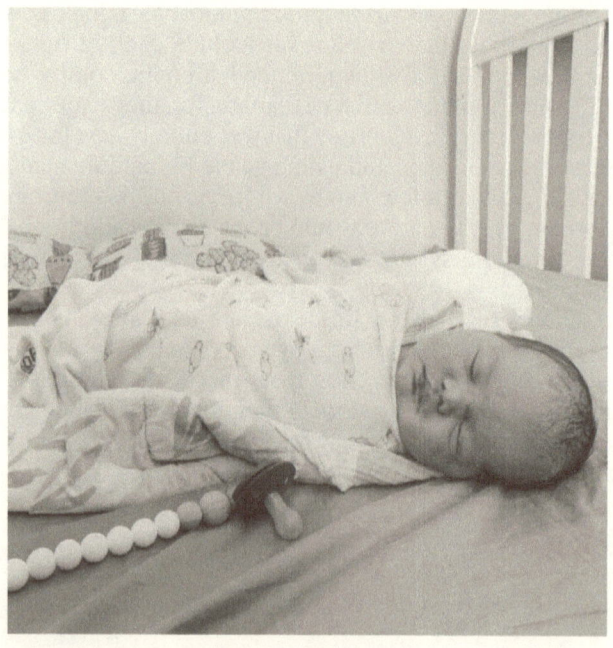

The Freebirth of Yusuke Pierce

By Porshia Pierce

FRIDAY, NOVEMBER 13TH

I was woken up throughout the night/early morning by what seemed to be random "intense" Braxton Hicks interspersed with continuous "normal" Braxton Hicks. These continued throughout Friday. I increased my magnesium and RRL (*Red Raspberry Leaf*) intake which seemed to help throughout the day. I knew this wasn't "true" labor, but baby had dropped significantly and I understood this was prepping him and my body for what was to come.

That night the random intense waves began again, still very irregular. This continued all through to the early morning with the pressure coming about 20-30 minutes apart. I woke up, took the kids to their Mamaw's, went to get breakfast at my husband's work, and called my nana to come help me do meal prep. Still, I knew this wasn't it yet, but that I needed to get my last minute things done.

We spent the entire day cooking and cleaning and stocking the fridge and freezer. Surges continued, but some 20/30 minutes apart, sometimes only one an hour. Many of these were intense enough for me to need to stop walking or talking and focus on them.

Saturday night/Morning of Sunday the 15th

By this point, I was exhausted. Surges came about every 15-20 minutes throughout the night, at this point I felt things might progress, but that things still weren't right. I spent most of the day resting and take naps while Matt handled the kids and the house. During the day, the surges became extremely intense but spaced out to be only every 30-45 minutes or so.

We decided to go up to the local taproom for the kids to play in the play area they have and just to get me out of the house. While there, I expressed to a couple of people that I "might be in very early labor, but it'll probably be another day or even a few." Surges picked up a bit while we were there, two of which became intense enough for me to ask Matthew to hold my hand through them while I breathed. I told him I thought it was time to go home and rest.

At home, I spent a little time on the yoga ball and stretching on the floor. I could tell baby still wasn't in the optimal position and decided maybe that was a factor in the prodromal labor I had been experiencing.

Sunday night/morning of Monday the 16th

I was woken every 15-30 minutes by intense surges I had to breathe and moan through. At about 4 am, Matthew asked if he should go to work and I replied, "don't leave me." So, he immediately texted to let them know. Both of the kids woke up around 6 am, and we got them set up in their room with cartoons. Surges were steadily coming 15-20 minutes apart and were very intense. I called my nana and asked her to bring us breakfast and play with the kids so that Matthew could be with me.

At this point, I've already had Matthew fill up the pool, but it was a bit too warm, so I got in the shower to let the water run on my lower back. Nana got there around 9 am, I could only take about three bites of food despite me starving it seemed, but the pressure was so intense I was too nauseous to eat more.

Eventually, we added cold water to get the pool cool enough for me to get in at first, but I quickly realized it still wasn't cool enough since I became so hot flashy during surges. I got out and tried to lay in bed and rest and did part of the Miles Circuit to help baby's positioning, because he still wasn't where he needed to be, and I could tell there was immense pressure being put on my left hip due to it. Miles Circuit definitely helped move him a bit and I was able to sleep in 10-15 minute spurts between the waves.

I finally got back up and moved back into the pool and stayed there for a while. Again I dozed off in between surges and the water offered so much relief. After a while in the pool, I started coming to terms with the fact that I knew I needed to get out and utilize some gravity to let things progress a little faster, but mentally I was not ready to push.

I had a moment and cried to myself and to Matthew and my nana. I texted a dear friend who was my doula for our first child and expressed my fears to her, which even at the time sounded silly coming out of my own mouth. I wasn't afraid of something going wrong or anything like that, I simply knew the immense pressure to come and how quickly things would probably progress, and my mind just wasn't ready yet. These spaced-out surges were intense, but familiar and offered a break in between, and I wasn't ready to lose that yet, but I also knew that I could only stall for so long.

Everyone encouraged me to have a good cry, come to terms with the emotions, and then decide how to proceed. I did exactly that. Right before I got out the kids, Mamaw called my nana and asked if they wanted to come play for a bit. We wanted them there for Yusuke's arrival, but they were going a little stir crazy so we decided to let my nana take them over there to play.

I got out of the tub and went back and forth from the bathroom and bed, somewhat convinced I might have him on the toilet right then and there until I finally laid in bed and tried to nap again. Nana had to run some errands after dropping off the kids and Matthew laid in bed with me and I encouraged him to fall asleep and I would wake him if things got more intense since he had been up with me all night.

While Matthew slept, it was just me. This was the "hard" part. I had mostly worked through the anxiety of things going from 0-100 in an instant and surges were still 10 minutes apart, but now it was time for me, in that silence, to meditate and talk to my baby and body. I'd never done this before. Never during the journey of bringing a child earthside did I truly have that moment when I decided ok, it's time.

Never had I really had the chance to listen to every little message my body was sending me and surrender to it. That was because I'd been in a place of assistance. Nurses, midwives, doulas, family, all had been present in previous births. And while for the most part they've respected my wishes and just observed, I still knew I was being watched. I didn't have that now and it was indescribable. I could freely labor with NO ONE watching. Not even my supportive, sweet husband who was now loudly snoring beside me.

I turned on a hypnobirthing music/meditation soundtrack and sat in a familiar position in my own bed. The same position I birthed Kenshin and Kojima in; an inclined, kind of side-lying position. I kept my eyes closed and quite literally felt the beats of the music and the rhythm of my own body sync. I let Yusuke know if he was ready, then I was too and that I would not hold him back any longer.

Immediately my surges changed. Now with each one, I felt my body quite literally ejecting my sweet boy downward further into my pelvis. I was able to fully surrender to quite a few surges until the pressure became so much I could feel myself beginning to tense up during them again and I would still experience the surge, but I would not feel him move downward. I knew this meant I had to get back into the water in order to let myself relax enough to allow my body to release my baby.

It was about this time that my nana arrived back. It'd been about an hour and a half since she had gone, I think. Who knows. Time has no concept or place in a birthing mother's mind. I asked her to please add hot water to the pool to get it back to temp, and I sat on the toilet trying to relax while I waited. Matthew asked if he had time to take a shower, and I assured him it was a good time but to hurry.

I got into the pool and the SECOND my belly hit the water, the downward surges began again. I got into that inclined side-lying position again and held my left leg up a bit to help open my pelvis more. Surges immediately went to 4 minutes apart, prior to that they'd been 10-15 minutes for our entire journey thus far. After about three or four of those surges, I told my nana who was sitting silently in the corner to please get Matthew and tell him he needed to hurry.

Two or three more surges passed, now they were about two minutes apart. (I only know this because my nana began timing them without telling me.) Matthew finally joined me, and I grabbed his hand. I remember him at one point saying, "You're going to hurt your own hand if you keep squeezing that hard!" I didn't realize how forcefully I was grabbing him.

Nana asked what I needed, I said, "everyone to be quiet." At this point she knew we were close, so she left the room and sat out in the living room.

A few more surges passed, (nana said these were now coming every minute according to her timing) and Matthew told me, "I'm going to go grab my drink."

I got a little mama bear at this point and told him, "No you are not! This baby is literally coming out of me! Ask nana to get it for you!" She immediately appeared around the corner with it and returned to her spot in the other room.

Matthew expressed that if the baby was about to come out, maybe I should leave the water because he wasn't comfortable and "had no experience" with that. I remember thinking to myself, "why do you need experience? I'm doing this, not you." And I actually smiled to myself because his concern was valid but seemed silly as I'm feeling a head descending into my vagina.

Luckily for his nerves, I didn't plan to birth in the pool anyway. I was definitely also more comfortable with "land" birthing, as it's familiar and felt more controllable to me. I told him, give me one or two more surges and then help me out. He grabbed two towels and helped me out of the pool.

I stood for a moment while he dried my legs and he draped the other towel around my shoulders. I immediately sat on the ground and he said, "Oh, you're staying in here?" I told him to sit with me. I resumed my familiar side-lying position, reclined back onto the side of the pool/half on Matthew's shoulder. The man wasn't ready, to say the least.

With our other children, at this point he would be literally hugging me, kissing my face, petting my hair, and telling me what an amazing job I'm doing...he wasn't. He was just sitting there while I clung to him and panted during surges. For a moment, in my head, I started to get upset and ask myself why he felt so distant... then I realized he had zero clue my body was pushing for me.

There wasn't a team of birth support huddled around telling me to hold my breath and push during surges. There was zero indication that he was familiar with to tell him that this was it, his baby was descending downward and he should be cheering me on.

Instead of pushing during these waves, I had been panting through them and allowing my body to eject my baby instead. This was totally unfamiliar to Matthew and he likely just thought I was doing funny breathing because of the pressure, haha. The moment I realized this, I felt Yusuke's head hit a point inside of my body that literally forced me to bear down with the surge. This happened twice despite me doing my best to pant through the urge and not push. I took this as a sign that I needed to change positions and follow instinct.

Matthew immediately asked, "Are you pushing?!" and I replied with a quick, "Hush!"

I moved from my side-lying position and now was on my knees, somewhat leaned forward onto one hand, while I kept my other hand on my vulva. The next wave came, I literally couldn't pant and my body forced me to give a push, my waters popped immediately. It wasn't a huge gush like with my other children and I knew this was because his head was already far enough down to practically be plugging the rest.

Matthew jolted up and said, "is that what I think it is?!" Again, I replied with a loud, "SSSHHHHHH!"

Matthew asked if he should get nana in the room so someone could "see what's going on behind you" again, I exclaimed, "NO! Now SSSHHHHH!" And thought to myself, "What does someone watching from behind do?!"

I again reminded myself this was all new to him, and only I knew what was going on within my body. There was no midwife there to vocally exclaim it for him on this journey. The next surge came, and I don't think my body has ever pushed like that in my life. 90% of it was FER (*fetal ejection reflex*), literally my body pushing for me, the other 10% I couldn't help but bear down.

There was no crowning. There was no, "his head his born" then shoulder rotation, then shoulders born, then body. With that ONE push I felt his entire head and body literally cannon ball out of me. My hand had still been flat against my vulva the entire time, so that's how

I knew for sure all of him shot out at once. One second I was literally closed and the next there was an entire baby slipping into my hands.

He slid perfectly into my hands, 10/10 best football catch I've ever performed, and within a second I had him on my chest. Matthew literally jumped backwards and up to his feet like someone threw a grenade at him. Yusuke let out a bellowing cry immediately.

I heard Matthew say, "Oh my god Porshia, PORSHIA!" And I snapped back with "What?!" And did a quick scan thinking something was wrong that I wasn't seeing. He said "NOTHING! YOU JUST DID THAT OH MY GOD YOU JUST DID THAT! WAIT WHAT TIME IS IT?! 4:54!"

I look up to see nana in the doorway replying to Matt, "She did do that! You just did that!" With a big smile on her face. Yusuke had already fallen back asleep on me at this point since the room was dim and there were no "professionals" aggressively wiping his vernix off and attempting to suction his nose and mouth. He sounded a little gurgly still, which I expected considering he came out so quick, meaning he didn't have the extra time for my vaginal canal to squeeze the fluid out quite fully.

Matt asked if I needed a suction bulb, I said no and used my own mouth to gently clear his nose and throat. He immediately let out another cry and fell back asleep. Perfect muscle tone, perfect color, perfect breathing, perfect reflex, everything about our sweet boy was perfect from the start.

We asked nana to go get the kids, and she ran out the door. I began trying to get him to latch and it only took him a few minutes, but he was very sleepy and wasn't suckling quite as much as I wanted him to. I assessed my bleeding, had Matt get me 2 ounces of orange juice and I added some Angelica Tincture to it since Yusuke still wasn't nursing strongly.

I had Matthew help me switch the chux pad under me, so that I could keep track of the blood until I was able to birth the placenta and by the time I lifted myself up and he slid the new pad under me, I felt my placenta detach so I gave a little push and out it came.

Matt had to leave the room now because his stomach couldn't quite handle it while I assessed my placenta to ensure it and the bag were whole and there were no tears, missing pieces or abnormalities. All were perfect. I got it into its designated bowl and Matt returned back in the room to hold Yusuke while I cleaned myself off and put on a 'mommy diaper.'

Yusuke and I moved to the recliner in the living room while Matthew cleaned everything up and the kids arrived back with nana. Nana and Matthew finished emptying the pool, cleaning up all blankets, towels and pads fairly quickly and within 15-20 minutes it looked like nothing ever happened besides a kiddie pool and some blankets drying on our front porch.

Nana got me a huge bowl of beef stew and some sausage balls, and I chowed down while Yusuke nursed. A little later Matthew helped Kenshin cut Yusuke's cord, we weighed him and got a diaper on him, and I returned to the recliner with him.

Life proceeded as normal for a family of 5. No overnight in the hospital. No one poking and prying. No one aggressively massaging my stomach or trying to inject me with artificial oxytocin. No discharge tests or forms or required parenting classes. No masks or walking through halls shared with sick people.

Just some good food, some baby snuggles, a GOOD night's sleep in my own bed, and the next morning waking up and loving on a new baby and our other two babes in our own home.

This is uncomplicated, unhindered, free childbirth as nature and physiology intended.

This is FREE BIRTH without fear.

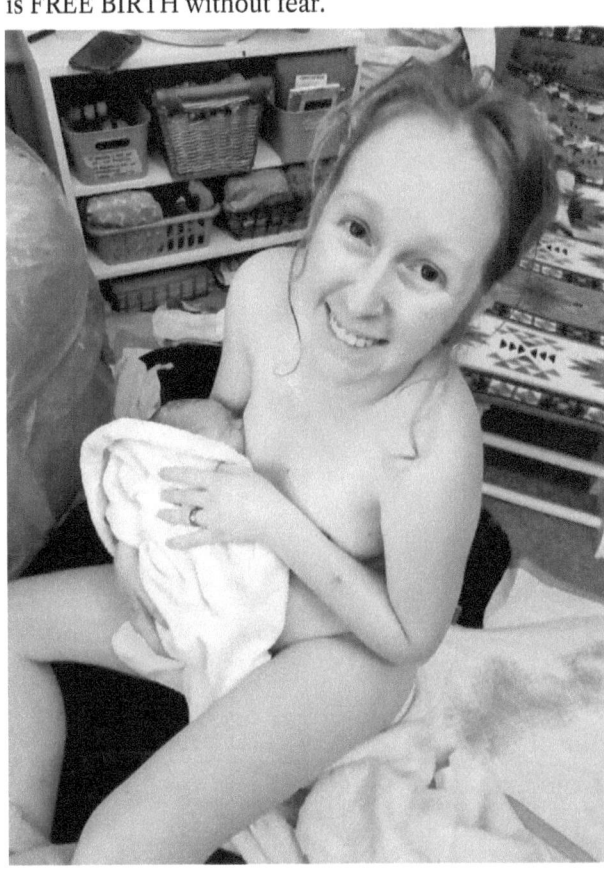

A Life-Changing Christmas Freebirth

By Lindsey Stark

I DISCOVERED UNASSISTED BIRTH a few months after the birth of my daughter in 2016. I had just given birth via VBAC in a hospital setting after having my dreams of a home birth ripped away from me due to a misdiagnosed placenta condition. While I was beaming from my success at my vaginal birth after cesarean, I was still coming to terms with the many interventions that took place during and after my birth.

I took to Facebook like so many of us do and joined several home birth groups where I came across a group dedicated to unassisted birthing. My initial thoughts were, "I can't believe these women are birthing at home WITHOUT a midwife!" I was shocked but intrigued, so I stuck around and read through the group.

These women were so brave and powerful, but I told myself I could never do something like that though I respected others' choice to choose it. I learned a lot through my time reading articles, studies, personal experiences, and stories from these women. It brought me further into my journey of researching home birth, interventions, risks, and benefits of all of these things, and the more I learned the more I thought, "Maybe these ladies are on to something."

Fast forward a few years, we decided to have another baby. After 2 losses and losing hope I found myself pregnant with a baby who was a fighter and finally stuck. I began prenatal care through a midwifery group that practiced in a birth center within a hospital almost 3 hours away. I had initially decided I would continue care with these midwives because my insurance covered everything.

The further I got into my pregnancy the more I knew I would regret not having a home birth. I discontinued care with the midwives at the birth center and decided to set up a consultation with a local homebirth midwife. From that point, my desires took a hard left turn, and I found myself contemplating doing something I never thought I would do.

The consultation with the midwife went great! She was wonderful, we had the same beliefs regarding birth, she was very hands-off like I wanted, and I trusted her. I decided to hire her and went on to have one prenatal meeting with her. I can't say enough good things about this midwife but, something in the back of my mind kept pulling me back to freebirth. Between my consultation and prenatal with the midwife, I felt myself being led to freebirth.

I could NOT stop thinking about it. I talked to my close friends, I talked to my husband and I sat with my feelings for weeks trying to sort through them along with my fears. It took me a while to really pinpoint why I was feeling led to this decision. I didn't take this choice lightly. I knew that it wasn't something to go into for the wrong reasons. I knew I had built up trauma and negative feelings from my past birth experiences and I needed to get myself in a place where I could listen to my intuition without feeling cloudy. Around 17 weeks I finally decided that freebirth was the right choice for me.

So many people ask me why I made this choice. Many assume it was a money issue - it wasn't. Some may even think I didn't click with the midwife I saw. I loved her. I knew that with this birth of my last baby I needed to have the birth experience that I had been yearning for since I started my journey into motherhood.

I needed my choices to be mine. I needed to feel supported. I needed to reach deep down within myself and pull out that voice that had been inside of me for years and finally let it speak. I knew I had to accept responsibility for my past birth choices to be able to accept responsibility for this pregnancy and birth to go on to trust myself and the process.

I did not feel that I could do that with a medical provider present. I didn't want the option to have anyone else in a position of 'authority' over me to look to when choices had to be made. I wanted full and complete authority over my autonomy, and freebirth was the way for me to achieve that.

I won't lie and say my husband came on board without a hitch. It took a couple of weeks for him to actually have a serious conversation with me about it after I made my decision. He had his fears like any normal person would, and I believe some of them were still with him up until the moment I gave birth. I see so many women struggle with this topic.

Their partner isn't supportive for whatever reason they have and the woman feels trapped into going on and giving birth in a way she doesn't feel comfortable with. I love my husband and I respect him, but ultimately, I knew that this was my choice to make and I would go on with or without him at that point. Thankfully, I didn't have to go on without him, and he came to understand how important this was for me and trusted me to make the best decision for our family.

I informed the midwife that I had made up my mind to freebirth and discontinued prenatal care. It was important to me that I had another woman well-versed in birth present who was not in the role of a provider, but rather as a support person and someone to lean on who understood my wants and feelings. I hired an amazing birthkeeper to walk my journey with me.

I went on to have a wonderful, healthy pregnancy. I've never experienced a pregnancy so void of stress - it was amazing. No prenatal appointments to drive to, no need to decline unnecessary testing or exams. Everything I did, I did it because I felt like it was important. I listen to my baby's heartbeat. I measured my fundal height.

I listened to my body and followed my intuition. It was very freeing. I took the time to realize my specific fears and learned how to work through them. I learned how to nourish my body to avoid certain situations, I prepared myself on what to do if the situation arose, and I educated myself on variations of normal and how 'different' is not always wrong or scary.

I had to let go of all of the lies I had been fed about birth and how my body was not sufficient enough to handle it without mainstream interventions. Physiological birth is defined as **"Birth that is powered by the innate human capacity of the woman and the fetus."** As I learned more about this process and the works behind it, I could feel my worries shrink down smaller and smaller.

I was fully prepared to go to 42 weeks or longer into my pregnancy but this baby had other plans. At **39 weeks**, while making my older children breakfast, I felt my water gush. It was tinged pink, and I knew that birth was close. I texted my birthkeeper to let her know. She advised me to rest, which I'm so grateful for now as I look back.

My waters were broken for well over 50 hours. Gushing here and there, sporadic waves on and off with no pattern to interpret. It was a hard couple of days, wondering when something more would happen. Waiting to meet my baby. Trusting the process fully. At one point, everything stopped completely. No more gushing, no more waves. I slept on and off, ate delicious food, I even started to bake a cake that evening. Once my cake came out of the oven the waves were back and intense. I decided to lay down and see where they took me.

My waves were 10 minutes apart when they started, and I slowly noticed that I was having to breathe through them. I laid in our cold, dark room with my sound machine on as I concentrated on my breathing. The sensations were like nothing I had ever felt before. I remember being so in my head as if I was having an out of body experience.

I could feel my baby working himself down through each wave and when the wave would end, he rested. I felt such a strong, connected energy to my baby at that point - as if I knew his movements were his way of communicating to me that he would greet me soon. Before long, I noticed that I was moaning through the waves and reminding myself to keep my body loose as my husband ran his fingers through my hair and breathed with me.

I needed to go to the bathroom, and by the time I was done I told my husband to start filling the birth pool and I texted my birthkeeper to let her know I needed her.

I labored on my hands and knees in the bathroom until the pool had enough water for me to get into. Not long after I climbed in my birthkeeper arrived and my sensations felt very powerful. I remember thinking to myself "Why is this taking so long?" I told myself to focus on the waves.

I reminded myself of my affirmations, I told myself that each wave had its purpose and that I needed to trust the process. I can remember hearing my husband tell me to stay loose and offering me sips of water as my birthkeeper applied counter pressure to my back. I felt so supported and so safe.

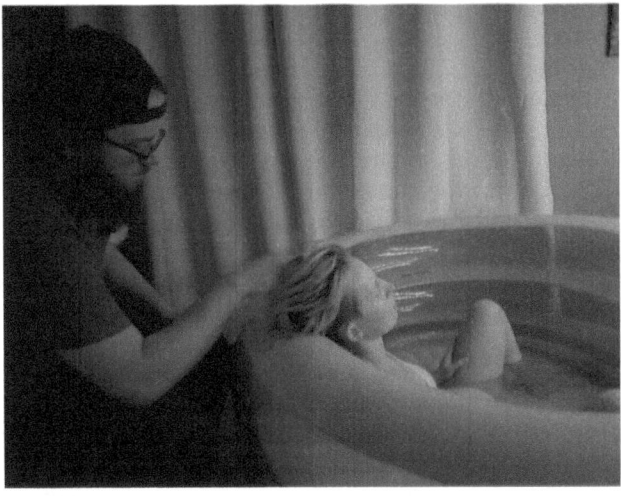

At one point I felt that I needed to get out of the pool and try to use the bathroom again. Once I did, I tried to squat on the toilet but it was unbearable to sit without counter pressure and I needed to be somewhere that my birthkeeper could reach me to apply it. I made my way into the living room and found myself on the couch.

I asked my husband for pillows and as soon as he rounded the corner to go get them I yelled for him to come back. I reached down and could feel my body opening up. I felt my baby drop down and my body began to push. This was the moment we had been working towards. My baby was ready to meet us!

I started to shake. I've never in my life felt anything like I did in that moment. I wanted to crawl out of my skin. I wanted to cry but I couldn't.

I remember thinking if I could cry it would make it better but, the tears never came. I needed a break, I asked for help. I told them that I couldn't do this anymore- please help me. Make this stop. So lovingly and calming my birth team told me that I WAS doing this. That I was safe. I was almost there.

I knew I didn't want to ruin my couch so I got down onto the floor onto my hands and knees but that didn't feel right. I tried to squat and lay back onto my husband but that didn't feel okay either. I flipped myself onto my belly with my left leg pulled up and right leg out and I roared my baby into the world.

I felt the ring of fire and about that time my husband told me he could see our babies head and then I felt it come out. Such sweet relief. My body gave me a small break at that point.

My husband began to tell me to push- he sounded panicky. My body didn't feel like it needed to push in that moment and before I could process what was being said I heard my birthkeeper reassuring him that it was okay for me to rest and that my body would continue to push by itself.

Another big wave came, and I could feel my baby rotate as his shoulders emerged, one more and he was in my husband's hands.

I flipped over onto my back and my perfect, sweet baby was placed onto my chest. He was so tiny! I began to rub his back and he started to cry. That first cry was something I'll never forget. I was so relieved. I laughed and said I was glad that was over when my birthkeeper informed me she had only been there an hour.

I couldn't believe it! It felt like an eternity. My husband helped me onto the couch where we marveled at this perfect creature that just came out of me. He latched onto my breast and nursed as he stared into my eyes. He was so alert and calm.

I had originally planned a lotus birth but, my after pains were intense and his cord was short. My placenta hadn't budged after an hour and in an attempt to get more comfortable we severed his cord so that I could move around more. I squatted in the tub, over the toilet, coughed, and pushed but my placenta wasn't ready to be birthed. I decided to rest and ended up taking a nap. 4 hours later I felt rested enough to try to encourage my placenta to be birthed.

I ended up squatting in the living room over a chux pad and gently tugged on the cord to get it out. I could feel that it was detached from my uterus and felt comfortable with my choice to tug it out. My birthkeeper helped my husband clean up, made sure we were comfortable and left us to snuggle our precious new baby alone.

I have never felt more powerful, more in control, more instinctual than I did throughout my last pregnancy and birth. My experience was truly life changing. It was that big for me. I learned things about myself that otherwise I may have been too afraid to fully understand had I not made the choices that I made during this time.

I would do it 1,000 times over again and will forever be grateful for this time in my life. All of the waiting, preparing, second guessing, trusting myself, trusting my baby, it all led up to this utterly perfect experience that I wouldn't trade for the world. I'm still in awe over our story, and I honestly don't believe that will ever wear off.

Warming Postpartum Recipes

Chicken or Vegetable Stock

THE PRAISES OF HOMEMADE bone and vegetable broth cannot be sung enough! This is a powerful food to ingest at any season. I highly recommend the inclusion of chicken, beef, and/or fish bones for the minerals and collagen.

Additionally, any time you chop vegetables, save the scraps! You can store them in a ziploc bag or container in the freezer and get it out any time you make stock for added nutrition and flavor. Herbs are a welcome, but optional addition, just avoid anything that might cause stomach discomfort in your baby or yourself. Stock is simple to make, especially if you have a crockpot or instant pot!

Simply take the chicken bones (can also use roasted beef bones, fish bones, vegetable scraps, etc.) from a single whole chicken (any bones can be used, so long as they roughly equal one chicken's worth) and add to the pot of your choice.

Cover bones with water and add a splash of apple cider vinegar (to draw out minerals from the bones).

Herbs may be added as desired.

For instant pot, set pressure time to 1.5 hours. Allow to naturally release.

For crockpot, cook on high for 3 hours or low for 8 hours.

For stovetop, simmer overnight or for about 8 hours.

The longer you simmer your stock, the more "gel" you will get when it's refrigerated. (Vegetable stock will not gel). This is good! You want your stock to gel. Freeze in ice cube trays and place in a Ziploc bag or container for easy storage. Can also be stored in mason jars in the fridge. Use or freeze refrigerated stock within a few weeks.

Ginger Tea

G*INGER IS BLOOD-BUILDING, DIGESTION-AIDING,* and *warms the body nicely. It also soothes sore throats with the addition of honey and helps boost your immune response if you feel any sickness coming on.*

Ginger tea is one of many hundreds of teas that can benefit you postpartum.

Using fresh ginger, peel and slice several thin pieces off of the root.

Boil 1-2 cups of water.

Add ginger and let simmer or steep for 5 minutes.

Sweeten with raw honey.

Add lemon for a nice citrus flavor or turmeric powder for anti-inflammatory purposes.

Beef Stew

Nutrient-dense, warm, and so delicious! Beef stew is one of my absolute must-haves postpartum.

Ingredients:

- 1 lb stew beef
- 3 carrots and/or parsnips
- 3 stalks celery
- 3 potatoes
- 1 yellow onion
- 6 cups water or bone or vegetable broth
- Herbs to taste could include any of the following: Bay leaf, oregano, thyme, rosemary, sage, salt and pepper, etc.

Method:

1. Optional first step: Sear thawed stew beef in bottom of instant pot (on saute) or soup pot on stove until just browned on the outside.
2. Add chopped onion and vegetables. Stir until onion is slightly translucent.
3. Simmer for 3 hours on low with lid on pot for stove, 3-4 hours

in a crockpot on low, or 25 minutes high pressure in the instant pot with a 10-minute natural release. Can be assembled and frozen before cooking for an easy, nourishing freezer meal.

"Pudding" Oatmeal

THIS IS A FAMILY-SIZED recipe (for my family of 7). You can easily cut the recipe down for smaller servings. Does not work in the microwave.

Not only is oatmeal filling and warm, but it's great for building and maintaining your milk supply! The addition of seasonal spices and eggs increases protein and makes this a hearty meal or snack for any time of the day.

Ingredients:

- 6 cups water
- 4 ½ cups Whole Rolled Oats (gluten-free if needed)
- ½ tsp sea salt
- 6 eggs (one egg per cup of water used)
- Spices to taste could include: Cinnamon, nutmeg, allspice, ginger, cloves, cardamom
- Optional add-ins: Honey, Maple Syrup, brown sugar, craisins, raisins, goji berries, other dried fruit, chopped dates, almonds, walnuts, pumpkin seeds, hemp heart seeds, other chopped seeds or nuts, collagen powder, cocoa powder, peanut butter, chocolate chips, carob chips, fresh berries or fruit, coconut pieces, cream, coconut or almond milk, etc.

Method:

1. Bring water and salt to a boil on high heat

2. Crack eggs into a separate bowl and whisk. Make sure the bowl has enough room for double the volume of the eggs.

3. When water is boiling, add oats. Bring temperature down to Medium heat.

4. After the oats have cooked for 2 minutes, use a large spoon to scoop 2-3 scoops of oats into the bowl with the eggs. Whisk until the eggs start to lighten in color from bright yellow to pale yellow. This is called "tempering" and will prevent the eggs from cooking too fast when added to the main pot.

5. Add tempered egg mixture to the main pot and stir for 2-3 minutes. If you've fully tempered your eggs, you won't get any visible stringy white strands of egg white. Otherwise, you may see some egg strands in the pot. These are not a problem unless you have picky eaters, in which case you could try to pick them out.

6. Remove oatmeal from the heat and add your choice of sweeteners and spices. You may want to create an oatmeal "bar" on the table with bowls of add-ins for people to make their own oatmeal creations.

Postpartum Belly Binding

WHAT IS POSTPARTUM BELLY BINDING?

Belly binding is a tradition in many eastern cultures. The practice involves using special knots to tie a long strip of cloth around the abdomen - sometimes after applying an herbal paste or essential oils to the abdomen - during the 40-day postpartum recovery period to support a woman's uterus and other organs after childbirth.

The Bengkung style of belly binding seen here is specific to the Malaysian culture. There are many methods and cultural practices of belly binding, but this is the one I'm most familiar with.

BENEFITS OF POSTPARTUM BELLY BINDING

- It helps to slim the ribcage, abdomen and hips.
- Pulls in the separated abdominal muscles (diastasis recti) back together.
- Encourages healing from pelvic/pubic separation (a partial bind during pregnancy can be especially beneficial for pelvic support).
- Supports relaxed and stretched out muscles.
- Reduce fluid and air retention in bowels/abdomen.
- Gets rid of the "empty" feeling after childbirth.

- Nurtures the mother in a time of vulnerability and healing.

- Prevents back pain. While wearing it, you are reminded to sit and walk straight, a good antidote to the "nursing-slouch".

- Decreases postpartum bleeding time by speeding up the process of getting rid of waste blood in a natural way.

- It's an ancient traditional natural way of healing after birth.

- In the case of a miscarriage or still-birth, belly binding can improve emotional healing as it speeds physical healing.

- It feels good!

BELLY BINDING IS ESSENTIAL

One of the essential components of the postpartum tradition of belly binding is the "warming" aspect. During the winter months, it's especially valuable to keep your body very warm. Your body will heal faster and more fully, your blood will circulate more efficiently, your milk supply will be better if your core is kept extra warm. Even in the summer, belly binding can be beneficial as it securely wraps your body and keeps out "wind" that many cultures believe causes illness and mental instability.

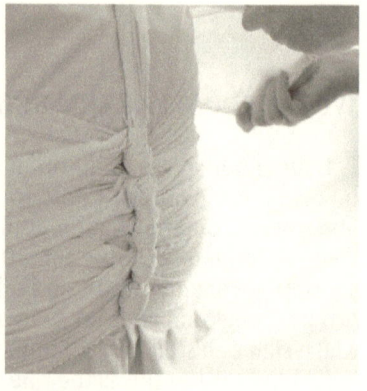

The more I belly bind women postpartum, the more I realize how needed it is. Women are instinctive nurturers. They take care of everyone around them but rarely do they have the opportunity to be taken care of themselves.

Postpartum belly binding is a ritual of nurture and healing that creates the feeling of being surrounded, loved, and noticed.

Belly binding is about more than weight loss, getting your pre-baby figure back, or even healing physically. It is about supporting your body in a time of vulnerability. It's about honoring the space of motherhood, the transition from woman to mother, mother of one to mother of many. It is about surrounding each other with the most basic and essential of human needs: acceptance and love.

When you receive belly binding, you receive warmth, understanding, and most of all, love that will lift you up in a time of vulnerability and healing.

CHOOSING A BELLY BIND

Here are some essential tips for choosing a postpartum belly bind method.

Decide whether you will hire someone who is proficient and knowledgeable in belly binding OR if you will learn from a reputable source. Yes, there are youtube videos, however, many of these videos teach incorrect methods that can potentially cause certain issues in the postpartum time. It is better to find and pay for a course in belly binding so you can be certain to get full and correct information, or to pay someone to come do the binding for you and teach you.

When binding yourself, choose a bind that covers you fully. There are many styles of belly bindings available now. A quick Amazon search will show you a myriad of vecro "abdominal binders", and Etsy has hundreds of styles also. How will you choose between them? You're looking specifically for a binder that will start below your hips and go up to your sternum to cover your full torso.

Most velcro binders will be too short. The length is essential for making certain you get full support and don't put pressure on your pelvic floor. I recommend a bengkung belly bind because it is customizable to your size and shape.

Choose a bind that is comfortable. Wearing a tank-top (with nursing access) underneath your bind may be essential for optimal comfort. However, some styles come with an extra panel of fabric to go underneath and make wearing more comfortable. Make sure you get a bind that is not too small, or too short.

Bind from the bottom of your hips to the top of your torso, NEVER bind from the top down. This includes the velcro binders. If you choose to get one of these, make sure you are attaching it starting at the bottom of the bind, at the hips, so you lift pressure OFF your pelvic floor rather than push it down.

For more information, take my Self-binding for Postpartum Women Course here:
www.learnbellybinding.com

Advice for Winter Births

From the women who wrote the stories in this collection.

Giving birth during the typically colder months comes with unique situations to navigate. The focus is often on holiday preparations, and schedules quickly fill up with parties, family obligations, and the desire to keep up with often-extravagant traditions.

Look at these tips from women who have expected babies during this busy season and enable yourself to sift through and keep the most meaningful parts, while giving yourself permission to let go of everything else and rest.

Trust in God and Pray.

Set boundaries and stick to them. Don't be afraid to say "no" or step back from events and gatherings in order to hold space for yourself and prepare your mind and home for your birthing time.

Get all the Christmas shopping done early. Wrap and ship in advance as needed.

Keep Christmas low key.

Take events one day at a time, depending on how you are feeling.

Spend extra snuggle time with your kids before the baby arrives.

Plan out your holiday dinner(s) and any seasonal baking projects in advance. Even if it's just sugar cookies made from refrigerated dough, make a plan so it doesn't get forgotten.

Putting meals in the freezer might be even more important with a December baby because everyone you know is crazy busy this time of year. Don't count on a meal train, even if you normally get one.

Do not feel bad if you want to skip family gatherings. I stayed home and rested while my husband took the oldest to a family celebration for a few hours. No regrets!

Once you have your baby, wear them in a wrap everywhere. It keeps the baby-passing and germ-spreading to a minimum, especially at family gatherings.

Make sure before you go to someone's house that they'll have space for you to privately nurse your baby. And listen to your baby's cues!

If your baby is overstimulated and hungry, it doesn't matter that Aunt Mae hasn't held him/her yet. Whisk that baby away and have some quiet time in a dark room.

Have lots of warm blankets ready for after birth and some hot tea on hand.

Honor your postpartum healing time. For one year, most things can be put aside so that you can get the most out of the physical healing you need.

Also By Bree Moore

"Reading 'Birth Becomes Hers' is like having a conversation with an extremely knowledgeable and intuitive best friend! Bree's warmth, compassion and understanding come through on every page as she shares her journey from hospital birth to midwife assisted home birth to free-birth.
In addition to Bree's excellent research, she also provides links to articles, podcasts and books that go deeper into the issues many women face when considering having an unassisted birth. Lastly, she allows others to share their own fascinating stories of the challenges and rewards of giving birth at home on their own terms."

-Laura Kaplan Shanley, author of "Unassisted Childbirth"

Find it on any retailer in ebook, print, and audiobook here:
https://books2read.com/u/b5wkKO

About the Author

Bree Moore first became involved with birth as a profession after the natural hospital birth of her first child. Her passion grew as she studied childbirth, drawn by the emotional and spiritual implications birth has on the life of both mother and child. She initially trained as a professional postpartum belly binder, helping women recover postpartum, and then later as a birth Doula. Bree finds great fulfillment in joining women on their journey on the path to motherhood and helping them discover their innate powers of creation through pregnancy and birth. She lives in Iowa, is wife to an amazing "baby-catching" husband, and mother to six children, four of which were born at home, unassisted.

https://www.facebook.com/birthbecomeshers
https://www.authorbreemoore.com
Instagram: @birth_becomes_hers

www.ingramcontent.com/pod-product-compliance
Lightning Source LLC
Chambersburg PA
CBHW020245010526
44107CB00002B/108